THE SURFER'S GUIDE
to
COSTA RICA
and
SW NICARAGUA

By Mike Parise

Art by Bob Towner

(Cool maps by Bob Towner,
amateurish map by Mike Parise)

Edition 7.0

SurfPress Publishing, California

www.TheSurfersGuides.com

THE SURFER'S GUIDE *to* COSTA RICA *and* SW NICARAGUA

By Mike Parise

Published by:
SurfPress Publishing
P.O. Box 492342
Los Angeles, CA 90049
www.thesurfersguides.com

All rights reserved. No part of this book may be reproduced or transmitted in any form or by any means, electronic or mechanical, including photocopying, recording, or by any information storage and retrieval system, without permission in writing from the author, except for the inclusion of brief quotations in a review.

Although the author and publisher have made every effort to ensure that the information was correct at the time of going to press, the author and publisher do not assume and hereby disclaim any liability to any party for any loss or damage caused by errors, omissions, or any potential travel disruption due to labor or financial difficulty, whether such errors or omissions result from negligence, accident, or any other cause.

Copyright © 2009 by Michael Parise
First Printing 1996
Printed in the United States of America

Library of Congress Cataloging-in-Publication Data
Parise, Michael
    The Surfer's Guide to Costa Rica & SW Nicaragua/by Michael Parise. — 7th ed.
    p. cm.
    Includes index
    ISBN 10 1449925103
    1. Costa Rica—Guidebooks. I. Title.
    2. Surfing
    3. Nicaragua

To Francesca

*"Dad, can we find a restaurant with fish
like they have in Tamarindo?"*

COSTA RICA SURF BREAKS

Table of Contents

Introduction	1
Background and Tips	3
Guanacaste and the Northwest	36
Nicoya Peninsula	57
Central Pacific	75
Pacific Southwest	98
Caribbean Coast	111
Southwestern Nicaragua	122
Index to Maps	130
Appendix	131
Index	135

Introduction

"Pura vida!" In Costa Rica it's the local slang for "great," "terrific" or "cool." In English it translates literally as "pure life." A country whose national exclamation is "pura vida" just had to have been created for surfing. And the same goes for its neighbors.

Take a trip to this part of Central American and you will quickly see why—warm water year-round, tasty and inexpensive food, affordable lodging, friendly locals, and a wide variety of waves with swells from two hemispheres in two oceans. With all that Costa Rica and Nicaragua have become popular destinations for traveling surfers worldwide.

Surfers travel for many reasons—to get away from crowds, cold water, and overly familiar waves; to get to uncrowded reefs and points, consistent and bigger waves, warm water and different cultures. We travel to empty our minds of everything but surf. Pure surf. Pure life. Justifying a surf trip is easy. Making it work often is not. Before every trip most surfers do some sort of research and planning to ensure that precious time and hard-earned money are put to best use, which means surfing the greatest number of the best waves, or maximizing wave count. For many that means ordering up a prepackaged surf tour on a credit card. Others want more control, spontaneity, privacy or adventure. They want to merge with the local environment and culture, and do it on their own terms. And get a lot of great waves.

Maximizing wave count starts with knowing where to find the waves, followed closely by knowing how to not waste time that could be spent surfing. The biggest time waster is getting to and from the breaks. Staying at a surf camp often solves that problem, and it would be convenient if there was a surf camp at every great break on the planet, or if the surf camps were all within walking distance of the breaks. But that's usually not the case. So an important part of surf travel planning is finding accommodations closest to the breaks you want to surf so you waste minimal time getting to and from the waves. That search is complicated by amenity needs (bringing a non-surfing companion? kids? need air conditioning?) and budget. Budget, of course, is the greatest determinant of wave count. The rich can surf anywhere, anytime, and for as long as they want. They literally buy waves.

The biggest time waster is not planning, and spending your precious surf trip time driving from break to break and hotel to hotel looking for the right accommodations at the right price at the right break. Imagine the typical frustration at home of you and your buds packed in the F150 checking all the local breaks, arguing about going north or south while the wind turns from offshore to sideshore to onshore and the line-ups get crowded. Now multiply that by the number of dollars your plane ticket costs. That number becomes the "aggravation factor" experienced by driving around a strange country seeking the right accommodations near the right breaks if you don't plan properly. Or buy a prepackaged trip.

Then again, "planning" usually goes like this: Go online. Find the surf spots. Research accommodations. Check the photos to see if the place is really in front of the break it says it is. Get frustrated because they never have those shots. Buy a travel guide. Try again to match up the hotels with the breaks. Call friends. Try to find that old issue of *Surfer*, or was it *Surfing*, no…it was *Transworld*… The research and cross-referencing takes forever and still leaves you wondering because the travel writers rarely, if ever, tell you which hotels are near the surf breaks, and the ads say all of the hotels have perfect surf right out front. I found planning a surf trips to be time consuming and frustrating. I needed a thorough guide to suit my needs. That's when I started writing this. That was in the early 1990s.

Everyone knows the best way to maximize wave count is to stay somewhere with a direct view of the surf. By sitting and watching a break you can jump on it when the combination of conditions – tide, wind and crowd – is just right. Since finding accommodations with surf right out front is ideal, I've tried to point out those hotels wherever possible. Unfortunately, there are very few hotels or even surf camps sitting right on top of good surf breaks. (In fact, most surf camps drive or boat you to the surf, just like at home.) Fortunately, there are way too many to cover in this book that are nearby one or many great, and often uncrowded breaks.

As mentioned, this book is a guide for surf travel. It is not much of a travel guide. There is little here on history, climate, flora, fauna, government, economy, sociology, arts or culture, except as related to your surf trip. It will help you maximize your wave count. It is not meant for the coffee table. It is meant to be used, traveled with, shoved in backpacks, splashed with rain, beer and saltwater, and hopefully, to end up dog-eared and scribbled up. It is printed in short runs for frequent updates and to provide room for your own notes.

Sorry, but no secret breaks are revealed. While over 70 breaks are described herein, every one has already been published for public consumption somewhere else. True, you would have to search quite a bit to put together the same list. It's also true that you will find suggestions as to where there may be spots yet to be discovered or talked about. Another truth is there are a few breaks that are pretty well known by the experienced Central America travelers but haven't yet been written up, like Chacocente (oops) so I'm holding off on those. The most important truth, however, is that every inch of the Pacific Coast has been discovered, and despite that, you can still find excellent, totally uncrowded waves.

Lastly, while this guide is updated regularly, it is impossible to keep up with all the changing details of every road and hotel, as they seem to change daily. So the book you hold in your hands is already out of date, especially when it comes to prices and even telephone numbers.

Thankfully, what doesn't change is the consistently good surf.

Background and Tips

"Smoke and ash from field-clearing fires curled up here and there in the middle-distance like riptides; the air smelled like burning wood and diesel fumes, and reminded me of every Central American trip I've ever taken. It was comforting and also a bit exhilarating. I've scored way more good waves to that acrid smell than I have to plumeria and gardenia."

- Matt Warshaw, *Surfer*, November 2004

Surfer's Paradise

At the risk of sounding cliché, Costa Rica is a surfer's paradise. You have seen it said in the magazine ads and you have probably heard it out in your local line-up. With little qualification, you are hearing it again here. Costa Rica has a zillion breaks with waves coming from all directions on two coasts. You don't need a wetsuit and the hazards are minimal. People are friendly. Comfortable lodging and food are plentiful and reasonably priced. There are populated breaks for those needing company or an audience, and they are usually bordered by empty breaks within walking distance. And when you really want to get remote there are plenty of world-class waves accessible only by boat or long hikes through tropical rainforest. Everything a surfer needs is in Costa Rica.

Friendly, Safe, Beautiful

When one thinks of Central America, visuals of highway ambushes, military violence, mass graves, torture, poverty and especially unpleasant prisons once came to mind. Assign those thoughts to other places, because Costa Rica is a beautiful, peaceful democracy known as "the Switzerland of Central America." For good reason: The standard of living is one of the highest of the Americas. The education and literacy rates are high compared to other countries of the Americas, and the economy is stronger. The people are happy, friendly and well mannered. And while crime has been on the rise, violent crime is rare, especially when compared to the U.S.

WARNING

Friendly, safe, beautiful, warm water, and all the other wonderful things about Costa Rica conspire to hide the biggest danger: The surf. Drowning is a regular occurrence at the beaches here, but unlike the occasional murder, it rarely makes the news. For example, Dominical alone had 20 drownings in 2001, including a 30-year-old surfer celebrating the first day of his honeymoon. Jacó, with smaller surf than Dominical had six drownings in 2005. Overall, there were 120 reported drownings in 2005, up from 85 in 2004. While most of the drownings are not surfers, the fact remains that unless you are an experienced surfer and a strong swimmer you should take extra caution. The better beach breaks, reefs and rivermouths all have dangerous rips and undercurrents, and there are almost no lifeguards to be found. So beware, and be a strong swimmer, or wait for small surf to venture out.

For the novice, here's some standard advice on how to avoid the most popular cause of drowning: "Rips." Riptides, rips, or rip currents occur at most beaches with waves. The experienced surfer spots them easily as the brown, sandy, rippled water interrupting an otherwise uniform blue/green shoreline. When waves break they push water up the beach, which then needs to return to the sea. Sometimes, the returning water gathers together forming a sort of river heading back out to sea, a rip current. Swimmers get caught in rips and dragged out past the breaking waves where the rip dissipates and releases the victim. Inexperienced swimmers drown because they don't understand how the rips work, so they panic and try to fight their way back to shore. Even experienced surfers have been known to drown after being caught in a rip, notably in Puerto Escondido, the mainland "Mexican Pipeline." The best thing to do when caught in a rip is to relax and let it have its way with you. It will eventually release its grip, at which point you swim in letting the breaking waves lend a hand by washing you ashore. Don't try to swim straight in as you'll be swimming back against the same rip that dragged you out. Instead, swim laterally, parallel to the shore to get around the rip (and hopefully not into another), and in. If you are a strong swimmer you can try swimming laterally out of the rip before it takes you all the way out. But it's not always the best use of your energy.

There is good news about rips. Experienced surfers know that the quickest way to paddle out to the lineup is in the rip itself. It's the express lane.

Tropical Diseases

People unfamiliar with Costa Rica invariably ask about needing vaccinations, malaria and other scary diseases made infamous by the tropics. Yes, there's malaria, dengue fever, tuberculosis and even leprosy lurking about these parts, but the infection rates are low, and most are dropping lower. Malaria, for example, dropped from about 5,150 reported cases in 1998 to 1,400 in 2001, and has dropped since. And leprosy has dropped from 10 to 20 annual cases to none since 2000. The diseases on the rise include tuberculosis and AIDS, the former being curable and the latter preventable. If you're prone to worry, worry about dengue, which is on the rise. It's carried by mosquitoes, so avoid stagnant water and ponds, especially during early mornings and evenings. (Mosquitoes, like sharks, feed at dusk and dawn.)

When to Go

When is the best time to take a surfing vacation in Costa Rica? Anytime. Since Costa Rica is bounded on one side by the Pacific, where it picks up anything from southern hemisphere to wintertime northwest swells, you will get waves so long as there has been a decent-sized storm somewhere in that ocean. And if not, check the other side of the country, the Caribbean, where it catches swell from the same weather that brings cold fronts down the Atlantic Coast of the U.S. in the winter, and swells from hurricanes that move into the Caribbean window in the late summer and fall. Regionalized, it goes like this:

> **The Pacific Northwest** (Guanacaste and Nicoya Peninsula): Picks up swell year-round. The summer gets bigger with the larger, more frequent southern swells. The summer is also the rainy season, which at times makes it difficult to impossible to reach some breaks. The

winter is dry. It gets good offshore winds from December through April; winds that can blow steadily for days on end. February and March generally have the strongest offshores, and some swell from the northwest Pacific. The north swells are generally smaller and weaker. Best months: May through September for size, December through April for conditions. September and October to beat the crowds.

Central Pacific: Best in summer with the Southern Hemisphere storms because it generally faces southwest and the Nicoya Peninsula helps block any northwest swells. Offshores often until mid-morning, followed by onshores until an evening glass-off (although it really doesn't get all that glassy). Best months: April through September.

Pacific Southwest: Generally the same as the Central Pacific with some exceptions. Rainier overall. Best months: April through September.

Caribbean Coast: Best in winter, December through February, when the cold fronts come down from the north into the Caribbean, and late summer (July/August). If you are looking for big, juicy surf, get to the Caribbean coast in the winter when it is most consistent. Or if the surf reports don't offer anything promising on the Pacific, head to the Caribbean and you may get lucky.

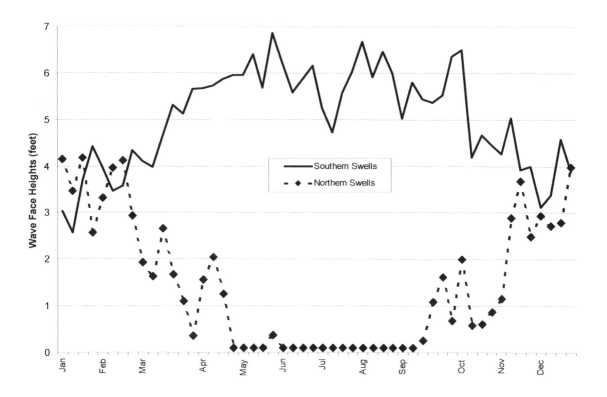

Data Source: Sean Collins—Surfline/Wavetrak. Mexico/Central America forecast is available every Monday, Wednesday and Friday at 1-900-976-SURF or at 714/310-976-SURF. To subscribe go to Surfline.com or call 1-800-940-SURF.

To sum it up, there are basically two seasons in Costa Rica: wet and dry. The dry season corresponds roughly with our winter, and the surf is, on average, smaller on the Pacific coast and larger on the Caribbean. The wet season has been dubbed the "Green Season" by the marketers and corresponds somewhat with our summer. Surf conditions reverse from the dry season, so the Pacific surf—which contains most of the surf spots—is bigger. But the rain (you wondered why it's called the *wet* season) causes many of the smaller roads to the breaks to become impassable due to mud. Now for the confusing part: Although it is in the Northern Hemisphere, the Costa Ricans call what we call the winter, "summer," and what we call the summer, "winter." No one has ever explained that well enough for me to feel comfortable passing the reason on in writing. It just is.

A final note on when to go... It's more expensive in the winter due to heavier tourism that prefers the drier weather. It's also more difficult to secure lodging, which means that you'll have less freedom to roam at will. It's especially difficult late December through March, and avoid Easter Week altogether as all of Costa Rica vacations at the beaches that week, and it's now become a popular college Spring Break destination, too. Airfares start dropping shortly after the Easter madness. (To check ahead on holidays see www.earthcalendar.net.) In the summer it's cheaper (you can often negotiate room rates to beat the published off-season rates) and less crowded, and even more so in the fall. The absolute cheapest time to go is between Labor Day and Halloween.

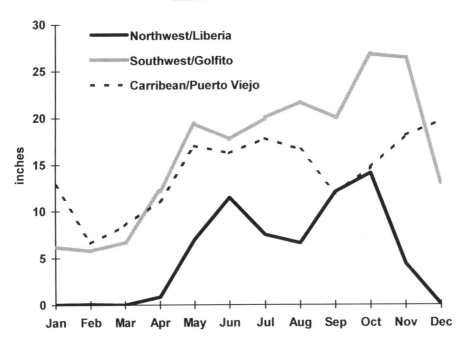

A Word on the Pacific Coast Tides

On the Pacific coast the tides can make a huge difference in the surf with swings of up to ten feet and more. Sometimes you will surf an overhead break at dawn for a couple of hours get out, have breakfast, go back and it will be totally flat. Other times, waves will appear from nowhere in a matter of a couple of hours, and disappear just as quickly. One example of this is seen at the reef right in front of the Tamarindo Diría, Pico Pequeño. On a full-moon high tide the place looks like a mushy, outside beach break. On low tide it can look like a hell-reef. (On my first trip there I was warned not to go out on low tide. The warning was backed up by a story about a guy who face-planted the reef. Fortunately, he and his buddies were doctors.) You can find tide tables on the Web at www.crsurf.com or www.centralamerica.com.

What to Pack

No matter how much surf travel experience you may have, if you are like me, the day of departure is always spent in a busy, nervous, anxious, state of adrenaline rush. This is due to the anticipation of good, uncrowded surf; the hurry to get last-minute jobs finished so you leave with a clear conscience (never possible); and most importantly, the only fear worse than a pintail-first sucking over the falls: forgetting to pack something important. Even as I write this sitting in the Los Angeles airport I know that I forgot my sunglasses—left in my car. I'm sure I forgot more, which wouldn't be so bad except that I used my own checklist! Which also means that the edition you are presently reading has a better checklist than the one I used when I first wrote this paragraph.

You really don't need much beyond your trunks and a board, assuming that you are good at and comfortable with leeching off of your buddies. Otherwise, like a good Boy Scout, you will want to be prepared. So in no particular order, get packing.

- **Airline tickets**: Or the receipt printout from your online order. Sometimes I carry mine around in my backpack for a week before I go just to make sure I don't forget them. If you are going paperless and getting your eticket at the airport, don't forget the credit card you used to make the purchase. Some airlines won't give you your eticket without you having the purchasing credit card in your possession.

- **Passport**: You are required to have a passport to get into Costa Rica, and it must be valid (not expire) for 90 days following your entrance. There was a time when you could get in with your real birth certificate and your driver's license, but that ended April 30, 2003. Friends may tell you that you don't need a passport, but don't believe them.

    A good idea is to also bring a copy of your passport. Whenever possible give policemen and others who need to see your passport the copy. American passports are valuable and go for a good price on the black market, so they get stolen.

    Don't wait until the last minute to apply for a passport; they are issued by a government bureaucracy. Check with the State Department's web site (http://travel.state.gov/passport_services.html) for general passport information and the specifics on Costa Rica (http://travel.state.gov/costa_rica.html).

- **Surfboards**: Since really big waves are rare, you most likely will not need a ten foot Brewer gun. But you may luck into some eight foot waves, so you would not want to be stuck with only your 5'6" fish. Bring your small wave board, whatever that may be, and bring your board for six foot barrels, just in case. Basic rule of thumb: bring the board(s) you have the most fun on.

    > **Renting Surfboards**: These days, you don't even need to pack a board as rentals are fairly convenient, especially if you are heading to Tamarindo, Jacó, Nosara, Dominical, Mal País and other popular surf centers. They have tons of longboards, mostly epoxy, and the selection of shortboards has gotten surprisingly good. Considering the hassles of packing and carrying boards along with the baggage fees the airlines charge, rentals are not a bad way to go, especially if you are a novice.

- **Fins** and **hardware**: If you removed the fins to pack your boards, don't forget to pack them along with the hardware (key or screwdriver) for securing them. Pack with your boards as you won't need fins if your board bag gets lost.

- **Clothing**: You might consider packing or wearing one respectable-looking outfit (long pants, a "non t-shirt" shirt, shoes, socks), because you never know when you might need it. The world is not fair and book is judged by its cover, especially in foreign countries. At the very least you might get better treatment by airline employees, especially when you need favors. (There isn't always a fee for surfboards as checked baggage.) At worst, you could find yourself in front of a judge. Otherwise, all you will need are trunks, t-shirts, and sandals. I also pack or wear a long-sleeved shirt for cool nights (rare), overly air conditioned airplanes and to fend off mosquitoes.

- **Beach towel**: The hotel towels aren't big enough to blow your girlfriend's nose. And beach towels make good board-packing material anyhow.

- **Wax**: You can buy wax in Costa Rica, but it costs twice as much as at home and shops are not always convenient. Bring tropical and base coat. You will need base wax if you decided to strip the wax from your board(s) before packing. Plan on one to two bars a week. You may want to double that for your buddy and other "bro's." (The only thing worse than a shoulder-hopper is one of those "hey bro, got some wax" guys who never, ever, have any wax. I save old bars of cold water wax just for those jokers.) And bring a wax comb too. If it turns out you brought too much wax, leave your leftovers with the locals. Wax is really expensive for them.

- **Extra leash** or two: (Assuming you already packed one with your board.) A spare in case you break yours, and the second extra leash for your buddy who never brings wax.

- **Ding repair kit**: Bring Solarez and sandpaper (sandpaper sponges pack well) for the little dings. If you are going to remote spots or plan on being more self-sufficient, bring the whole kit—fiberglass cloth, fiberglass roving, razor blade, sanding resin, catalyst, masking tape, 60 and 100 grit sandpaper—for gashes and broken fins. Or just pick up one of the Surfco Quick Fix packs that have everything. There really is no need to pack much repair stuff, since there are shops and ding repair joints nearly everywhere now (see Appendix), especially near the more crowded areas. Now, after all that, know that post 9/11 airport security has been confiscating resin and other flammable liquids from luggage. I have never had ding repair stuff confiscated at U.S. airports, but on the way out the Costa Rican security take my resin every time. Who knows what they do with it.

- **Duct tape**: Quite a bit lighter than a ding repair kit. If you are traveling in a pack, have one guy bring the tape and another the ding repair kit.

- **Soft racks** (or foam tubing) *and* **bungee cords** *and* **cinch straps** (good ones): Many rental cars come with racks, but none have straps. The soft racks or tubing will be handy once you've unpacked your boards, but they won't handle board bags. Cinch straps are for your packed boards from and to the airport. (Good cinch straps can be found online at www.justsurfusa.com). Bungees are for the anal guys who need even more security. Know that the rental car racks are bare metal with no cushioning for surfboards. Either be prepared to tape spare towels (they will get muddy from road muck) around the racks, or bring your own soft racks or foam tubing (secure them with tie wraps).

Pack soft racks, cinch straps and bungee cords in your board bag. If the airline loses your boards your straps may as well go along for the ride.

The quality of the racks has grown worse over the years. It used to be that, while the racks were "bare-bones," they were sturdy and worked. It seems now that racks are harder to come by, and the ones you're likely to get will be wimpy. I rented a Daihatsu Terios few years back. The racks that came from the factory were rated for 75 pounds. We had two double board bags and one hard case—more than 75 pounds. We spent half of our driving time stopping to slide the racks back on the roof to keep them from coming off completely. (We did, however, find a benefit of the wimpy racks on our last night. I tried to squeeze under the awning at a hotel we were checking out near the airport, but I miscalculated and hit it square. The boards were saved because the racks were ripped clean off the roof of the car. Needless to stay, we stayed at that hotel.)

- **Trunks**: Two to three. If you bring only one pair you'll rip 'em, lose 'em, or both. And with a few pairs you will always have dry boardshorts for walking around.

- **Sunglasses**: Cheapies

- **Hats**: Two—A trucker cap to look cool and a wide-brimmed hat to keep the brutal sun from roasting you. If you are fair-skinned you should look into one of the many surfing caps designed to wear in the water. This goes double if you do a boat trip to Witches and Ollies. I've seen many end up with blistered lips after the Witches boat trip. Not only is that painful, but you can forget about extra-curricular activities for awhile as you'll look like a leper. (Not that it stopped or even slowed one good friend from diving right into the Del Rey. What people won't do for "love" and money!)

- **Swiss army knife**: Pack in your checked luggage. Airport Security will not let you carry it on the plane. If your knife doesn't have pliers, pack one of those nifty multi-tools, too.

- **Spanish-English dictionary**

- **Flashlight** and extra **batteries**: There's a shortage of electric power in Costa Rica, and sometimes there is none at night. Don't forget extra batteries; they're expensive here.

- **English-Spanish dictionary**

- **Sunblock** lotion: Lots of the highest UV rating you can find—you will quickly learn to appreciate SPF 50. Buy the cheap stuff for your body (and the no-wax buddy); you will use gallons of it. Buy the expensive stuff for your face. The cheap stuff stings your eyes more, ruining the first hour of every session. Look for waterproof, rubproof, sweatproof, UVA and UVB protection. Wear a long sleeved rash guard and you'll save on sunblock. You'll also get less grease on your surfboard. Get sunblock **chapstick** too.

- **Rash guard(s)**: For the sun, not wetsuit rash. I pack two since they are light. Extra t-shirts work, too. Long sleeve rash guards are best. As mentioned above, you will save on sunscreen (which only lasts an hour or so anyhow), you'll get into the water quicker (since you'll have less area to cover) and you won't suffer the embarrassment of having your buddy lather up your back. (Not that there's anything wrong with it.)

- **Mosquito repellent**: Deet is the super-power stuff. Its warnings, however, include things like, "Do not use on face... Wash treated clothing... Avoid contact with plastics..." So it is a bit scary. An unlikely and healthier alternative is Avon Skin-So-Soft moisturizing stick. Avon has no warnings about your skin peeling off like a boiled chicken—and it leaves your skin feeling oh-so-soft too! But it doesn't work as well as Deet when the Costa Rican Air National Guard comes out. Avon now has a cream that works well and doubles as sunscreen. Long pants and shirtsleeves work well too.

- **Caladryl** and **cotton balls**: You're screwed. You're gonna get eaten no matter what. Especially if you are out near the beach early near dawn or dusk.

- **Cruex**: Balls don't take to warm, moist, tropical climates well. Bring Cruex to prevent or cure jock itch.

- **First aid kit**: Start by buying *Sick Surfers Ask the Surf Docs & Dr. Geoff,* by Drs. Renneker, Starr and Booth. Read it, especially the part about cuts. Get cut in the ocean and you stand a good chance of getting an infection. The more you surf the more you will get cut. And you will be surfing more than usual, hopefully. These are the tropics where infections are more likely. Back to the kit... antibiotics (check with your doctor for a good prescription), antiseptic (betadine is good), Neosporin, a variety of waterproof bandages, gauze, lots of tape, snake bite kit (if you are camping), antibacterial soap, Advil, aspirin (for pain and fever), Pepto Bismol, tweezers (to pull out urchin spines and pieces of fiberglass), Q-tips for cleaning cuts and the sand out of your ears, hydrogen peroxide to pour into cuts, scissors and lots of soap and fresh water for washing out cuts.

Unusual for a typical first aid kit, but invaluable for a surfer's first aid kit is duct tape. I once took in a four-inch slice on the fourth day of a ten-day trip thanks to the reef at Cabo Blanco. The cut didn't absolutely require stitches, but no typical bandage would have held it shut either. My buddy Mark Chapman recommended duct tape, and sure enough it worked. Trip saved.

- **Super Glue**: In addition to the obvious uses, Super Glue works great as a bandage. Clean and disinfect the cut, then pull the skin together and glue it. It works like stitches.

- **Wetsuit**: Wetsuits are practically unnecessary. But a vest or maybe a spring suit may be a good idea in the winter if you are going to Witches where the water is cooler (but not cold). The cushioning of a vest is also handy if you get sore ribs. And if you never use 'em, they pack well as board protection.

- **Reef booties**: A good idea if you decide to head for the reef breaks like Salsa Brava, Cabo Blanco and others. (In fact, for Salsa Brava you should seriously consider a helmet.) Booties are also good in the event that you cut your foot and need to hold bandages in place and protect the wound from more damage.

- **Credit cards**: Visa and MasterCard are most widely accepted. American Express is much better at solving disputes. I have found erroneous charges on my statement six months after returning home from Costa Rica.

- **Cash**: The lower-priced eateries and hotels don't take credit cards or traveler's checks. In fact, nobody really takes traveler's checks, except banks, and the banks are a big hassle. You can find ATMs in the bigger cities, but they still are not as common as back home. You may want to exchange some money into colónes as soon as you arrive at the airport in Costa Rica, despite the fact that they take American dollars nearly everywhere now. (In fact, there's been a movement to adopt the dollar as Costa Rica's currency.) Don't exchange in the U.S. as the rate is terrible. It's not so great at the airport in Costa Rica, either. Outside of the San José airport you will find that most of the hotels, stores and restaurants will exchange at or near the official rate. Anyway, using colónes will be your best bet for accuracy.

- **More money**: Bring more money than you think you will need (but don't tell your "can I borrow some wax, bro?" buddy). Travel has a way of nickel-and-diming you to death. And if it's flat you'll want the extra dough for more cervezas. Lastly, if you don't have a credit card <u>be sure to set aside $26 (or more, it fluctuates) for the departure tax they charge at the airport</u>.

- **Calculator**: For calculating the exchange rate. Bring a small, cheap one that fits in your pocket.

- **Address book**: You never know when you may need to call someone back home or send a postcard to your boss.

- **Driver's license**: International would be great but not required unless you are staying more than 90 days. (You wish.) At that point getting a Tico license—which is pretty easy and cheap—makes sense.

- **Hiking boots**: Or something to hike in that can get wet, muddy and protect your ankles. Don't pack them; pack your sandals instead. Wear your boots on the plane to save packing space and luggage weight. Hiking boots are not essential if you don't plan on doing any hiking. But if you are walking at night in the rural areas much, they are good mosquito and snakebite protection.

- **Map**: You can get free maps from the travel agencies and rental car companies, but you will want, need and appreciate the detail you will not find in those free maps. Spend a few bucks on a good map. See "Guides and Maps."

- **Compass**: My bud Arnold Onaga insists that I put this on the list. No matter how good your map is, you're gonna get lost. With the way the roads twist and turn I doubt that a compass will help keep you from losing your way, but at least it will get someone else actively involved in helping you try to get back on track. (Most importantly, Arn will now stop bugging me about the friggin' compass.)

- **This book**

- **T-shirts** to give to the kids. One travel plan is to pack clothes you were going to give to charity, and leave them in hotel rooms as you wear them and travel around. You will lighten your load as you go, not have any dirty clothes to bring home and wash, and you'll be doing a good deed because the Costa Ricans are predominantly poor.

- **Surf stickers**: Costa Rican kids like stickers so much they will stop you on the street for them. Stickers are like cash. Even the airport porters like them. Keep them handy for when you ask directions or other favors.

- **Camera**: If you're not yet digital, bring lots of film and extra batteries. Both are expensive in Costa Rica. Consider bringing an extra camera as well. There is a lot of rain. I got the batteries in my camera wet the first day of my first trip, wasting it (until I got it overhauled back home for over a hundred bucks). Pack your film in your carry-on bag; don't check it. The new security scanning machines can damage film.

- **Binoculars**: The breaks are often not easily visible. (Actually, this a luxury item.)

- **Powerbars**: Or whatever (Clif Bars are good as they don't melt or get sticky from the heat), and bring lots. While sodas (Costa Rican "cafes") and other places for cheap grinds are plentiful, they are not near every break, and you will want to surf the breaks where they are not (i.e., not crowded). Powerbars make a good dawn patrol breakfast since the eateries don't open that early. Then again, bananas work great, they're cheap and you can get them anywhere.

- **Books**: *Da Bull, Life over the Edge,* and *In Search of Captain Zero.*

- **Tide chart**: Available at www.crsurf.com.

- **Earplugs**: You will be in the water a lot. An infection will ruin it.

- **Toilet paper**: It's not Huntington Pier; restrooms are few and far between, and those on the road often have none. Forget TP and you can always use your beach towel. Wet sand works too. Or you can pack toilet paper.

- **Paper** and **pen** to write down directions and take notes in this book. Better still, bring a journal book and keep a diary and scrapbook of your trip. In time you'll be glad you did.

- **Watch or alarm clock**: So you don't miss your flight back. On second thought...

- **Sandwich bags and trash bags**: Trash bags are good for wet or muddy clothes, and double as raincoats. Use sandwich bags to pack goop—sunscreen, insect repellent, K-Y, whatever your goop-thing is—so if a leak develops your bitchin Bad Boy tank top won't get ruined.

- **iPod, headphones, charger and radio adaptor**: If space matters, and it does for me, and noise cancellation matters, and it does for me, and sound quality matters, and boy it does for me, then you might want to check out the in-ear Ultimate Ears (www.ultimateears.com). They pack well, sound fantastic and don't draw undo attention to your stuff. The radio adaptor is for the car. For some reason they seem to work better down there, so don't let sound quality hold you back. Besides, they're tiny. (Don't bother bringing a cassette adaptor; most rental cars have CD players.)

- **Airline tickets** and **passport**: Just checking.

A final note on what to pack… You really don't need to pack anything. You can buy it all when you get there if you want. Costa Rica is no longer the remote Third World outpost it used to be. So you really could travel light and buy as you go. Of course, shopping takes time you might rather spend surfing.

How to Pack Your Boards

Make preparations in advance for your boards. If you start early you will get a better deal on a surfboard travel bag if you don't already have one. Also, it takes time to pack boards properly. If you wait until the last minute you will be sorry.

Preparation starts with buying the best board bag you can afford. If you buy a good travel bag *and* have padded day bags *and* removable fins, then you're set. If not, you should buy bubble wrap, tape and foam fin blocks (they fit around and between your fins and are available at most surf shops or online at www.justsurfusa.com) if you don't have removable fins. Before packing your boards remove the old wax. It's hot as hell down there, so by the time you get to the beach old wax can melt all over everything in your board bag.

Consider getting a water resistant bag because you are likely to encounter rain. Packed board bags are heavy enough when they are not waterlogged. When waterlogged they are a torture to drag around. And they don't dry quickly in the tropics, so they get stinky.

The goal in packing is to make a padded lump out of your board even before you put it in the bag. Tape a towel, old wetsuit or a couple of tee shirts around the nose and tail of your board and make it bulky, or use foam nose and fin blocks. Put the foam blocks on and tape the bubble wrap over it. Bubble wrap the whole thing. Put the wad into your board bag along with your leash, cinch straps and foam tubing (for securing your bag to the car roof), and your vest or short john, if you're bringing one. It used to be that you would pack everything in your board bag—clothes, towels…everything that would fit and provide extra protection. But the airlines have weight limits now, and they tend to treat the heavier, bulkier bags worse than others. So you want maximum protection with minimum weight. Not too difficult with today's board bags and some extra supplies. Feel good when your boards arrive with no dings, as it will happen eventually.

Don't discard the bubble wrap when you unpack as you'll need it for the return trip. It will be a pain dragging it all around, along with the board bag, but it will be worth it.

You may want to try the hard cases from Santa Monica Surf Cases. I used them for awhile, with pros and cons. I hesitated to buy one because they seemed heavy and like they would be cumbersome once you unpack your boards. I was right. With your boards out of the case, the case itself takes up much of the trunk of your rental SUV, or half a Costa Rican hotel room. As expected, the hard cases are strong—I never got a single ding using a hard case. And it can be fast and easy to pack and unpack your boards as you don't have to think about padding or anything, just shove your boards in and go. But they are big and heavy compared to conventional board bags, and conventional bags have come a long way.

A word on traveling with surfboards.... Virtually all airlines now charge for surfboards as oversized or "unusual" baggage. Charges range from $25 on Southwest (which doesn't fly to Costa Rica) to $100 on Continental, for each board. And with the new security measures in place they always check inside your bags, so lying about the number of boards in your bag no longer works as well. To add insult to injury, they also give you a warning that should the flight be full your boards might not get loaded. (That's where lighter bags come in handy.) It's all at the airline's discretion. And it means that you should be prepared to stay at or near the airport should your boards get bumped to make room for Michael Jackson's cosmetic cases. (Surfing lawyers, please sue the airlines.)

Another word.... Keep a close eye on your sticks, tip porters generously, and you may get to your destination at the same time as your beloveds. Once, on a trip to surf Southwest France (before the crowds) I actually watched helplessly through a window at the Frankfurt, Germany terminal as some goon pulled my brand new swallowtail off the baggage cart and sent it off to Venice, Italy, as I learned three days later after waiting out that time at the Madrid airport. I tried to tell the gate agent what was happening while it was happening…a waste of travel breath. Three days in a hot airport while the surf is going off can feel like a stay in the Turkish prison in *Midnight Express*.

Traveling with surfboards sometimes seems like trying to paddle out at a big, consistent, walled-up beach break: Endless Bummer. Then, all of a sudden, while waiting in line at the ticket counter, that working stiff from Chicago asks you, "What's in that bag?" and you realize that, hey, you're on a surf trip, and a warm wave of stoke massages you silly.

By the way, when you arrive in the Juan Santamaria Airport in San José, look for the "Oversize Baggage" (*Equipaje Especial*) sign. That's where your surfboard bag will appear. (Juan Santamaria is a well-organized airport, with polite and helpful officials and assistance easy to locate. That's on the arrival end. When it's time to leave it can be a horror it's so crowded and disorganized.)

Locking it all up

Most air travelers like to lock their bags. With the security screening put in place after 9/11 all locks were off—either you took them off or the security people cut them off, unless you have TSA-certified locks. These are locks approved for security screening, as they can open them, but supposedly, thieves can't. Who knows? But at least it makes it so one can't just open your bag at will, which is more protection from thievery than none. Find places to buy these locks at www.travelsentry.org. I also go to eBags.com.

Airlines

There are now a ton of flights going into Costa Rica, so it's very convenient. In fact, a New York City surfer can get into the lineup just as fast as a Malibu surfer, it's that easy. From the U.S. you can take America West, American, Continental, Copa, Delta, LACSA and Mexicana, depending on your departure point. I try to stick to the domestic carriers for fewer hassles, like stopovers added to the itinerary after you've booked, losing your seat to overbooking or having your seat assignments changed without warning. For all airlines, fares are lower May through November.

It used to be that you had one airport option if flying from the U.S., the San José airport, or Juan Santamaria (SJO). That wasn't a problem if you were heading straight to the Central Pacific. But if your destination was Guanacaste you were looking at what was a six hour drive to the Tamarindo area, and more if heading to the Nicoya area beaches. Now you can fly directly into Liberia's Daniel Oduber International Airport, cutting your drive to Tamarindo down to an hour.

As mentioned previously, all airlines charge excess or oversize baggage fees for surfboards. They have limits on the number of bags, maximum weight for an individual bag, and maximum total weight for all of your bags. For example, LACSA's limit is two bags weighing a total of 100 pounds with no single bag weighing more than 50 pounds. Exceed these numbers and pay extra. Or travel first class for higher limits. Or book through a surf tour operator sometimes board fees are included in the package.

Like everything, those fees are going up, and that is to be expected. But to make matters worse (for some), some airlines will not accept longboards. But wait, there's more! Some airlineswon't accept any surfboards at all during what they call "blackout" periods. Blackout periods vary by airline and from year to year, so always check ahead.

Below are the most popular airlines from the U.S. and their one-way board fees. Again, be sure to call ahead for restrictions (e.g., length, weight, number of boards) as they change all the time. That said, what the agent tells you on the phone and what really happens when checking in at the airport are often different.

Airline	Board Fees Each Way	Phone	URL
American Airlines	$75	800-433-7300	www.aa.com
America West	$80	800-235-9292	www.americawest.com
Continental	$100	800-525-0280	www.flycontinental.com
Copa Airlines	$50 per leg	800-FLY-COPA	www.copaair.com
Delta Air Lines	$80	800-221-1212	www.delta-air.com
LACSA	$50	800-225-2272	www.taca.com
Mexicana	$45 per leg	800-531-7921	www.mexicana.com

Travel Agencies or Surf Tour Planners

For the very best deal, don't bother trying to package your own surf trip. Use one of the experienced surf tour operators. It's almost always the best deal, especially when you package airfare with car rental and a few hotel nights. Also, while it's not guaranteed, you are usually in better hands. You are less likely to be taken advantage of and more likely to get help if you need it. This is especially important when it comes to car rentals. And naturally, most of the surf travel outfits are staffed by surfers, so they either have firsthand knowledge or they at least know what you are looking for and how to help.

One of the best is Mike Brooks' Costa Rica Travel and Real Estate (www.crtre.com, or toll free 866-502-3883). "CRTRE" is a full-service travel agency that offers discounted airfare, hotels, condo and house rentals, 4x4s, fishing, adventure tours, surf camps—the whole deal. What sets them apart are service and knowledge. Mike lives in Costa Rica half the year, and has vacation hosts there year 'round offering what he calls a "free concierge service" where they'll book hotels, surf camps, rental cars, private transfers and adventure tours at not additional service charge to his clients. They'll also give info on good restaurants and of course, surf breaks. It's all a local phone call away. Mike Brooks is a long-time surfer who has been in the business of sending people to Costa Rica for years and has also run surf camps and resorts there. I've been booking through Mike for awhile now and have never been let down—great prices and smooth sailing every time.

You also should consider Alacrán Surf Tours (866-ALACRAN, www.alacransurf.com). This is a Costa Rica based agency started in 1997. They offer the same services as the US-based agencies, except they're Ticos, so they are right there all the time. And yes, they're surfers, just like most of the U.S. agents, and great guys.

Boat Tours

While most Costa Rica touring is done by car, you can also go by boat. Boat touring has been on the rise, so check the Internet for the latest. One boat tour that's been around since the mid-nineties is the Lohe Lani. The Lohe Lani is a 60' catamaran that typically schedules once-a-month six-day trips, September through April. The trips carry up to six passengers at $190 per person per day (2003 price), including meals and fruit drinks (no alcohol on board, but they will take you to shore-side resorts if you suffer withdrawals). They also arrange private charters. The Lohe Lani is headquartered at the Costa Rica Yacht Club in Puntarenas, but you book with "Dave" in Dana Point, California (see Appendix). I can't vouch for the stoke level of the trip as I've never gone. Sounds cool though. Here's what Paul Stout from Florida had to say about his trip in June of 1998:

> *"We had fun to great surf everyday. The only time we surfed with people other than those from our boat was at Pavones. In fact, Pavones was also the only place where we even saw other surfers in the water during the trip. In addition to Pavones, we surfed Playa Valor, Boca Damas, a "secret spot" on the Osa Peninsula, and a place on the southern end of Playa Hermosa. Overall, I would highly recommend the Lohe Lani as a way to go for hassle-free, uncrowded waves, as well as comfortable cruising and accommodations. The captain (we had Pedro, a native) and the two crewmembers (two locals from the Puntarenas area) were great. We surfed about 4-5 hours each morning starting shortly after daybreak, and then would steam to the next spot (trolling for fish/dinner along the way). You could surf more each day (if your body could take it) if you traveled less, or if you traveled more at night. Traveling at night is complicated/difficult due to floating debris in the water. Traveling by boat certainly beat the hassle of driving long distances on rough, wet roads, stopping for meals, finding new hotels each night, etc. and then finding the surf flat and/or crowded. One drawback, or at least challenge, with the boat trip is that it can be tough to figure out the best breaks/lineups when you are at a spot for the first time, since you do not see the waves from the beach. Getting back out to the boat in big beach-break at lower tides can also be an effort."*

A more recent edition to the sleep aboard boat tour lineup is The Giuseppina, a 48 foot trawler-like yacht. They just got going in 2004, and focus on shorter, customized trips mainly to Witches and Ollies. More on these guys in the Witches Rock section. Or just call them at 506-305-1584.

Guides and Maps

You are going to need a good road map. There are some directions given here and there, but to give detailed directions to every spot would require a couple hundred extra pages, and you wouldn't want to pay for those. The best Costa Rica map I have found is published by International Travel Maps (345 West Broadway, Vancouver, B.C., Canada V5Y 7P8; tel. 604-

879-3621; fax 604-879-4521) and is available at better map and travel stores or you can buy it on line at www.surfmaps.com or www.maps.com. Buy the best map you can find. Spend the money; you will save it in gas money ten times over. And the time you will save will get you more waves, and like the MasterCard ad campaign says, that's priceless.

Your best fold-up-to-pocket-size surf map and guide is *The Surf Report* available at www.surfmaps.com or www.surfermag.com. It is a concise guide to surf destinations focusing on the breaks, and includes brief information on how to get there, accommodations, climate, equipment needs, etc. It costs $7 and is a great bargain in my opinion.

If you are really into Costa Rica, you might want to subscribe to *"Surfos: La Revista de Surf de Costa Rica."* It's the bilingual and only Costa Rica surfing magazine. The U.S. address is: SBO#60, P.O. Box 025292, Miami, FL 33102-5292. Email: surfos@racsa.co.cr.

And if you're really, really into Costa Rica, then you'll want to look at it from God's view—space. WorldView Ventures publishes the most extensive and up-to-date collection of satellite image prints and art pieces of Costa Rica that I know of (tel. 858-354-6778, www.SatPrints.com), and they are awesome. The prints are priced at $37.95 each, are printed on high-end, glossy paper, and come 24" x 36". One of the coolest things about looking at maps like these is that there are no crowds anywhere!

Accommodations

While Costa Rica is a beautiful country with lovely, genteel people, it is still a developing country, so you should not expect the same standards as you may have experienced back home. Then again, the prices are a lot lower. (Although they have been going up, a lot.)

If you are not opting for the highest priced hotels, you will find the rooms are smaller, darker, dingier, and simply not in as good condition as you may be used to. The mattresses usually are not firm and many have lumps. Pillows are flat or packed with foam rubber. Room service is rare. Bed sheets are not crisp. Most rooms have bugs, even at the nicest resorts. Furnishings are often shabby. And don't expect to find air conditioning, TV, telephone, hot water, free shampoo, towels worth stealing or even a toilet in every room. Do expect to get what you pay for most of the time since price is a good indicator of quality and amenities.

And look before you rent. In developed countries, such as the U.S., most travelers do not check out the rooms before making a decision on a hotel. Experienced international travelers know better. Always ask to look at the room before checking in. You don't want to check in, unpack your vehicle, and drag everything to the room only to find out that it is too much of a dump even for a surfer. Often you will find that you can get a better room by simply asking. Checking out rooms and negotiating rates are normal and accepted practices in Costa Rica.

Speaking of negotiating…Always try to negotiate the best room and rate. The longer you are staying the better deal you can negotiate. One-night stands aren't worth much. And paying cash helps sweeten the deal.

If you definitely do not want to rough it, don't waste your time looking for bargains. Use this guide and the internet to find the higher-priced hotels with the most amenities. This approach will save you time and make your trip more enjoyable. And compared to Tahiti, Fiji, Australia, Hawaii, Biarritz, Maldives, Cabo, Barbados, et al., you will still be saving a lot of money. Travel during the off-season, roughly May through November, and you'll save 20 percent more, on average, at most hotels.

Most of the decent hotels have web sites, so you can make your reservations and other inquiries online. (And you should try to make reservations. There is a shortage of hotel rooms during the busy seasons, and even with the recent building boom they still are not keeping up with demand.) Many URLs and e-mail addresses are listed here, and you will find increasingly more hotels on the Internet every day. As with everything else, don't expect a prompt reply to your e-mail. Many hotel operators check their e-mail infrequently. And others are in parts of the country with unreliable service, like Pavones.

One of the amenities that comes in handy is a pool, especially if you are staying in a hotel without air conditioning. It is hot and humid in Costa Rica, and a convenient, quick dip in a pool is appreciated.

A biggie is air conditioning. A/c is first thought of as relief from the heat. But it's also good protection from mosquitoes. And you'll find mosquitoes anywhere where it's rainy and hot, like Costa Rica.

With the rapid growth experienced these past 10 years, there are now quite a few houses and condominiums available for rent. This home-away-from-home approach can be a great alternative to crowded hotels with limited privacy. Be forewarned, however, that burglaries are on the rise. In some places, like Jacó, break-ins are nearly epidemic. Check with the owner or management before reserving and try to work out some sort of insurance against theft. If it's a problem at that property you'll likely get none. And the owner will know if it's a problem.

Finally, as a surfer's guide, most of the accommodations listed here are near surf or boats to surf (e.g., Witches and Ollie's). This is not to say there is nothing else worth seeing or experiencing in Costa Rica. But you will need to buy another guide (see Appendix for other travel guides) if you plan on experiencing some of the non-surfing attractions.

Driving

Your current driver's license will do unless you are staying more than 90 days.

If this is your first time driving in Costa Rica do not try to make the drive from or to the airport at night. The roads are dangerous at night, as are the other drivers, especially the truckers. Heck, they're bad enough in the day! (I still have a vivid picture in my mind of dead bodies at the side of the clear stretch of road outside Tamarindo at 7:00am on a Sunday morning while heading out for an Ollie's trip.) Even the most experienced Costa Rica travelers I know spend the night at a hotel near the airport rather than attempt the drive to the beach at night. (I used to stay at the

Hampton Inn just outside the airport. You can't beat it for convenience as they have free airport pickup, free Continental breakfast, free local calls, and it's right next to most of the car rental agencies. But the price has gone up quite a bit, so I'm on to other options, like the Hotel Mango, Hotel Herradura and the Best Western Irazú.)

The *Tico Times* reports that people are killed on Costa Rican highways at the rate of one every 15 hours. Most of the accidents occur between 8 p.m. and 4 a.m., and alcohol plays a role in 31 percent of cases.

Look for sticks and stones in the road, especially near bridges. There aren't many caution or warning cones or signs in Costa Rica. Instead, they improvise with sticks, tree branches, rocks or anything handy to warn drivers of ditches, holes and other hazards. So if you see stuff in the road, don't just race around or over it, slow way down and check things out.

Don't drink and drive. I know it sounds cliché, but the penalties are severe.

The roads in Costa Rica are legendary in their conditions, ranging from freeway quality to war zone quality. The Ministry of Public Works and Transport (MOPT) has been on a "zero pothole" campaign for a few years now in an attempt to improve the 4,000-kilometer, pothole-wreaked national road network, and they've done a great job. It is a battle that will never be won entirely, but it has made a huge difference. In the meantime, the potholes they are not catching are big, deep and dangerous when driving fast. Be careful—flats and broken suspensions take time from surfing. Rolling your vehicle means crushed surfboards—no surfing. Assuming you survived.

Fixing the potholes has created another problem: No shoulders. Or more accurately, steep, undercarriage-tearing drop-offs at the edges of the roads. Followed by deep ditches for rain runoff. If you veer off of the pavement even slightly you are nearly guaranteed an accident, probably a rollover, especially if you whip the wheel to get back on the road or slam on the brakes. (If you do run off the edge, don't do anything but take your foot off the gas and let the car roll to a stop or a safe speed to ease back onto the road. Braking or turning is what causes the accidents.)

Buy gas whenever your gauge goes under half full. There are not many gas stations near the beach and the rest are not open at night. A good map will have the gas stations marked (see "Guides and Maps"). Gas costs about twice as much as in the U.S., and double that for gas sold out of the can in the remote areas.

Yield to pedestrians everywhere—crosswalks, intersections, even the side of the road. They have the legal right of way. Be extra polite. You are a guest, but you will quickly become an unwanted guest if you are rude. You do not want to become an unwanted guest in another country.

Exceed the speed limit and you will pay a fine. The cops are all over the highways and they will get you. The lowest fine is more costly than the most expensive Costa Rican meal. I like food more. And given the road and rental car conditions, you won't save much time anyhow. The cops use radar, so maybe a radar detector will save you. Otherwise, if an oncoming car is flashing its headlights at you, expect to find a cop over the next hill or around the next turn. I have been told repeatedly that it's a bad idea to bribe the police in Costa Rica. It could get you in bigger trouble than just a ticket. And the bribe could cost more than the ticket. But lately, the cops have been doing everything possible to convince me to bribe them. (I get pulled over every time I go.) They tell you the ticket will be $100 and you'll have to pay at the bank, which has long lines and is hardly ever open. So why not take care of it right then and there? The rental car agents tell you to take the ticket, it's less than $20, and it's mailed to the rental car agency. But the cops just argue until I give up and hand them from $20 to $40 to get on my way. Highway robbery, yes, but they always are pleasant, offer a "pura vida" and guide me safely back onto the highway. In the end, it's not a big deal. By the way, the maximum speed limit is currently 90 km/hour on highways, and 40 km/hour in cities. This is for all of Central America.

Police corruption sometimes works in your favor, and sometimes it doesn't. Here's a story from a friend who wants to stay anonymous. This happened March 2000.

> *"I got pulled over next to the airstrip in Nosara at 11:00PM, had to blow into a breathalyzer. They said anything under 100 and I could go no problem. I blew a 64, and they demanded 20,000 colones ($67). We didn't have it so they took our car. Pain in the ass to get it back. It was a DWI check from hell, set up right on the blind turn-off by the airstrip on the way to town, Tropicana Disco. I heard that there were a lot of drinking related crashes in the months before I got nabbed, so I guess they were cracking down. But it seemed they were only stopping Gringos. The funny thing is that once they got my jeep, they hightailed it back to Nicoya (where the station is). The locals were saying this was total BS as these traffic cops were from Nicoya (about an hour away). They said they were just looking to bust people and fleece them. The traffic cop with really hairy ears was the ring-leader—a major dick! Corruption is seeping in down there slowly but surely."*

Screw up driving and you will ruin your surf trip, at the least. Look around the car rental lot while you are filling out papers and you will undoubtedly see a few totaled 4x4s. They will tell you that surfers rented those cars.

Renting Cars

Oh boy, second to the surf, this is the topic of most discussion, starting with four wheel drive (4x4s) versus cars. Cars are cheaper and best suited for getting to the more popular breaks, and are pretty good for the dry season. But you will undoubtedly want to try the more out-of-the-way spots—most of the very best breaks are out-of-the-way—which require four-wheel drive, especially in the rainy season.

Probably the most popular 4x4s rented are the Suzuki Sidekick/Vitara 4-doors. They will get you just about anywhere. The Suzukis are a bit tinny and rattle like coffee cans, and you will too after a week of driving these roads. They're also a bit cramped for four guys, but you can do it;

perfect for three. A little bigger and better than the Suzuki (and becoming more prevalent) is the Toyota RAV4. Range Rovers, Landcruisers, 4-Runners and Pathfinders are more comfortable, especially on potholed roads, but cost more and can be more difficult to negotiate tight dirt tracks. There are also bunches more that are pretty cool, like the new Kias and Mitsubishis. Check them all out online before reserving your car.

At some agencies the Daihatsu Terios has become a replacement for the Sidekick, or that's what some would like us to believe. Don't. It's smaller, doesn't have the same 4WD options, and has less power. It's an inferior vehicle but costs the same. What's worse is that the Terios dangerous due to its narrow wheelbase, resulting in lots of rollovers.

Ask for surf racks, but don't expect to see them on your vehicle when you get there, at least not what you may expect. Usually "surf racks" means "bare metal bars on the roof." Sometimes it means nothing. The rack situation often depends on who you rent from and the car you rent. Some companies, like Toyota, charge extra for the racks.

There have been many reports that some car rental agencies try to get more money from renters by claiming the renter damaged the vehicle when in fact the car was already damaged when it was picked up, just not properly noted. With the anticipation of surf, most newcomers to Costa Rica are too anxious to thoroughly check out their rental vehicle before hitting the road. You, of course, won't make that expensive mistake. *You* will inspect the car with a fine tooth comb for damage because you know that it's worth the extra 10 to 15 minutes. *You* will make sure that all dents, scratches and other problems (check the tires for tread, air conditioning, even test the 4wd) are noted on the rental form. *You* won't blow it.

If when inspecting your car you find that it has bald tires, get them replaced. Every time that I've asked the rental car agent to replace the tires they've done it. Sometimes it takes a little urging, but it sure beats getting a blowout on a mountain road with a semi barreling down on you. You may get new tires; you are more likely to get tires from another rental that are in better condition. Either way you'll be better off.

I've heard bad reports about Exotico and Jeeps "R" Us; good reports on Dollar (at the airport), Poas, Prego, Mapache and Tricolor (good personal experiences with the last five); good and bad on Adobe, Avis and Economy (although lately I've received mostly good reports on both). It's difficult to recommend with complete confidence a rental car company because service can be erratic due to changing ownership and other factors. For example, I had a great experience with CRUSA once; the next year they were gone. I had great service from Adobe for a few years, then things changed to the point that even one of the tour operators, TourTech, dropped them.

Here's a typical story straight from a letter I received a couple of years ago:

> "You should think of taking Exotico Rental off your list. They ripped us off on our last trip down. Besides not having the vehicles promised (I know it's common), they said our agent (Morris) didn't confirm the rentals. It was funny though, my name was right on the

list behind the guy taped on the wall! They (Exotico) also overcharged on my friend's credit card bill. Morris dropped them soon after our experience."

I used Dollar exclusively for a while, but recently I've been using Tricolor and Mapache, mostly Mapache. Nothing against Dollar, I've just been getting decent cars at good rates and great service from Mapache lately.

Repairs, even minor ones, can be quite expensive. Once I scratched the fender on a barbed-wire fence in Matapalo. I admit the car was pretty well scratched. Since I'm like you, I dropped the car off at the last minute on my way to the airport leaving myself vulnerable to the rental company—Adobe—insofar as the costs of the repair. When I got my American Express bill, I learned exactly how much it costs to fix fender scratches in Costa Rica (at Adobe): $277.94. And since they knew that I author this guide, it may have been a special rate. Be careful and you'll save money.

A good bet is to arrange your travel with a tour operator who specializes in surf travel to Costa Rica (see Appendix or any surf magazine) and get a "fly/drive" package which includes airfare and car rental at a discounted rate. The relationship between the tour operator and the car rental firm often increases your chance of getting good service. But, as you read above, that's no guarantee.

Avoid the San José Airport car rental tax. If you book your car in advance, be sure to negotiate an agreement that you will not be charged the 12 percent tax now levied against car rental companies who pick up passengers at the airport. Otherwise, take a taxi. It's cheaper, but it's a pain strapping and unstrapping your board bags to the taxi roof.

Buses

As with most of the world outside the U.S., bus transportation in Costa Rica is cheap and plentiful and makes economic sense if you're traveling alone or with one other person. A great option to and from the airport in San José is the Fantasy Bus, which picks up right at the Hampton Inn near the airport. You can reserve your seat online at www.graylinecostarica.com. Passengers are permitted one hand bag and one suitcase. Additional luggage (e.g., surfboards) depends on space availability, but there's no additional cost. Here's some of the (often changing) schedule and prices.

    Jaco Beach at 8:30 am - Cost US$21
    Manuel Antonio, Quepos at 8:30 am - Cost US$25
    Tamarindo and nearby beaches at 7:00 am - Cost US$25
    Puerto Viejo and Cahuita at 7:00 am - Cost US$25
    Samara at 7:00 am - Cost US$25

The bus leaves early from the airport, so you really can't just fly in and hop on the bus to the beach as the flights don't arrive early enough. So if you add the cost of a hotel room to the bus it probably makes sense to take a cab, especially if you can buddy up.

Local Air Transportation

For air transportation within Costa Rica there is scheduled service by Sansa, TravelAir and Paradise Air. Sansa is cheaper and carries shortboards for $10 each, but nothing over seven feet. Always check first as to whether they can take boards and what the size restrictions may be. If you have a group of five to seven, you might consider a charter flight with Aero Costa Sol Air Taxi. (See Appendix for information on contacting air lines.)

Locals

Here you don't have to worry about locals paddling over and snapping a fin off your board. This is a friendly country with well-mannered people. Everybody is pretty mellow and violent crime is rare. As one Tico put it, "This is a nation of thieves, not killers." (Oh yeah, don't leave valuables on the beach or in your car. And leave the bling at home.) When in doubt, say "pura vida," and the locals will love you.

But just because the Ticos are not violent doesn't mean that you should take advantage of their peaceful nature. As with anywhere else, show respect. It's their country, and it may not be long before they really learn how to be "locals."

Crime

It's sad, but crime has been on the rise. According to *The Tico Times*, between 1990 and 2002, property and sex crimes both doubled, and homicides grew from 4.8 to 6.3 per 100,000 inhabitants. (The U.S. homicide rate was 5.8 per 100,000 in 2002, dropping from 10 in the early 1990s.) So while nearly all of the homicides are between Ticos, you should exercise the same cautions here as anywhere else. Then add some extra diligence to compensate for sticking out as a tourist, as tourists have increasingly become the targets.

Keep your goodies locked in the hotel safe. Expect that anything you leave in your car or take to the beach could get stolen. The old, "I can watch my towel from the line-up" doesn't work. The thieves will rifle through your beach towel and take what they want even while you are trying to paddle in to stop them because they know they have time to get away. Locked car? Hah! Just break the damn window. Anyhow, why bring valuables to the beach? what more do you need than your surfboard?

Some areas are worse than others, especially the more crowded beach cities. Jacó and Tamarindo both seem to be experiencing more crime than other areas. Hotel rooms and houses are routinely burglarized in Jacó. Tamarindo had a brazen, guns blazing armed robbery in 2003. (Following that the local business owners got together to hire more police.) Late in 2004 a 21-year-old San José woman was stabbed, raped and left for dead in the woods outside Tamarindo, having been abducted outside the Mambo Bar at 3 a.m.

If you decide to spend any time in San José you should know about an ongoing scam. Enterprising thieves will distract you by squirting you with a sticky goop (it's actually melted ice cream). A "good Samaritan" will offer to help you out with paper napkins or otherwise. While you are busy cleaning up with your newfound friend, his friends will take off with your backpack or other valuables. Be careful in San José.

Here's another scam experienced travelers already know of that's become more popular lately in Costa Rica: The flat tire scam. You stop your car somewhere for food or who knows what. After getting back on the road one of your tires starts thumping until you discover you have a flat. Just as you get to work fixing it other "good Samaritans" pull over to help. They proceed to stealthily relieve you of your luggage or other valuables. By the time you figure out something's missing you're well down the road thinking "what nice people" and they're long gone.

Sometimes they don't even need to scam. Some Topanga locals I know went to down for a month long trip. One of the locals, Larry, is a professional cameraman, so he had thousands of dollars worth of equipment, and at that point in their trip, priceless video. They stopped for food, parking the car right in front of the restaurant, which had an open front like every other restaurant in Costa Rica. When they returned with their full bellies they found an empty trunk. The thieves broke into the back of their car right in front of their eyes. It's easier than you would think when every tourist is driving the same kind of car as thieves either learn the break in secrets or even build a collection of single car model keys.

I know all this sounds pretty bad and may cause you to rethink a trip to Costa Rica, but I've never had a thing stolen. Nada, zippo, nothing. Well, a wave or two. Anyhow, folks have asked me to recommend that readers try Pacsafe products (www.pacsafe.com). I haven't tried them yet, but it's worth a look.

For more on crime warnings see the State Department Travel Advisory at the end of this chapter or online at http://travel.state.gov/costa_rica.html.

Symbols, Ratings, Shorthand & Excuses

You will find the following symbols in the hotel listings to help organize things:

    $$$ = most expensive, over $100
    $$ = $50 - $100
    $ = $20 - $50
    ¢ = less than $20
    $$$$ = more than most expensive
    A/C$ = air conditioning costs extra
    bath$ = private bath or shower costs extra
    bung = bungalow
    pp = per person
    s = single (one bed)
    d = double (two beds)
    t = triple (three beds)

q = four (four beds)
apt = apartment
AE = American Express
DC = Diner's Club
MC = MasterCard
V = Visa

Telephones

To dial Costa Rica from the U.S. you'll need to first dial the international "011" instead of the typical U.S. long distance "1". The area code for all of Costa Rica is 506. No need to dial a country code from the U.S. In this guide you'll find 800 numbers and other area codes. For the most part, the 800 numbers only work when calling from the U.S.

The phone system in Costa Rica is pretty good, but it's not as good as in the U.S. or Europe. Land line (hard wire) coverage is somewhat limited. For example, Pavones still doesn't have land line phone service. Cellular or wireless coverage is fairly good, so those areas not reached by land line use cellular. Again, Pavones is a good example. Coverage is one problem; glitches are another. Getting connected to the wrong number happens more often than you would expect, but don't get discouraged.

When phoning home from Costa Rica it's cheaper to use a calling card than a credit card or to call collect. If you don't need a written record of your calls for tax purposes or something, then don't bother with any of the above. Buy a prepaid calling card, or *tarjeta telefónica* (tahr-<u>heh</u>-tah tell-eh-<u>fone</u>-ee-kah) at the first opportunity. They are sold at markets everywhere. The instructions are easy and the calls to the U.S. are cheap, about 50 cents a minute. Don't forget to do the scratch-off on the card to reveal your card number. Also, renting a cell phone is a good idea. Pick one up when you rent your car; it's a pretty good deal and comes in very handy.

Sales Taxes

"Luxuries," such as staying in hotels and eating in restaurants, cost extra in Costa Rica. The hotel room tax is 16.39 percent. Restaurant tax is 25 percent, including the tip. But not all hotels (especially cabinas) or restaurants (especially sodas) will charge you tax, especially the lower-priced ones or if you pay cash. Luckily, there is no tax on car rentals.

Food

Depending on who you talk to, the food in Costa Rica is either ordinary or wonderful. It is ordinary in that it is not haute cuisine inspired by the latest culinary trends, nor is it exotically spiced. It is wonderful in that it is remarkably and consistently tasty and healthy. And important for surfers, it is inexpensive and the portions are big. Personally, I love the food in Costa Rica. It is not so unusual that you have to wonder whose pet you may be eating, and you never have to worry about missing surf because you are regretfully re-reading surf magazines on the can.

In Costa Rica you will eat better for less than most any other surf destination, especially if you stick to the local food. Let me qualify that: If you like fresh seafood, rice, beans, fresh fruit, coffee and beer you will eat and drink well. Look for "*sodas*" for hearty meals at good prices. A soda is a Costa Rican café, or cheap restaurant. The food is as good as at most of the more expensive restaurants, but you get less atmosphere and more flies.

Unlike many countries, it is easy to get a hearty meal for breakfast—rice, beans, eggs (AKA "*gallo pinto*"), fresh fruit, coffee and juices. The only letdown from breakfast is that it usually costs as much as lunch—and why shouldn't it given the hefty servings? Lunch is usually a rice dish of some sort, like seafood rice, or you can easily find hamburgers if you get the calling. Dinner is grilled food time, such as grilled local fish, and more rice. Fruit and salads are plentiful, and the coffee is wonderful. And don't fret if the food isn't spicy enough for you; found at every eatery is the local hot sauce, and it's good.

If you are worried about getting sick, here are some tips that pretty much apply to most travel situations. Stick to the busy eateries whenever possible. They turn their food over faster, and it's a sign that their regular customers aren't dying off. It's safer to eat the well-cooked food—that, should be common sense. So salads, fresh vegetables, fresh salsas and fruit can be suspect. Stay away from cream sauces and dressings served at room temperature, especially those made with eggs, like hollandaise (which you won't see much in Costa Rica). Depending on the strength of your stomach you may want to avoid cheeses. Monday is not the best day to order fish as you'll probably be eating Friday's catch, or worse. And to be really safe, you might consider taking Pepto-Bismol as a preventative for your first few days up to a week, rather than waiting until you really need it. (That's a tip from experienced Latin America surf traveler Bobito Sancho, AKA Bob Towner. He thinks Pepto-Bismol is a Mexican aperitif.)

If you get traveler's diarrhea be sure to drink plenty of fluids as dehydration is a serious risk. Flat soft drinks work well. If the diarrhea persists beyond a couple of days or includes blood or mucus in the stool, get medical help as it could be serious, amoebic dysentery or worse.

Tipping in Restaurants

As mentioned above, tips are included in the bill at restaurants. That said, tipping is now somewhat expected in most tourist areas, especially if you get good service.

Drinking Water

Generally speaking, the tap water is safe to drink. It is safer in the cities than the rural areas, except Puntarenas and Limón, where you should never drink the water. It is recommended that you carry your own bottled water to be safe, and because it's damned hot all of the time and you will dehydrate if you don't. When you buy bottled water inspect it before taking it to the cash register. The purified water sometimes has UFOs in it (unidentified floating objects). Look very closely. I usually don't discover the UFOs until I've downed half the bottle. I haven't had the same bad luck with bottled spring water. Anyway, check it first.

Surfing Water

In 1996 Costa Rica initiated a program to recognize those beaches deemed by experts to be the cleanest, best ecologically protected, and safest beaches in the country. There are now roughly 37 beaches awarded the Ecological Blue Banner Distinction (*Bandera Azul*), up from only ten in 1996. Officials from local, private and public sector institutions, including the National Water & Sewage Service, the Health Ministry, the Costa Rican Institute of Tourism, Ministry of the Environment and the National Chamber of Tourism, present the award. Some of the more popular surfing beaches awarded the Blue Banner include Playa Hermosa, Langosta, Sámara, Carrillo, Eserillos Oeste, Bejuco, Manuel Antonio, Playa Negra, Zancudo, Punta Cocles and Cahuita. In a step backwards, Tamarindo lost its Blue Banner in 2005.

Medical Emergencies

It's not fun to have a medical emergency at home, and it's usually worse to have it in a foreign land. Fortunately, Costa Rica has a pretty good healthcare system. Unfortunately, the care you need isn't often near the surf breaks. Some resources for emergency medical care in the Appendix. I suggest you refer to a "real" travel guide, like *The Lonely Planet*, for more comprehensive information. This next story from Andrew Drake illustrates why.

> *"I was out at Dominical in six to eight foot beachbreak and found myself in a position of having a set wave about to break right in front of me, leaving me no options but to bail my longboard and dive under. Upon surfacing my board shot up from underwater after going under the wave and hit me square in the face above my upper lip and below my nose, opening a huge gash in the process. I was almost knocked out, everything was a blur for about 10 seconds. Then I regained my vision got my board and went in belly first on the next wave. Upon reaching the shore a friend offered to take me to the hospital in my rental car, which I was very grateful I had. I was in Dominical when this happened and we were headed for San Isidro, but after really seeing the wound once the bleeding somewhat stopped we realized it was pretty serious and required care only available in San José. After making this decision it dawned on me that we were going to have no idea where to go, then I realized my* Lonely Planet *guide was in the car where it recommended the Clinica Biblica in San José. This is the oldest private clinic in Costa Rica and is a full service hospital. They attended to me immediately, took me off for x-rays to be sure that no face bones were broken and then one of their plastic surgeons came in and started work on me. He took two pieces of broken bone from my face plate out and then stitched up the inside muscle with eight stitches, then three in each nostril, and then 14 to close the whole thing up. The doctor I had was as good as there could have been; I don't think anyone in the states would have done any better of a job. My doctor was trained in Florida, which made me feel good. I was very relieved to have been able to get to San José, for I don't think the free clinic in San Isidro was up for my job. So I would definitely recommend the Clinica Biblica and maybe try and find a few more."*

As bad as all that sounds, Andrew only had to shell out $450 for what turned out to be a pretty good job. (Costa Rica is a mecca for cheap plastic surgery.)

Miscellaneous

Let friends or family know your travel plans as well as you know them yourself. It may be helpful should bad fortune befall you. The Costa Rican government is not responsible for communicating with your relatives in case of emergency or worse. As one official put it, informing an embassy or family members of a death "isn't the law... it's a courtesy."

State Department Travel Advisory

You should check the State Department's web site (below) before your trip for the latest information. They update at least once each year.

Costa Rica - Consular Information Sheet, Updated May 26, 2005
Call 202-647-5225 for the latest updates, or check the Internet at: http://travel.state.gov/travel

COUNTRY DESCRIPTION: Costa Rica is a middle-income, developing country with a strong democratic tradition. Tourist facilities are extensive and generally adequate. The capital is San Jose. English is a second language for many Costa Ricans.

ENTRY AND EXIT REQUIREMENTS: On December 31, 2005, the U.S. Government will begin to phase in new passport requirements for U.S. citizens traveling in the Western Hemisphere. By December 31, 2007, all U.S. citizens will be expected to depart and enter the United States on a valid passport or other authorized document establishing identity and U.S. citizenship. The Department of State strongly encourages travelers to obtain passports well in advance of any planned travel. Routine passport applications by mail take up to six weeks to be issued. For further information, go to the State Department's Consular website: http://travel.state.gov/travel/cbpmc/cbpmc_2223.html.

For entry into the country, Costa Rican authorities require that U.S. citizens present valid passports that will not expire for at least thirty days after arrival.

Costa Rican authorities generally permit U.S. citizens to stay up to ninety days; to stay legally beyond the period granted, travelers will need to submit an application for an extension to the Office of Temporary Permits in the Costa Rican Department of Immigration. Tourist visas are usually not extended except under special circumstances, such as academic, employment, or medical grounds, and extension requests are evaluated on a case-by-case basis.

In a modification to a legal requirement that foreigners carry their passports on their persons at all times, Costa Rican migration authorities have stated that U.S. citizens may carry simply photocopies of the passport data page and of the Costa Rican entry stamp on their persons, and leave the original passport in a hotel safe or other secure place. (U.S. citizens must still, however, present their passports for entry into and exit from Costa Rica.) Due to the high incidence of theft of passports, travelers who do carry their passports on them are urged to place them securely in an inside pocket, and to keep a copy of the passport data page in a separate place to facilitate the issuance of an emergency replacement passport.

There is a departure tax for short-term visitors. Tourists who stay over ninety days may experience some delay at the airport. Persons who have overstayed previously may be denied entry to Costa Rica.

In an effort to prevent international child abduction, many governments have initiated special procedures for minors at entry and exit points. These often include requiring documentary evidence of the child's relationship to the accompanying parents and, if one of the parents is not traveling with the child, permission from the non-traveling parent for the child's travel. Having such documentation on hand may facilitate entry and departure.

Dual U.S./Costa Rican citizens are required by Costa Rican authorities to comply with entry and exit laws that pertain to Costa Rican citizens. This means that dual citizen children (children who hold both U.S. and Costa Rican citizenship), who might normally travel on U.S. passports, will be required to comply with entry and exit requirements applicable to Costa Rican children. Some American parents may not be aware that their child acquired Costa Rican citizenship through birth in Costa Rica or because the other parent is Costa Rican. American parents of minors who may have obtained Costa Rican citizenship through birth in Costa Rica or to a Costa Rican parent should be aware that these children may only depart Costa Rica upon presentation of an exit permit issued by the Costa Rican immigration office. This office may be closed for several weeks during holiday periods. Parents of dual citizen children are advised to consult with the Costa Rican Embassy or Consulate in the U.S. about entry and exit requirements before travel to Costa Rica. For general information about dual nationality, see the Consular Affairs home page on the Internet at http://travel.state.gov.

The most authoritative and up-to-date information on Costa Rican entry and exit requirements may be obtained from the Consular Section of the Embassy of Costa Rica at 2112 "S" Street, N.W., Washington, D.C. 20008, telephone (202) 328-6628, fax (202) 234-6950, or from a Costa Rican consulate in Atlanta, Chicago, Houston, Los Angeles, Miami, New Orleans, New York, San Juan (Puerto Rico), San Francisco, or Tampa. The Embassy of Costa Rica also maintains a web site: http://www.costarica-embassy.org/, as does the Costa Rican immigration agency: http://www.migracion.go.cr.

SAFETY AND SECURITY: On both the Caribbean and Pacific coasts, currents are swift and dangerous, and there are no lifeguards or signs warning of dangerous beaches. Several American citizens drown in Costa Rica each year.

Adventure tourism is increasingly popular in Costa Rica, and many companies provide white-water rafting, bungee jumping, jungle canopy tours, deep sea diving, and other outdoor attractions. In recent years, several Americans have died on Costa Rica's flood-swollen rivers in white-water rafting accidents. Others have died trying to reach the mouths of active volcanoes after being assured by tour guides that this dangerous activity is safe. Americans are urged to use caution in selecting adventure tourism companies, and are advised to avoid small, "cut-rate" companies that do not have the track record of more established companies. The government of Costa Rica has passed legislation to regulate and monitor the safety of adventure tourism companies; enforcement of these laws is overseen by the Ministry of Health. To be granted official operating permits, registered tourism companies must meet safety standards and have insurance coverage.

Demonstrations or strikes, related to labor disputes or other local issues, occur occasionally in Costa Rica. Past demonstrations have resulted in port closures, roadblocks, and sporadic gasoline shortages. These protests have not targeted U.S. citizens or U.S. interests, and are typically non-violent. Travelers are advised to avoid areas where demonstrations are taking place and to keep informed by following the local news and consulting hotel personnel and tour guides. Additional information about demonstrations may be obtained from the Consular Section at the U.S. Embassy, or on the Embassy website.

For the latest security information, Americans traveling abroad should regularly monitor the Department's Internet web site at http://travel.state.gov, where the current Worldwide Caution Public Announcement, Travel Warnings and Public Announcements may be found.

Up to date information on security can also be obtained by calling 1-888-407-4747 toll free in the United States, or, for callers outside the United States and Canada, a regular toll line at 1-202-501-4444. These numbers are available from 8:00 a.m. to 8:00 p.m. Eastern Time, Monday through Friday (except U.S. federal holidays).

CRIME: Crime is increasing and tourists are frequent victims. Criminals usually operate in small groups. While most crimes are non-violent, criminals, including juveniles, have shown a greater tendency in recent years to use violence and to carry handguns or shoulder weapons. All criminals should be considered armed with firearms or knives. Criminals, if challenged or threatened, will quickly use their weapons. U.S. citizens are encouraged to exercise the same level of caution that they would in major cities or tourist areas throughout the world, and to be aware that the same types of crime found elsewhere are also found here, whether of a violent nature (e.g., robbery) or furtive (e.g., identity theft). Local law enforcement agencies have limited capabilities and do not act according to U.S. standards, especially outside of San Jose.

Americans should avoid areas with high concentrations of bars and nightclubs, especially at night, and should also steer clear of deserted properties or undeveloped land. For safety reasons, the Embassy does not place its official visitors in hotels in the city center, but instead puts them at the larger hotels in the outlying suburbs. Americans should walk or exercise with a companion, and should bear in mind that crowded tourist attractions and resort areas popular with foreign tourists are also common venues for criminal activities. Travelers should avoid responding in kind to verbal harassment, and should avoid carrying large amounts of cash, jewelry or expensive photographic equipment.

In recent years, several Americans have been murdered in Costa Rica in urban, rural and resort locations. U.S. citizens have been victims of sexual assaults both in cities and in rural areas. In some of these cases, the victim has known the assailant. There have been several sexual assaults by taxi drivers. Travelers should be careful to use licensed taxis, which are red and have medallions (yellow triangles containing numbers) painted on the side. Licensed taxis at the airport are painted orange, rather than red. All taxis should have working door handles, locks, meters (called "marias"), and seatbelts. Passengers are required by law to wear seat belts. Passengers should not ride in the front seat with the driver. If the taxi meter is not working, a price should be agreed upon before the trip begins. When traveling by bus, avoid putting bags or other personal belongings in the storage bins. Thieves will take property from the bins when the bus makes its periodic stops. A good rule to follow is always to have your belongings in your line of sight or in your possession at all times.

There have been reports that unsuspecting patrons of bars and nightclubs have been drugged and later assaulted or robbed. Americans should always be aware of their surroundings, and should not consume food or drinks they have left untended. Americans may find it safer to seek entertainment in groups to help avoid being targeted, especially in urban areas.

Although unusual, there have been a number of kidnappings reported over the past several years, including the kidnappings of Americans and other foreigners. Some of these cases have been so-called "express kidnappings," in which victims are held for several hours as the kidnappers transport them to various automated bank teller machines in an effort to take as much money as possible from the victims' bank accounts. Carjackings have also increased, and motorists have been confronted at gunpoint while stopped at traffic lights or upon arrival at their homes. Late model sports utility vehicles and high-end car models are popular with carjackers. One method of initiating kidnappings and carjackings is to bump the victim's car from behind; the unsuspecting victim stops, believing he or she has been involved in a minor car accident, and is taken hostage. Americans should remain vigilant to these types of incidents, and use caution if bumped from behind on an isolated stretch of road.

Another common ploy by thieves involves the surreptitious puncturing of tires of rental cars, often near restaurants, tourist attractions, airports, or close to the car rental agencies themselves. When the travelers pull over, "good Samaritans" quickly appear to change the tire - and just as quickly remove valuables from the car, sometimes brandishing weapons. Drivers with flat tires are advised to drive, if at all possible, to the nearest service station or other public area, and change the tire themselves, watching their valuables at all times. Travelers can reduce their risk by keeping valuables out of sight, by not wearing jewelry, and by traveling in groups. Travelers should also minimize travel after dark. Before renting a car, travelers should ask the rental company their specific policy regarding damage to a tire or wheel rim due to driving on a flat tire. Some rental car companies may cover the costs of the damaged tire and wheel rim if the occupants feared for their safety and drove to the nearest public area to change the flat tire.

Travelers should purchase an adequate level of locally valid theft insurance when renting vehicles. One should park in secured lots whenever possible, and should never leave valuables in the vehicle. The U.S. Embassy receives reports daily of valuables, identity documents, and other items stolen from locked vehicles. In many of these cases, the stolen items were hidden under the seat, in the glove compartment, or secured in the trunk. Thefts from parked cars commonly occur in downtown San Jose, at beaches, in the airport and bus station parking lots, and at national parks and other tourist attractions.

Money changers on the street have been known to pass off counterfeit U.S. dollars and local currency. Credit card fraud (either using stolen credit cards or the account number alone following copying of the number) is on the rise. Travelers should retain all their credit card receipts and check their accounts regularly to help prevent unauthorized use of their credit cards. Avoid using debit cards for point-of-sale purchases, as a skimmed number can be used to clean out an account.

The loss or theft abroad of a U.S. passport should be reported immediately to the local police and to the Consular Section of the U.S. Embassy. If the police will not accept the report, as sometimes happens when only the passport is stolen, the traveler should in any case report the theft to the U.S. Embassy to help avoid use by criminals or other identity theft.

U.S. citizens can refer to the Department of State's pamphlet, A Safe Trip Abroad, for ways to promote trouble-free travel. The pamphlet is available by mail from the Superintendent of Documents, U.S. Government Printing Office, Washington, D.C. 20402; via the Internet at http://www.gpoaccess.gov/, or via the Bureau of Consular Affairs home page at http://travel.state.gov.

ASSISTANCE TO VICTIMS OF CRIME: Persons, who are victims of crime while overseas, in addition to reporting to local police, should contact the nearest U.S. Embassy or Consulate for assistance. The Embassy/Consulate staff can help crime victims find appropriate medical care and contact family members or friends. They can also explain how to transfer funds from the U.S. Although the investigation and prosecution of the crime is solely the responsibility of local authorities, consular officers can help a victim of crime to understand the local criminal justice process and to find an attorney if needed.

Costa Rica has a 911 system for reporting emergencies. Crimes that are no longer in progress should be reported in person at the nearest police station. In the event of a traffic accident, vehicles must be left where they are, and not moved out of the way. Both the Transito (Traffic Police) and the Insurance Investigator must make accident reports before the vehicles are moved. Although sometimes slow to respond after notification, these officials will come to the accident scene.

MEDICAL FACILITIES: Medical care in San Jose is adequate, but may be more limited in areas outside of San Jose. Doctors and hospitals often expect immediate cash payment for health services, and U.S. medical insurance is not always valid outside the United States. A list of local doctors and medical facilities can be found at the website of the U.S. Embassy in San Jose, at http://usembassy.or.cr. An ambulance may be summoned by calling 911. The best equipped ambulances are called "unidad avanzada."

MEDICAL INSURANCE: The Department of State strongly urges Americans to consult with their medical insurance company prior to traveling abroad to confirm whether their policy applies overseas and whether it will cover emergency expenses such as medical evacuation. U.S. medical insurance plans seldom cover health costs incurred outside the United States unless supplemental coverage is purchased. Further, U.S. Medicare and Medicaid programs do not provide payment for medical services outside the United States. However, many travel agents and private companies offer insurance plans that will cover health care expenses incurred overseas, including emergency services such as medical evacuation.

When making a decision regarding health insurance, Americans should consider that many foreign doctors and hospitals require payment in cash prior to providing service, and that a medical evacuation to the U.S. may cost well in excess of $50,000. Uninsured travelers who require medical care overseas often face extreme difficulties. When consulting with an insurer prior to a trip, ascertain whether payment will be made to the overseas healthcare provider or whether the traveler is reimbursed later for expenses incurred. Some insurance policies also include coverage for psychiatric treatment and for disposition of remains in the event of death.

Useful information on medical emergencies abroad, including overseas insurance programs, is provided in the Department of State's Bureau of Consular Affairs brochure, Medical Information for Americans Traveling Abroad, available via the Bureau of Consular Affairs home page.

OTHER HEALTH INFORMATION: Information on vaccinations and other health precautions, such as safe food and water precautions and insect bite protection, may be obtained from the Centers for Disease Control and Prevention's hotline for international travelers at 1-877-FYI-TRIP (1-877-394-8747) or via the CDC's Internet site at http://www.cdc.gov/travel. Incidents of dengue fever and malaria are rising in Costa Rica. For information about this and about outbreaks of infectious diseases abroad, consult the World Health Organization's website at http://www.who.int/en. Further health information for travelers is available at http://www.who.int/ith.

TRAFFIC SAFETY AND ROAD CONDITIONS: While in a foreign country, U.S. citizens may encounter road conditions that differ significantly from those in the United States. The information below concerning Costa Rica is provided for general reference only, and it may not be totally accurate in a particular location or circumstance.

Costa Rica has one of the highest vehicle accident rates in the world. Even the most experienced drivers are challenged by the disregard for traffic laws and driving safety. Traffic laws and speed limits are often ignored; turns across one or two lanes of traffic are common, and pedestrians are not given the right of way. Although improving, roads are often in poor condition, and large potholes with the potential to cause significant damage to vehicles are common. Pedestrians, cyclists, and farm animals may use the main roads. Traffic signs, even on major highways, are often inadequate. All of the above, in addition to poor visibility because of heavy fog or rain, makes driving at night especially treacherous. In the rainy season, landslides are common, especially on the highway between San Jose and the Caribbean city of Limon. All types of motor vehicles are appropriate for the main highways and principal roads in the major cities. However, some roads to beaches and other rural locations are not paved, and some out-of-the-way destinations are accessible only with high clearance, rugged suspension four-wheel drive vehicles. Travelers are advised to call ahead to their hotels to ask about the current status of access roads.

Travelers should avoid responding in kind to provocative driving behavior or road-rage. In case of an accident, travelers are advised to remain in their car until police arrive. Travelers are further advised to keep all doors locked and to drive to a well-populated area before stopping to change a flat tire (see "Crime," above).

Costa Rican law requires that drivers and passengers wear seatbelts in all cars, including taxis, and police are authorized to issue tickets. Traffic enforcement in Costa Rica is the responsibility of the Transit Police ("Transitos"), who are distinguished by a light blue uniform shirt and dark blue trousers. They use light blue cars or motorcycles equipped with blue lights. They often wave vehicles to the side of the road for inspection. Drivers are commonly asked to produce a driver's license, vehicle registration and insurance information. Third-party coverage is mandatory in Costa Rica. Infractions will result in the issuance of a summons. Fines are not supposed to be collected on the spot, although reports of officers attempting to collect money are common. Persons involved in vehicular accidents are advised not to move their vehicle until instructed to do so by a Transit Officer, who will respond to the scene together with a representative of the National Insurance Company (known by its local acronym, INS.) Accidents may be reported by dialing 911.

For additional general information about road safety, including links to foreign government sites, see the Department of State, Bureau of Consular Affairs home page at http://travel.state.gov/travel/tips/safety/safety_1179.html.

AVIATION SAFETY OVERSIGHT: The U.S. Federal Aviation Administration (FAA) has assessed the Government of Costa Rica's civil aviation authority as Category 1 - in compliance with international aviation safety standards for oversight of Costa Rica's air carrier operations. For further information, travelers may contact the Department of Transportation within the U.S. at 1-800-322-7873, or visit the FAA's Internet website at http://www.faa.gov/avr/iasa/index.cfm.

Since 2000, several American citizens have died in domestic air accidents. Local investigations have judged pilot error to be the cause in the majority of the accidents. Private air taxi services have been involved in a disproportionate number of crashes. The Government of Costa Rica's civil aviation authority has responded by dedicating additional resources to the oversight of the pilots, procedures, and aircraft of air taxi operators.

CUSTOMS REGULATIONS: Costa Rica customs authorities may enforce strict regulations concerning temporary importation into or export from Costa Rica of items such as cars, household effects, and merchandise. These regulations can be quite complicated and include the application of local tax laws. In addition, Costa Rican customs officials often require documentation that has been certified by the Costa Rican Embassy/Consulate in the country of origin. This is especially true for automobiles that are to be imported. The Government of Costa Rica has instituted strict emissions requirements for these cars and will not release them without an emissions statement from the country of origin. It is advisable to contact the Embassy of Costa Rica in Washington or one of Costa Rica's Consulates in the United States for specific information regarding customs requirements before shipping any items. Their website is located at http://www.costarica-embassy.org.

In many countries around the world, counterfeit and pirated goods are widely available. Transactions involving such products are illegal and bringing them back to the United States may result in forfeitures and/or fines. A current list of those countries with serious problems in this regard can be found at
http://www.ustr.gov/Document_Library/Reports_Publications/2005/2005_Special_301/Section_Index.html.

CRIMINAL PENALTIES: While in a foreign country, a U.S. citizen is subject to that country's laws and regulations, which sometimes differ significantly from those in the United States, and may not afford the protections available to the individual under U.S. law. Penalties for breaking the law can be more severe than in the United States for similar offenses. Persons violating Costa Rican law, even unknowingly, may be arrested, imprisoned, fined and/or expelled.

Soliciting the services of a minor for sexual purposes is illegal in Costa Rica, and is punishable by imprisonment. The Costa Rican government has established an aggressive program to discourage sexual tourism and to punish severely those who engage in sexual activity with minors. Several U.S. citizens are serving long sentences in Costa Rica following conviction of crimes related to sexual activity with minors. These acts are also illegal under U.S. law, even if the act takes place abroad.

Under the PROTECT Act of April 2003, it is a crime, prosecutable in the United States, for a U.S. citizen or permanent resident alien, to engage in illicit sexual conduct in a foreign country with a person under the age of 18, whether or not the U.S. citizen or lawful permanent resident alien intended to engage in such illicit sexual conduct prior to going abroad. For purposes of the PROTECT Act, illicit sexual conduct includes any commercial sex act in a foreign country with a person under the age of 18. The law defines a commercial sex act as any sex act, on account of which anything of value is given to or received by a person under the age of 18.

Under the Protection of Children from Sexual Predators Act of 1998, it is a crime to use the mail or any facility of interstate or foreign commerce, including the Internet, to transmit information about a minor under the age of 16 for criminal sexual purposes that include, among other things, the production of child pornography. This same law makes it a crime to use any facility of interstate or foreign commerce, including the Internet, to transport obscene materials to minors under the age of 16.

Penalties for possession, use, or trafficking in illegal drugs in Costa Rica are strict, and convicted offenders can expect lengthy jail sentences and fines. In addition to the criminal penalties they may face, tourists who purchase or sell illegal drugs or use the services of prostitutes greatly increase their risk of personal harm. Several Americans have died in Costa Rica in recent years in incidents related to drug use or patronage of prostitutes.

Under Costa Rican law, suspects in criminal cases may be held in jail until the investigation is completed and the prosecutor is ready to proceed to trial. This pretrial detention can last two years, and in some cases, longer.

SPECIAL ISSUES:

Borders: There have been disagreements regarding navigational rights in the Nicaragua-Costa Rica border area. Nicaragua and Costa Rica signed a three-year agreement in September of 2002 to defer presenting these issues before the International Court of Justice (ICJ) for resolution. Meanwhile, the governments of Nicaragua and Costa Rica have agreed to work towards an amicable solution and to jointly fund community development projects in the border area.

Land Ownership, Expropriations, Squatters, Shoreline Property: U.S. citizens are urged to use caution when making real estate purchases, and should consult reputable legal counsel and investigate thoroughly all aspects before entering into a contract.

Irregular Land Registrations: Due to irregular enforcement of property laws, investors should exercise extreme caution before investing in real estate. There is a long history of investment and real estate scams and frauds perpetrated against U.S. citizens and other international visitors. There have been numerous instances of duly registered properties reverting to previously unknown owners who have shown they possess clear title and parallel registration.

Expropriations: A few cases remain in which U.S. citizens have yet to be compensated for land expropriated by the government in the 1970s or 1980s. Unexecuted expropriation claims cloud title in other cases. However, changes to Costa Rican law in 1995 place more restrictions on the government's ability to expropriate land and require compensation prior to expropriation. The new law also provides for arbitration in the event of a dispute.

Squatters: Organized squatter groups have on occasion invaded properties in various parts of the country. These squatter groups, often supported by politically active persons and non-governmental organizations, take advantage of legal provisions that allow people without land to gain title to unused agricultural property. This phenomenon is particularly common in rural areas, where local courts show considerable sympathy for the squatters. Victims of squatters have reported threats of violence, harassment, or actual violence.

Restrictions on Shoreline Property: The Maritime Terrestrial Zone Law governs the use and ownership of most land up to 200 meters from the waterfront (mean high tide level) on both coasts of Costa Rica, including estuaries and river mouths. The first 50 meters from the waterfront is public land and normally may not be developed. The next 150 meters can be privately developed and occupied under five-to-twenty year concessions from the local municipality, provided the land has been zoned for the intended use. Strict residency requirements apply to foreigners who seek concessions.

Investments and Loans: Persons planning to make investments in Costa Rica are advised to exercise the same caution they would before making investments in the U.S., including consulting their investment advisor and tax accountant. Several U.S. citizens have lost appreciable amounts of money in local investment or lending schemes that "sounded too good to be true." Some of these are believed to have been "Ponzi" schemes with few or no assets behind the "investment" or "loan." Persons offered an investment opportunity in Costa Rica promising interest above that generally available may wish to check with the Costa Rican government's Superintendencia General de Valores, which lists investment opportunities that are legally registered and authorized to offer investments. That office can be contacted at (506) 243-4700 or http://www.sugeval.fi.cr

Lottery and Sweepstake fraud schemes: The Embassy has received several complaints from U.S. citizens in the United States who said they were victims of sweepstake or lottery fraud originating in Costa Rica. In these schemes, the victims are contacted by criminals (who may even claim to be employees of the U.S. Embassy) advising them that they have won a lottery or sweepstake, but that they must provide personal funds to secure the winnings or to pay local taxes or administrative costs.

DISASTER PREPAREDNESS: Costa Rica is located in an earthquake, hurricane and volcanic zone. Costa Rica is also a country of microclimates and travelers to Costa Rica should check the projected rainfall amounts for the area in Costa Rica they intend to visit. Serious flooding occurs annually on the Caribbean side near the port city of Limon, but flooding could occur in other parts of Costa Rica as well, depending on the time of year and projected rainfall in that region. General information about natural disaster preparedness is available via the Internet from the U.S. Federal Emergency Management Agency (FEMA) at http://www.fema.gov/.

CHILDREN'S ISSUES: For information on international adoption of children and international parental child abduction, please refer to the Department of State's Internet site at http://travel.state.gov/family/family_1732.html or telephone Overseas Citizens Services at 1-888-407-4747. This number is available from 8:00 a.m. to 8:00 p.m. Eastern Time, Monday through Friday (except U.S. federal holidays). Callers who are unable to use toll-free numbers, such as those calling from overseas, may obtain information and assistance during these hours by calling 1-202-501-4444.

REGISTRATION / EMBASSY LOCATION: The Department of State invites American citizens to register their travel on the Internet-Based Registration System (IBRS) on line at: https://travelregistration.state.gov/ibrs/ or http://travel.state.gov. IBRS provides a convenient means for American citizens traveling or residing overseas to provide important contact data, useful in the event of emergencies, and to instantly receive up-to-the-minute travel and safety information for the regions or countries on their travel itineraries, on the website or through optional email lists. Even American citizens who have registered previously but did not do it using the IBRS online program may now wish to register online to update their records. U.S. citizens may also register in person at the Embassy, which is located in Pavas, San Jose, and may be reached at (506) 519-2000; the extension for the Consular Section is 2453. The Embassy is open Monday through Friday, and is closed on Costa Rican and U.S. holidays. For emergencies arising outside normal business hours, U.S. citizens may call (506) 220-3127 and ask for the duty officer.

Guanacaste and the Northwest

Guanacaste is home to two of the best waves in Costa Rica, Ollie's Point and Witches Rock. They are also two of the most difficult to reach. There are no hotels anywhere nearby, and after taking the trouble to reach them you will likely find them crowded, especially Ollie's. But you'll never have the complete Costa Rica surf experience without surfing these spots. In fact, Witches ranks as one of the best beach breaks in the world, and Ollie's one of the funnest points. So you gotta go.

Portrero Grande (Ollie's Point)

Incredible and famous right point at a rivermouth with fast, fun and semi-hollow waves that wrap down the cove forever. One of the best rights in Costa Rica, or anywhere for that matter. Best on low to mid tide, but that depends on the sand situation. With enough sand it can stay good on higher tides. There are a few rocks at the main take-off spot, otherwise there are no hazards. (Well, there are some sting rays near the beach and croc's in the rivermouth, but since you'll arrive by boat you may never get that far.) For a good look at this wave rent *Surfer* magazine's *South of the Border* video or *Endless Summer 2*. I hear the left point at the south end of the bay breaks, but I haven't seen it break and I've been to Ollie's when there's been solid swell. Takes any good southern hemi swell.

Getting There: The only way to get to Ollie's is by boat or seaplane as there are no roads in. You can rent a boat from Playas del Coco (from San José about 270km or a 4-5 hour drive) or Playa Ocotal (a few kilometers down the road from Playas del Coco), or hook up with one of the guided trips from experienced outfits like Witches Rock Surf Camp, The Giuseppina and others. (More on those two below and later in the book.) The hike in is humanly possible, as is anything else, but not recommended. If you do figure out how to get in you'll find that there's nothing there once you get there, no facilities of any kind (except those you'll see floating offshore in the way of boats). To reserve a boat out of Playas del Coco call Papagayo Sport Fishing (tel. 506-670-0374, fax 506-670-0446) or Sea Raven Boats (506-670-0840 or 506-382-8405). You can also head down to the dock at Playas del Coco and ask around for Gerardo or Wilbert (one of my favorite captains—he surfs). Another plan is to stay at the El Ocotal Beach Resort where they have two 32' twin diesel boats that carry up to six. The cost for a boat is higher than in Coco—$325 for six hours—but the boats are faster and plusher than most others. Shop and you will find cheaper boats. Trips typically start at about $200 for a boatload of surfers for a day, which is eight hours. The cheaper the fare, the less you get, like a smaller boat that beats you up in the wind chop and no food or beverages. Some trips include lunch, sodas and beer. Be sure to plan your boat in advance; it's not a last-minute deal. The boats leave between 6:00AM and 8:00AM, so get set up the day before (or sooner) to be sure. If you don't want to hassle finding a boat yourself, most of the hotels in Playas del Coco or Tamarindo or seemingly anywhere in Guanacaste will set you up. Everyone seems to know someone who will get you to Ollie's and Witches.

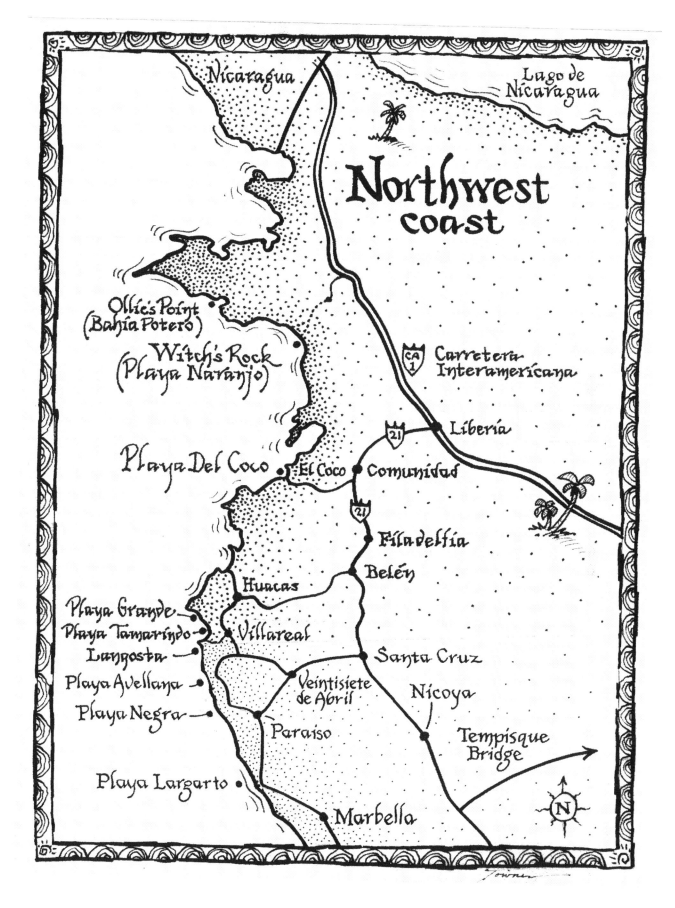

Playa Naranjo (Witches Rock)

"Even when it sucks it's good," is the way one surf traveler describes it. Well, not really. But the experience of being there is nearly as awesome as the surf, which can be truly awesome. If you don't believe it, rent *Endless Summer 2*.

Playa Naranjo is a 2-3 mile stretch of beach with hollow sand-bottom beach-breaks throughout, but the best are in front of the quite obvious Witches Rock (Peña Bruja). Witches Rock is where an estuary meets the ocean creating sandbars. The fast hollow lefts and rights that make Witches famous are perfected by offshores, which come December to April and can get very strong. The offshores blow the warm surface water out to sea and cause a bit of upwelling, so the water can get a little chilly here, at least for Costa Rica, so you might bring your spring suit or short john just in case. I've been there when the water dipped into the high sixties, or at least it felt it. While it doesn't get big often, it can get very big. I've seen 15-20' faces (I didn't get off the boat), and heard of it getting even bigger. And when it gets big, it pounds hard. Best on WSW swells and upcoming mid to high tides. It walls up on low tide.

Have you heard about "Shredder?" As the story goes, he's a 14-foot crocodile who lives in the estuary and occasionally paddles out into the line up just to stir things up. I haven't heard of any attacks, and I've never actually seen him, but just thinking he may be there gives me the willies. He may be a rumor to keep the crowds down.

Getting There: Witches is in the Santa Rosa National Park (entrance fee $6). If you drive in the rainy season (May through October), it's accessible only by 4x4. Even in the dry season I can't see getting in (and out) without 4-wheel drive. If you are staying in Tamarindo, it's a 150-mile round trip. I suggest you go by boat; it's the primo ticket. See "Getting There" for Ollie's Point (above) for boat options, or look into the Witches Rock Surf Camp (see "Where to Stay").

Tales abound of surfers stranded in their attempts to drive in or out. It's a difficult 12km drive (once in the park) followed by a 20 to 30-minute hike which, depending on the tide, may include a paddle across the estuary (keeping eyes peeled for croc's). And it's hot as hell. If you drive in during the dry season, you can drive all the way into the camping area only during low tide because you have to cross the estuary at least twice. Then, depending on the sandbars, Witches typically closes out at low tide, so after driving in at low tide you'll have to wait for high to surf. Then wait for low to get out. At least that's the routine some years.

Another option is to take a 4x4 taxi from Liberia for about $40 each way. Then there's Rica Roadtrips (506-653-0874). They specialize in drive-in and camping trips to Witches (and other spots around Tamarindo). You can find them in Tamarindo across from Mamma Mia's and nearby Tamarindo Adventures.

At the park entrance you can get a decent map of the park. Keep in mind that the mosquitoes are bad at night and you are a long way from the things you'll need. So if you are camping, go totally prepared, since there is no place to buy anything. Do not forget a mosquito net, and bring lots of water.

If you decide to drive in or camp, know that as remote as this place is there are still thieves. Don't leave anything valuable in your car and find other campers to help watch your stuff. Here's a good one…. I met a German surfer (yes, German) at the campground who had his trunks and a t-shirt stolen a few days earlier. The day following the crime, he ran into a Tico on the beach wearing his stolen duds. The German made the Tico give him his trunks and t-shirt back right then and there, leaving our thieving Tico to walk home naked. Wiener burn.

Where to Stay for Ollie's Point and Witches Rock

For the most part, you don't "stay" around here unless you camp. You can stay in Playas del Coco—a busy fishing port and popular destination for middle-class Ticos—or Ocotal, just like for Ollie's. Surfer Kerry Douglas of Sheffield, Massachusetts recommends staying at Rancho Armadillo. It is on a hillside a little out of town overlooking Playas del Cocos. As Kerry puts it, "The manager, Juan Carlos, is a sweet guy who will cook great stuff for you and do anything to make you happy—go there!" Or as previously mentioned, you can stay in Liberia or one of many inland towns and take a taxi to the surf.

Probably the best way to get the full-on Witches/Ollie's experience is to hook up with the Witch's Rock Surf Camp. Consider this: father/son team PK and Joe Walsh packed up and moved their lives down to Costa Rica for one reason, to surf Witches. Their story is an inspiration to any surfer who has considered that maybe, just maybe slaving your life away for someone else so you can squeeze in the occasional surf at the local break full of angry poseurs just isn't the way to spend your one and only life.

Their story starts in San Diego, California, where they bought a school bus, turned it into a motorhome, sold everything, and hit the road to Costa Rica with the goal of finding a way to surf Witches Rock every day of the year. They made the most of the trip, surfing the whole way to their destination of Playas del Coco, where they opened the Global Headquarters of WRSC. The Tamarindo operation followed shortly thereafter. Today, PK and Joe have a finely tuned operation that makes sure everything you never thought of is covered.

You can choose to either just hook up for a boat trip, or plan your whole vacation around the WRSC, with seven and nine day "Surfer Specials." For example, if you go for the "9 Day WRSC Surfer Special" you get lodging at the surf camp on the beach in Tamarindo (private bath, hot water, air conditioning); guided surf tours to local breaks (Negra, Avellanes, Marbella, Langosta, Playa Grande); and <u>four</u> trips to Witches and Ollie's. Breakfast is included, and lunches are provided on the boat trips. Like I said, everything is covered. They even have a back-up boat in case yours breaks down. (It happens.) They never send more than two boats out, which helps keep the crowds down. It's great for a group of surfers who just want to surf and surf and surf and surf. And perhaps have a beer or three to wash down "nachos as big as your head." If you are a beginner, you're covered too, as the WRSC surf school gives lessons for beginners and intermediate surfers alike. The lessons are held right in front of WRSC in the forgiving beach breaks of Tamarindo. The instructors are all well-experienced and are trained in CPR.

Another place to "stay" is on a boat, specifically, the previously mentioned Giuseppina—a 48 foot trawler-like yacht powered by two 135 HP Cummins turbo diesels that give it a cruising speed of about 10 to 12 knots. It has three staterooms to sleep six and is outfitted with a kitchen, bathroom and other amenities. They will go out for one day excursions, but the better plan is to go for at least one overnight stay right there at Witches, or Ollies if you like. They also do snorkeling, fishing and other tours, but you should just check in with Jeff or Fay to get the rest of the story (506-305-1584). Rates start at $800/day, including food, and go up from there.

Lodging Name	Rates High	Rates Low	A/C	Priv Bath	Hot H2O	Facilities	Comments
Coco (El) Cabinas $ Playas del Coco tel. 506-670-0110		$20s $30d	Not all	All	No	Restaurant	Office in Coco Mar Restaurant. A/C$. On the beach. Boat tours.
Coco Palms Hotel $ Playas del Coco tel. 506-672-0367		$70d	Yes	All	Yes	Restaurant Bar Pool Satellite TV	DC, MC, V. Tours. Bargain. One block from Coco Beach.
Flor (La) de Itabo Hotel $$ Playas del Coco tel. 506-670-0438 www.flordeitabo.com	$45-75s/d $85t $95-140q $120-160six	$45-75s/d $85t $95-140q $120-160six	Most	Yes	Yes	Restaurant Bar Pool Casino Volleyball	AE, DC, MC, V. Luxurious. TVs in rooms. Has a children's play area. Apartments have kitchens but no a/c. Sportfishing trips (maybe to surf?), rents bikes, tours.
Luna Tica Hotel $ Playas del Coco tel. 506-670-0127, 506-670-1106		$18s $22d $30t $38q	Fans	Yes	No	Restaurant Bar	Credit Cards. Includes breakfast. On the beach. Surf trips and fishing tours. Rents cars. Popular restaurant.
Ocotal (El) Beach Resort and Marina $$$ Playas del Coco tel. 506-670-0321 www.ocotalresort.com	$85s $97d $135t $180 bung	$70s $80d $120t $150 bung	Yes	Yes	Yes	Restaurant Bar Pools Dive shop Tennis Gym Jacuzzi	AE, DC, MC, V. Surf trips to Witches and Ollie's. Beautiful, luxurious, on the bluff with great views. Mainly patronized by rich fishermen and SCUBA divers. Satellite TVs, telephones, coffee makers and refrigerators in rooms. Meal plans available. Room service. Some rooms have jacuzzis. Rents cars, fishing charters, tours.
Pato Loco Inn $ Tel. 506-670-0145 www.costa-rica-beach-hotels-patoloco.com	$45-$55s $45-$55d $60-$70t	$35-$45s $35-$45d $45-$55t	Not all	All	All	Restaurant	No credit cards. $A/C. Boutique hotel away from the nightlife about ½ mile from the beach.
Rancho Armadillo Lodge $$ Playas del Coco tel. 817-483-2028, 506-670-0108 www.ranchoarmadillo.com	$80s $90-127d $127t	$65s $75-106d $106t	Yes	Yes	Yes	Restaurant Bar Pool Satellite TV	Private estate farm. Rates include three meals daily and beverages including alcohol. Boat to Witches Rock. Diving and tours. Satellite TV in rooms. A mile from town.
Witches Rock Surf Camp $$$ Tamarindo Tel. 506-653-0078, 506-653-0239 www.witchsrocksurfcamp.com	$1615s $1120pp/d $940pp/t one week packages	$1290s $895pp/d $790pp/t one week packages	Yes	Yes	Yes	Restaurant Bar	The hot ticket. <u>Highly recommended</u>. Boat trips to Witches and Ollie's, other guided surf tours, snorkeling and other fun, breakfast and lunches all included. Surf school packages for beginners through "established" surfers. A good deal!

Bahía Tamarindo

The beach resort of Tamarindo (including Playa Grande) is the unofficial surfing capital of Costa Rica. Well, Jacó really is, but Tamarindo is close. As a resort, Tamarindo offers much to do between surf sessions or when it's flat. If you want to see people on your trip, go here.

Surfers staying in the town of Tamarindo seem to follow the same surf schedule: Get up late, surf outside of town in the morning (e.g. Playa Grande, Avellanes, Negra.), wander about town, surf in town in the evening. As a result, the late afternoon/evening go-outs are usually very crowded, especially with locals who can get a good attitude going for the occasion, and the kooks from the surf schools.

A problem with this whole area is that there's not much in the way of low tide surf spots. Some of the reefs break on low tides, but they get sketchy, so you need to be a good surfer or know the reef well. And the beach breaks wall up, even with offshores. Any way you look at it, low tide can be frustrating.

Playa Grande

North of Tamarindo, but in the same bay on the same long stretch of beach and better exposed to south swells. One of the best beach breaks in Costa Rica, especially with good winter offshore winds, Playa Grande is known for its barrels. Like most beach breaks, it's fickle, depending on tides, swell direction and sandbars, but it is one of the most consistent waves in Costa Rica and does get big and powerful. And like most beach breaks that get big and powerful, Playa Grande is also the site of frequent tourist drownings. So you should be a good swimmer and surfer if you decide to paddle out here on anything but the smaller days.

Playa Grande is accessible from Tamarindo by either driving back toward Villareal and turning north toward Huacas, then back toward Matapalo and the beach, or by taking a long paddle and hike. To hike you need to first cross the estuary that borders Tamarindo to the north. It usually is worth taking the time to go to Playa Grande because it's almost always bigger than Tamarindo, especially on south swells that pass Tamarindo by, and less crowded if you stay away from the main peak. Playa Grande is nice in the winter with the offshores to groom those hollow peaks as it blows out early, often and easily. Breaks best on higher tides. The best peaks are just south of the Las Tortugas Hotel.

If you find Grande to your liking and think you want to buy some real estate there look up Tom Battaglia from Century 21 Coastal Estates (506-653-0400, tom@c21tamarindo.com). Tom's a Malibu transplant who knows the ins and outs of buying real estate here, and there are lots of them. He used to work out of the Tamarindo office, but he sold everything worth buying there so he's moved on to Playa Grande. His office is right there at the main break.

Where to Stay for Playa Grande

Rather than traveling in and out from Tamarindo, there are now a host of options at Playa Grande. The oldest and best known hotel is right on the beach: the aging Hotel Las Tortugas, which is also the closest hotel to the surf. But for the price it has become a bit rundown, and the hospitality leaves a bit to be desired, especially if your room's ceiling leaks. The restaurant is also rather expensive relative to the rest of Costa Rica. At Las Tortugas you will find other surfers looking for a more peaceful experience along with turtle-lovers and other "ecoids," since this is a world-famous nesting area. (Apparently, turtles like beach breaks.) A better option is the RipJack Inn, formerly El Bucanero. It's just 75 meters from the beach, but nicer and less expensive all around than Las Tortugas. The nice thing about the Playa Grande area is that you can walk to the surf from any of the area's hotels, they're all that close, even those in Salinas.

Lodging Name	Rates High	Rates Low	A/C	Priv Bath	Hot H2O	Facilities	Comments
Cantarana Hotel $$ Playa Grande tel. 506-653-0486 fax 506-653-0491 www.hotelcantarana.com	$60-75s $85-100d	$50s $70d	All	All	All	Restaurant Bar Pool Boat-taxis Kayaks	Visa. Prices include breakfast or breakfast and dinner. It's a little farther from the beach than some of the other options, but still in walking distance and it's a very nice place—great for the family or wife/girlfriend. Right on the estuary.
Casa & Casitas Linda Vista $$ Tel. 530-477-0996 (US), 506-653-0474 www.tamarindo.com/kai/	$60d $130q $10pp extra	$60d $130q $10pp extra	Fans	All	All		3-acre estate on a hill overlooking Playa Grande with 3 fully furnished homes for rent. 500 yards from the beach. Secluded.
Ferrari's Surf Resort $$ Tel. 506-653-0682, 203-415-2989 (US) www.ferrarissurfresort.com	$50 and up per person, depends on package	$50 and up per person, depends on package	All	Not all	All	Recreation area	No credit cards. In town about a 15 minute walk to the beach. Private and shared rooms. Shared kitchen, too. Walk to Kike's Place and Horno de Lena pizza. Can get board rental or surf lessons as part of the package deal.
RipJack Inn $$ tel. 506-653-0480, 800-808-4605 US and Canada www.ripjackinn.com	$75d $10 per extra person	$55d $10 per extra person	All	All	All	Restaurant Bar Satellite TV in bar	Formerly El Bucanero. Rooms renovated in 2004. After Las Tortugas, this is the closest hotel to the main break. Coffee makers in rooms. Board rentals, surf lessons, yoga. Great sunset viewing happy hour.
Playa Grande Inn $$ Tel. 506-653-0719 www.playagrandeinn.com	$60-95	$40-85	All	All	All	Restaurant Bar Pool Conference room	Owned by pro surfer John Logan. Formerly Rancho Diablo. Walk to surf. Trips to Witches and Ollies. Travel agency on site. Satellite TV in bar.
Tortugas (Las) Hotel $$ tel./fax 506-653-0423 www.cool.co.cr/usr/turtles	$50-60s $70-95d $100-150q	$40s $45-55d $75-85q	All	All	All	Restaurant Bar Pool Jacuzzi	No credit cards. Right on beach at Playa Grande. Rents surfboards, boogie boards, bikes, canoes, horses. Tours. Rental cars arranged. Also ask about rental apartments and homes.

Villa Baula $$ tel. 506-653-0493 www.nicoya.com/ villabaula		$80 bung	Fans	Yes	All	Restaurant Pool Playground	Has an eco-tour focus. On the beach at the south end of Playa Grande, just across the estuary from Tamarindo at what locals call "Casitas." Kind of a long way from everything else. Big pool.

Tamarindo

If you know nothing at all about surfing in Costa Rica, start your trip in Tamarindo. While Jacó is a bigger, busier resort with more surfers and surf shops, Tamarindo is a great way to get your feet wet, especially if this is your first Central America trip. For starters, it's an easy surf trip, especially for beginners and families. There is a variety of breaks in walking distance from the wide selection of hotels, so you don't even need a car. Or if you decide you need to rent a car you can get one right there in town. There are a bunch of surf shops carrying a great selection of rental boards, so you don't even need to bring a board. Tamarindo is easy.

Tamarindo is also crowded and touristy, for Costa Rica, and growing all the time. It has its own web site (www.tamarindo.com), pizza delivery service (Pizzeria Casera—653-0009) and even a Burger King. For the most part the growth has been managed well by the local businesspeople and residents, but at times it seems it's gotten out of hand.

There are more surf shops in Tamarindo than Malibu. They're constantly popping up and moving around, so it's difficult to stay current, but here's the basic lowdown. The oldest and probably best known is **Iguana Surf**. The original Iguana Surf is up on the road to Langosta. A newer annex is across the road from the main beach. If you need a board to rent or buy—longboard, shortboard or softboard—their selection is pretty good. They rent by the hour, day or week, as do many of the other surf shops. They also rent bicycles, videos, sun umbrellas, tents, racks, kayaks, arrange estuary tours and even boat taxi services to the breaks that may have be unreachable due to muddy roads, like Avellanes or Playa Negra. In between all those activities you can also log on to the Internet or check e-mail. They bill Iguana Surf as having "Everything you need to enjoy your stay," and they do a pretty good job. Heck, they'll even pull your car out of a ditch if you are stupid enough to back into one (thanks guys!).

You'll see **Tamarindo Adventures** on the road to Iguana Surf. You can't miss it. It has a two story surfboard for a sign. It's probably the biggest and best-stocked surf shop in Costa Rica. Right across the road from Tamarindo Adventures is Blue Trailz, which opened in 2003. This shop has a great selection of high quality boards to rent, and underscoring the international nature of Tamarindo, Blue Trailz is owned by a Belgian couple, Wim and Marjan. And don't miss the Robert August shop at the Tamarindo Vista Villas. Here you can rent epoxy Robert August longboards, like the Wingnut model and RA's signature "What I ride." It's small, but has most of what you need, and it's the closest walk to the rivermouth surf.

There are probably a dozen broadband **Internet** cafés in town. @Internet has been there the longest. It's in the little strip mall on the left just as you turn to go up the hill toward Langosta. But you really don't have to search for an internet café; they're everywhere.

Tamarindo is big enough to have medical services, which you'll find at the "Medico" in town. See Appendix for emergency phone numbers.

Getting there: To drive to Tamarindo from the San José area, take the Interamerican Highway north and look for the sign for the Tempisque Bridge. After crossing the bridge follow the signs to Nicoya, Santa Cruz, 27 de Abril, then Tamarindo. This route includes some dirt road driving on the stretch between 27 de Abril and Villareal. You can avoid that by continuing north from Santa Cruz to Belén and hanging a left. It's an easy drive with lots of signs. You can do it in about four to five hours, depending on traffic and stops.

There's also an airstrip two miles outside of town with daily service from San José (45-minute flight) by SANSA and Travelair, and even direct flights on Delta. Private charter services are available too. And there's an international airport in Liberia, a 45-minute drive, which now has regular service from Miami and Atlanta.

Tamarindo Rivermouth (El Estero)

This is the first break as you drive into town, accessible from anywhere in Tamarindo, but most directly via the trail across from El Milagro. Best on upcoming medium tide and a strong northwest or combo swell, but it's good on souths too. Rights and lefts. The rights peel from outside the rivermouth just off the reef and get fast and hollow, especially with winter offshores. The lefts go into the rivermouth from the south, fast and hollow, too. But it all depends on the sand bars, of course, and they're good four out of five years.

Given its proximity to the hotels of Tamarindo, the rivermouth can get very crowded. But sometimes you can get it to yourself because everyone else is at Playa Grande, other spots or sleeping in.

Tamarindo Beach Break

Pretty typical beach break. Can be great, and often crowded, especially in the evenings when the locals and surf schools come out, but you can find the occasional peak to yourself. On the other hand, it sure is convenient if you're staying in Tamarindo. Like all of Tamarindo, it doesn't break when the swell is small and the tide is high. Best on mid-tide. Best waves are just north of Hotel Doly.

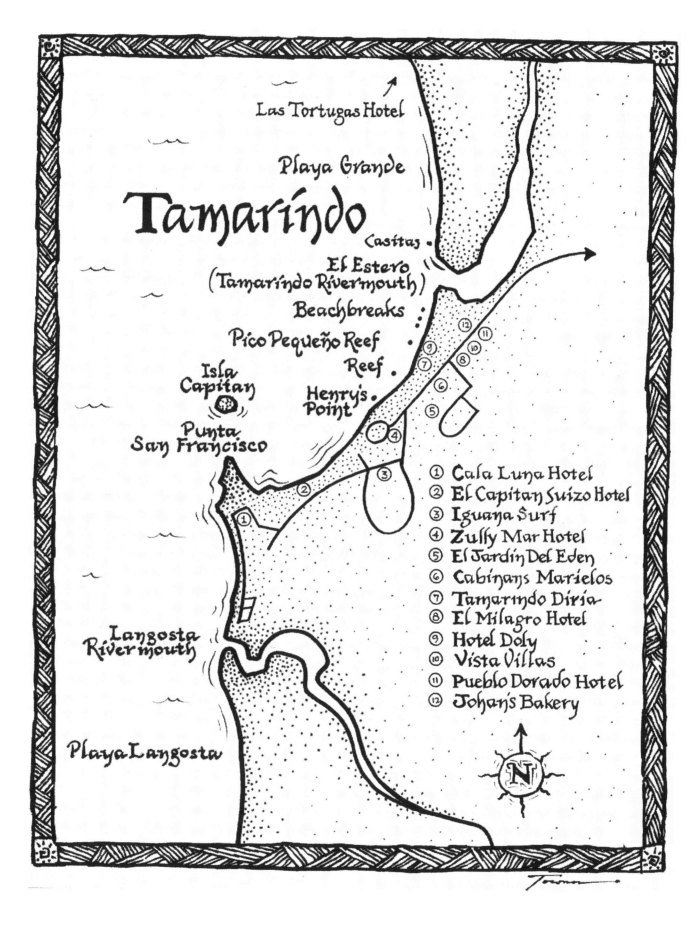

Pico Pequeño

Directly in front of the Tamarindo Diría sits a small, lava finger reef. Off that reef breaks a beautiful right that ranges from mushy to howling tubey, depending on the swell and tide. Works best on mid-tide and it does need some swell. Low tide gets sketchy because it gets too shallow, and it's a lava rock bottom. It does not handle a crowd well, and there's always a crowd. But if you stay at the Diría, or the Hotel Doly next door to the north, you can watch it while having a beer and catch it just right—tide and crowd.

Henry's Point

Rocky lava reef in front of the Zully Mar Restaurant. Mediocre at best.

Isla Capitán

Talk about perfect offshore reef barrels… Everyone who has ever come to Tamarindo has gazed at the lefts breaking off the north side of the little deserted island out in Tamarindo Bay, and wondered why no one surfs it. Get to the right vantage point and you'll see rights breaking off the south side of the island, too, but the lefts are much better. Just hop in a boat or paddle 20 to 30 minutes from the beach in front of Casa Cook's and Capitán Suizo. If you stay at Cala Luna or Sueño del Mar Bed & Breakfast the paddle is way shorter as they are out near the point. Breaks best at higher tides. Something else cool about Isla Capitán: At low tide the rights and lefts wrap around the island and break over a little reef into each other like clapping hands. And you can ride these waves into each other. Do it for fun on a low tide blown out afternoon.

More Tamarindo

Tamarindo, just like the rest of Guanacaste, has outside reefs that break regularly, but no one ever surfs them. There are also a few of places to surf in between Tamarindo and Langosta. They are all a bit spooky. It's very rocky there as the whole area is one big lava reef. You'll probably watch some great lefts peel off the point at the south end of Bahía Tamarindo, but the lava reef situation is too hairy for most.

Playa Langosta

A left and right at the rivermouth, and a longer left on the reef outside. When it gets big it breaks way outside and can get scary. It also gets sketchy on low tide. Again, it's the lava reef. Mid-tide is best. It's a personal thing, because my brother Roger loves the place, as do others (although it's rarely crowded). Crocodiles have been spotted in the line-up from time to time. Across the river are the Langosta beach breaks, which can get great. Also across the river is a right called La Piedra del Zapo.

Alas, Langosta ain't what it used to be. There are now hotels, bed and breakfasts and condos right there—including the disgusting Barceló, a monstrosity built by a Spanish hotel corporation that, if left to its own will destroy every beach in the world. What was once one of the greatest rivermouth beaches anywhere is now just a big, sandy playground for pasty tourists. It sucks.

Getting There: 2-3km south of Tamarindo. It's a long walk around the point at the south end of Tamarindo Bay, or a short drive out of town, although "town" is getting closer to Langosta every day. By car, head toward then past the Cala Luna and Villa Allegre until you see the public beach sign (Sol y Playa) which is now the official Langosta parking lot. If you keep going, please just plow your car into the Barceló Hotel lobby.

Where to Stay Around Tamarindo

Where do you start? Tamarindo grows so fast you can't keep up with it. There are a number of great places for a surfer to stay comfortably or cheaply in Tamarindo itself. And if you want to style it, Tamarindo probably has more upscale hotels than any other resort in Costa Rica. So here are a few options, starting with one of the best surf "camps" anywhere.

The Witches Rock Surf Camp was mentioned earlier in the Witches section. But since it's really in Tamarindo it's appropriate to reintroduce it. First, however, let's clear something up. WRSC is no "camp." And while I wouldn't call it a resort either, no one roughs it here. For the full story on WRSC go back to the Witches section. Here I'll just say I think WRSC is a great choice for Tamarindo, probably the best for most surfers, unless you're looking for the full upscale pampered vacation. And if the WRSC on the beach is full, then they'll put you up at one of the many other Tamarindo lodging options they manage these days.

The Tamarindo Vista Villas is probably the best known hotel for surfers in Tamarindo, especially since hosting E's Wild On a couple years ago. You'll find it on your left as you come into town, right across from the Paris bakery and the Rivermouth rights and next door to El Milagro. The Vista Villas combines location, ambiance, cleanliness, amenities and the best view of the surf to make this a great option for the surfer not on a budget. It's got everything you need: Pool with a swim-up bar, great restaurant, the Robert August Surf Shop, board rentals (including a great selection of Robert August models), surfing lessons, tours, Witches/Ollie's trips, TVs with VCRs and video rentals, kitchens in (some) rooms with a big fridge, lots of space, big bathrooms, patios with surf views and a poolside patio for gathering at day's end to watch sunsets. The crowd here tends to be a bit older due to the prices, which have gone way up, especially in the busy season. There's live music and karaoke at the poolside Monkey Bar on many nights, which has also become one of the hot spots in town and the place to have a drink with (i.e., buy a drink for) surf legends. The Vista Villas is good choice for families, couples or a dude trip (mostly older dudes), especially if you like the camaraderie of fellow surfers, as it's a sociable place.

There's a good reason why the Vista Villas works so well for surfers: The ol' SurfnMoose. (Yep, that's his name.) In the early '90s SurfnMoose, a surfer/chiropractor from Santa Cruz fell in love with Costa Rica on his first trip and bought the land the hotel sits on a whim. At the time Tamarindo was truly an outpost, nothing like what it is today. SurfnMoose had a vision to build the perfect surfer hotel, and he did it. It helped that he picked the best piece of property in town for a surfer hotel. It also helps that the SurfnMoose is an outgoing, service-oriented guy, as his personality is reflected in the atmosphere and the great treatment you get from the staff. As a surfer, the SurfnMoose built the hotel brick by brick with surfers in mind, and that thoughtfulness is reflected everywhere. For example, most rooms have a closet just for surfboards. Where else to they have that?

If traveling with the wife or girlfriend and romance is on the menu, check out El Jardín del Edén, the most romantic hotel in Tamarindo. It's really a "Garden of Eden;" some rooms having great views of the surf from luxurious (for Costa Rica) hillside rooms that have big patios, blow dryers and great hot water. Unfortunately, trees block the views from many rooms. They also offer good kiddie deals (see below) and cash discounts, but in general, it's on the higher-priced side. If money is no object, head straight to Cala Luna, which is outside town near Langosta. Other great "keep-your-girlfriend" hotel choices include the Tamarindo Diría and the Cala Luna.

A very cool bed & breakfast choice out near Langosta is Villa Alegre. Come here and you'll want to sell it all and open your own in Costa Rica. Hosts Barry and Suzye, a couple from the L.A. area did just that. When you meet Barry you will know from his grin that he scored. They built their paradise just south of the hustle and bustle of Tamarindo, and they've done a fantastic job. The rooms are spacious and comfortable, each with a different theme. The patio and the pool face the surf so you can check out Langosta throughout the day. Whether you are traveling with buddies, your honey or your family (kids can stay down the hall), you will get totally stoked at Villa Alegre.

The popularity of Costa Rica as a tourist destination has grown to the point where there are now condominiums and vacation homes for rent, at least in the busier areas like Tamarindo and Nosara. In some ways it's sad, because it signals the advanced stage of tourist development. But it's also good, because renting a condo is a great option to a touristy hotel. There are lots of property management companies who rent condos in Tamarindo. A good one to contact is RPM (www.tulin.com/costarica, 506-653-0738). Their office is in the same location where the iguana-in-the-surfboard-bag scene took place in *The Endless Summer 2*.

Lodging Name	Rates High	Rates Low	A/C	Priv Bath	Hot H2O	Facilities	Comments
Aparthotel Montebello $$$ tel. 506-653-0085 www.tamarindo.com/montebello/	$80-90s $80-90d $145q $15pp extra	$60s $60d $90q $12pp extra	All	All	All	2 Pools	Credit cards. Five furnished apartments with cable TVs, some kitchenettes and telephones up the hill 200 meters from the beach.
Arcoiris Cabinas $$ Tel. 506-653-0330 www.hotelarcoiris.com	$40-50	$20-40	Fans	All	Yes	Restaurant	Italian owned. Bungalows with patios. Vegetarian restaurant. Room service. Cool place with a cool vibe. Been here forever. Well, since 1993. Yoga, dojo/gym, massages.

Cala Luna $$$$ Tel. 506-653-0214 www.calaluna.com	$167-193d $334-386q $418-520six $25 extra bed	$139s/d $249q $311six $25 extra bed	All	All	All	Restaurant Bar Pool Guarded parking	Credit cards. Includes continental breakfast. The best place for privacy. Long walk to much of the surf. Villas have private pools. All have TVs, CD players, sunken tubs, private patios. Top-notch upscale resort. <u>Highly recommended</u> if you have the dough.
Capitan (El) Suizo Lodge $$$$ tel. 506-653-0353, 506-653-0075, 800-948-3770 www.hotelcapitansuizo.com	$140-195 add $20 per person	$120-165 add $20 per person	1st floor only	All	All	Restaurant Bar Pool Ping-pong	Credit cards. Includes continental breakfast. Swiss owners and restaurant. Upscale (but getting rundown) hotel on the beach south of the hustle and bustle of Tamarindo. Decent break right out front, but the management is not very surfer-friendly. All rooms have telephone, lock box and fridge. First floor rooms have a/c; upstairs fans, terraces and breezes. Diving, horses, kayaking, boat trips, laundry service. Overpriced. A/C$
Coral Reef Cabinas ¢ Tel. 506-653-0291		$6s	No	No	No		Cash only. Good budget option. Tiny rooms but the surf's right across the street. International crowd of interesting characters.
Doly Hotel ¢ tel. 506-653-0017, 506-653-0151		$30d $26t	Fans	Not all	No	Restaurant Bar	On the beach. Spit and you'll hit the Tamarindo beach breaks and Pico Pequeño; it's that close. Simple but clean. Shared and private baths.
Bella Vista Village Resort $$ tel./fax 506-653-0036 www.tamarindo.com/bella/	$65 s/d $10 per extra person	$50 s/d $10 per extra person	No	All	All	Pool Bar	Credit cards. Private casitas with three beds, full kitchens, phones and fans. Discounts for extended stays of a week or more. In the hills behind Tamarindo 600 meters from the beach and the crowds.
Colina (La) Hotel & Condominiums $$$ Tel. 506-653-0303 Fax 506-653-0301 Email: lacolinatamarindo@yahoo.com www.la-colina.com	$125d $280q add $20 per extra person	$75-88d $160-170q add $20 per extra person	All	All	All	Bar Pool	Credit cards. Good view of the surf. Nice apartment-like suites with full kitchens, TVs and patios. 10 minute walk to the surf. Arranges tours and all rentals. Quiet place. The only problem is there's no restaurant, but you can eat across the street at Jardin del Eden. Tell Hans we sent you. <u>Recommended</u>
Frutas Tropicales ¢ Tel. 506-653-0041	$28d $36t	$22d $30t	Fans	All	All	Restaurant	Credit cards, TV, security box. Across the street from the surf. Great little restaurant.
Jardín del Eden Hotel $$$ Tel. 506-653-0137 Fax 506-653-0111 www.jardin-eden.com	$80s $105-120d $145apt surfer special $80 to 4	$60s $70-80d $100apt surfer special $60 to 4	All	All	All	Restaurant Bar 2 Pools Swim up bar Jacuzzi	Credit cards. Includes breakfast. Beautiful hilltop location; 120-meter walk to beach. Very nice hotel with beautiful ocean views from private balconies in some rooms. Safes, phones, TVs and minibars. Great food and a cozy bar. Kids under 4 free, 5-12 $15, additional adults $20. <u>Highly recommended</u> if you have the dough.

La Botella de Leche Hostel ¢ Tel. 506-653-0944	$15	$15s	Fans	No	Yes	Surfboard racks Community kitchen Rec room with TV	Hosteling International member. About 100 yards from the beach. Central a/c, lockers, internet access, laundry, free coffee
Marielos Cabinas ¢ tel. 506-654-0141	$13s $20d $21t $25q	$13s $20d $21t $25q	Fans	All	Not all	Communal kitchen Room safes	Visa. Budget Cabinas (14) in downtown area. Some bathrooms have no doors.
Milagro (El) Hotel $ Tel. 506-654-4042 www.elmilagro.com (if in Spanish, search Google and click "translate")	$70-80s $75-85d $10 add'l person	$50-60s $55-65d $10 add'l person	Not all	All	All	Restaurant Bar Pool Kiddie pool Room safes	Credit cards. Directly across from the walkway to the rivermouth surf and Witches Rock Surf Camp (who also books rooms here when they are full). Includes continental breakfast. Upscale restaurant. Tours arranged. A/C$ $10 extra.
Nahua Garden Suites $$ Tel. 506-680-0776 Fax 506-680-0776	$85s/d	$65s/d	All	All	yes	Small pool	5 condos. No credit cards. Rooms have kitchens with appliances. Discounts for weekly and monthly stays.
Costa Real Resort $$$ Tel. 506-653-0182 Email tamarindocostareal@email.com		$60-$95 inc tax	All	All	All	Restaurant Bar Large pool Tennis court	Includes breakfast. Cable TV. Japanese style bungalows with kitchens. Secluded, but a mile from the surf. On your left just before you reach Tamarindo.
Pasatiempo Hotel $$ Tel. 506-653-0096 Fax 506-653-0275 www.hotelpasatiempo.com	$60s/d	$40s/d	Fans	All	Yes	Restaurant bar Pool Boutique	AE, MC, V. Some rooms sleep up to 5. Sports bar with satellite TV and live music. Local hot spot. Been here forever. 10 minute walk to the beach, but a very nice place.
Pozo Azul Cabinas $ Tel. 506-680-0147		$24-33d	Not all	All	No	Pool	No credit cards. Some kitchenettes with refrigerators and hot plates. Some with clothes washing sinks. A/C$.
Pueblo Dorado Hotel $$ Tel./fax 506-222-5741		$40s $50d $60t	All	All	Yes	Restaurant bar Pool	AE, MC, V. Close to surf—just across the road from the rivermouth and the bakery—a real plus. Rents kayaks. Small rooms, good value.
Rodamar Cabinas ¢		$6pp no bath $9pp w/bath	Fan	Not all	No	Restaurant	Cash only. Bargain place that's right across from the surf next to Frutas Tropicales, a great little place to eat. Camping too.
Sueño del Mar $$ Tel. 506-653-0284 Fax 506-653-0001 www.tamarindo.com/sdmar		$75d $95 suite	Fans	All	Yes	Restaurant	AE, MC, V. Bed & Breakfast near Langosta. Prices include breakfast. Kitchenettes.
Sunset Hill Condos $$$ Tel. 506-653-0738 www.tulin.com/costarica	$130d $155t	$115d $135t	All	All	All	Pool	Credit cards. Way up the hill with great views of the surf. Privacy and security. Condos with full kitchens, TVs and VCRs.
Tamarindo Bay Resort Club $$ Tel. 506-680-0883, 506-223-4289, 506-233-1952 fax 506-255-3785		$93 up to 5	Not all	All	Yes	Restaurant Bar Pool Disco	40 cabinas with kitchens. Waterskiing, scuba and snorkeling trips, cruises. Rents surf and boogieboards. This is the place where you saw Diffenderfer put the iguana into Wingnut's board bag. That said, it's a pretty dreary place, and it's a bit of a walk to the surf.

Tamarindo Diría Hotel $$$$ Tel. 506-653-0031, 506-290-4340 Fax 506-653-0032, 506-290-4367 www.tamarindodiria.com	$132-154s $150-172d $207t $244q	$106-127s $124-144d $171t $200q	All	All	Yes	Restaurant Bar Pool Tennis Gift shop Casino Game room	AE, MC, V. Upscale, touristy place. Price includes breakfast buffet. Good place for a surfer traveling with a girlfriend/wife or family favoring resorts. On the beach in front of Pico Piqueño. Easy walk to all Tamarindo spots. Fishing and other tours. Good food. Cable TV, phones. Armed guards.
Tamarindo Vista Villas $$$$ Tel. 800-292-3786, 506-653-0114, 800-282-3786 fax 506-653-0115 www.tamarindovistavillas.com	$89-169d $99-109t $159-219q $209-259 8-person suite	$84-124d $94t $144-174q $194-214 8-person suite	All	All	All	Restaurant Bar Pool Swim up bar Video rentals Surf shop	Credit Cards. Surfer owned and built with surfers in mind. Internet access, board storage, full kitchens with coffee makers. TVs and VCRs. Good pool/bar/restaurant/ social area with the sunset surf views. Views of the rivermouth from some rooms. Patios. Skyrocketing prices. <u>Recommended.</u>
Villa Alegre Bed & Breakfast $$$$ Tel. 506-653-0270 www.villaalegrecostarica.com	$170-230	$150-195	Fans	Not all	Yes	Pool	Rates include a gourmet breakfast. Overlooks Langosta. Also rents small villas. Cool owners, <u>highly recommended</u>. Tell 'em we sent ya.
Witches Rock Surf Camp $$$ Tamarindo Tel. 506-653-0078, 506-653-0239 www.witchsrocksurfcamp.com	$1615s $1120pp/d $940pp/t one week packages	$1290s $895pp/d $790pp/t one week packages	Yes	Yes	Yes	Restaurant Bar	Credit cards. The hot ticket. <u>Highly recommended</u>. Boat trips to Witches and Ollie's, other guided surf tours, snorkeling and other fun, breakfast and lunches all included. Surf school packages for beginners through "established" surfers. A good deal!
Zully Mar Hotel $$ Tel. 506-653-4140, 506-653-0140, 506-653-0023 Fax 506-653-0028, 506-653-0191 www.zullymar.com	$65-69s $71-79d $79-89 $14per extra person	$56-61s $61-69d $73-82t $14per extra person	Not all	All	No	Restaurant Bar Pool Secure parking	AE, MC, V. A bargain favorite. 50 yards from Henry's Point near the circle. Some rooms have small refrigerators and cost more. All are basic and worn. A/C$. Arranges rental cars. Close to the Tamarindo nightlife. Crowded, noisy pool, but fun for kids.

Playa Avellanes

About a half-hour (dry season) drive south of Tamarindo is a great collection of rights and lefts, reefs and beach breaks. The first break (coming from the north down, although you probably won't come that way, you'll likely walk up from the parking lot at the south end of the beach) is a big reef with great, juicy rights called **Little Hawaii**. The reef gets shallow on low tide, so watch it. Other breaks include a reef just south of the river mouth, a left at the far south end of the beach in front of the parking lot (watch out for that reef at low tide, too), and other beach break peaks in between. Everything breaks best at mid-tide. The left in front of the parking lot is good at high tide with a decent swell. One nice thing about Avellanes is that it's a big beach with lots of breaks, so it's easy to avoid crowds.

One way to get here is to drive into Paraíso and head north out of town by making a right after you pass the soccer field. Follow the signs toward the Hotel Playa Negra, but pass the turnoff for the hotel (and the excellent break) and keep heading north passing the Mono Congo Lodge. You'll know you're close when you see signs for Gregorio's. Pass Gregorio's and you'll see the beach then the parking lot. It can be difficult to impossible to drive here during the rainy season, although the roads improve every year. You can also drive in from Tamarindo without going around through Paraíso. With the improved road to Tamarindo and the frequently graded roads to Avellanes the drive in and out has become a breeze in the dry season, and frankly, the most traveled route. Just head out of Tamarindo to Villareal, hang a right, and follow the signs to Avellanes or Cabinas Las Olas. If you don't plan on staying at Cabinas Las Olas, keep driving and you can't miss Avellanes. (Well, you can, and probably will, but that's about as good as it gets in Costa Rica.) It's about a 10-mile drive from Tamarindo.

You used to be able to drive on the beach at Avellanes. Now you can't, and that's a good thing for the beach. In exchange for the beach driving privileges, there's now a pretty cool little café setup at the parking lot. It's a great place to hang, not to mention eat. Gregorio's soda is only a five minute walk away and is a lot cheaper.

Where To Stay For Playa Avellanes

A favorite place is Cabinas Las Olas. The price is right, especially for small groups, the people are cool, and the restaurant serves great eats. The managers surf and can hook you up for Witches and Ollie's trips. It is not directly on the beach, but it's close, and the 300-yard walk is not bad. You can also camp right on the beach next to the main parking lot. Another favorite is the Hotel Iguanazul (see "Where to Stay for Playa Negra"), even though it's a little bit of a drive. Actually, there are lots of places between Avellanes and Playa Negra that are good headquarters for both spots. You won't find the conveniences of Tamarindo, but you will find more privacy and get a better feel for the country.

You also might want to check out Cabinas El Leon. I haven't visited the place myself, but John and Colleen Quintana from Dana Point did, and here's what they had to say in 2002: "…our favorite spot to stay…includes big and beautiful breakfast…spotless rooms…nice place for the wife or girlfriend, with nice bathrooms, sheets, towels, etc." As with much of Costa Rica these days, the owners are Italian. Cabinas El Leon is easy to find; it's near the last turn just before you reach the beach when driving in from the north (Tamarindo).

Lastly, no need to plan ahead or try to make reservations if you have the most basic needs or are planning to camp check out Cabinas Iguana Verde right there on the beach. Food, shelter and surf only steps away.

Lodging Name	Rates High	Rates Low	A/C	Priv Bath	Hot H2O	Facilities	Comments
El Leon, Cabinas $ Playa Avellanes Cell phone 506-381-1361		$35d	Fans	Yes		Restaurant	Reader recommendation. Near Cabinas Las Olas, but a little closer to the main beach. Breakfast included. Built in 1999.

Gregorio's Cabinas ¢ no phone		$20d/t	Fans	One	No	Restaurant Bar	200 yards to Avellanes. Local flavor.
Iguanazul Hotel $$ Playa Junquillal Tel./fax 506-658-8123 Tel. 506-658-8124 www.iguanazul.com	$60-80s $70-90d $80-100t	$47-64s $55-72d $64-81t	Not all	All	All	Restaurant Bar Pool Volleyball Ping-pong	Credit cards. Includes continental breakfast. Secluded, beautiful, cliff top setting, but you'll be driving a short way to the surf. All rooms have 2 double beds and ceiling fans. One of the best views anywhere. Rents horses, bikes, videos, mopeds, bodyboards. A/C$. Phones in rooms. Sportfishing and nature tours. Discounts for longer stays. Tell Roberto we said hola. Highly recommended.
Lagartillo Beach Hotel $$ Tel. 506-257-1420 Fax 506-221-5717	$45-60d	$45-60d	Fans	All	No	Restaurant Pool	Good food. About 200 yards to the beach.
Cabinas Las Olas $ Tel. 506-658-8315 Fax 506-658-8331 www.cabinaslasolas.co.cr	$60s $70d $80t	$50s $60d $70t	Fans	All	All	Restaurant Bar Secured parking Gift shop	Surfer-owned. About 300 yards from the beach. Great walk-to-surf choice. Parking with security guard. Laundry. Spaced out cabinas give lots of privacy.

Playa Negra

"Negra," one of the best and most consistent breaks in the country, is the spot seen in *The Endless Summer 2* and the old *Surfers' Journal* article with Wingnut, Mark Martinson and Robert August. Looks like a cakewalk in the movie and photos, but isn't. About 5km south of Avellanes, this beautiful rock-reef right gets fast, hollow, and juicy, especially at low tide, and holds size well—in fact, it can get quite big. It's always bigger than the other spots in the area. Lots of barrels. At low tide it gets sketchy, especially when it's small; at high tide it doesn't break on smaller swells. Difficult access when the roads are muddy, as is this whole area. Negra is almost always crowded—with aggressive, tuned-in locals as well as expats and travelers—and being a well-publicized reef with a hotel in front, surf camps nearby and housing developments going up on both sides of the break isn't helping to cut that down. There are really only two take-off points, about 15 meters apart, so it doesn't hold a crowd well. About the only time the crowds dwindle is on high tides with small swells as there's not much of a wave then. But it's a good opportunity to learn the break.

Learning the break is important because this is not a good spot for beginners. The wave comes in and jacks up on the reef fast, so getting pitched on the take-off is a regular part of a Negra surf session, even for the experienced. Beginners get scorn to go with their embarrassment and wave-beatings.

A bit south is another right called **Callejones**. It's an option when Negra gets crowded. And yet another break (beach break and a left reef) to the south is **Junquillal**, which breaks best at higher tides, which isn't saying much because it usually closes out. There's a left that breaks off of the reef at the south end of Junquillal, but it's sketchy and not that good anyhow. There are lots more breaks in the area that you'll never hear about and quality unsurfed offshore reefs all over the place. Spend some time, explore, and get rewarded.

Some of those breaks to the south of Playa Negra are the outside reefs at **Playa Blanca**. Directly in front of the Hotel Iguanazul is a reef with a good, long left and a shorter right. Breaks best on lower tides, but breaks on any tide with enough swell, especially when it's more out of the west. Access is difficult unless you stay at the Iguanazul, and even then finding a way off and on the sharp lava reef shoreline isn't a treat. If you stay at the Iguanazul you'll watch this wave break every day and rarely see anyone surf it. A little further north and much further outside is a right breaking reef. The shape can be excellent, but that too is for well-experienced surfers only.

Getting to Playa Negra: Drive into Paraíso, turn right just past the soccer field, and follow the signs to Hotel Playa Negra or Pablo's Picasso. There's parking right near the break at the Hotel Playa Negra. You can also stay in Tamarindo and drive in and out fairly easily. In the dry season it will take you about 30 to 45 minutes, depending on your vehicle, driving skills, and frequency of live obstacles, like Brahma bull cattle drives. In the wet season you may not be able to drive in at all. You can get ferried by boat from Tamarindo—drop off in the morning, pick up in the evening. Ask at the surf shops. There's also daily bus service from Tamarindo to Playa Negra and Avellanes.

Where to Stay for Playa Negra

Right in front of the break is a cluster of cabinas built in 1996 and appropriately named the Hotel Playa Negra. It has a restaurant, pool, jacuzzi, pool table, and one of the best breaks anywhere right out front. The rooms (palapas) are clean and comfortable with three beds in each, but a bit crowded when full. A pretty good setup. The restaurant is the hangout between surf sessions. This is kind of a drag if you are a guest at the hotel because you're paying to stay where you can get on the surf as soon as it gets good or uncrowded, while everyone else hangs out and waits for the same thing, ensuring quick crowds. To make matters worse, people sometimes camp on the beach right in front of the break.

There are quite a few surf camps in the area now, but it all started with the venerable Pablo's Picasso. Here you'll find pretty good American food served in surfer-sized (huge) portions. Like the sign says, "Sandwiches as big as your head." You'll also find boards for sale, relatively cheap digs and a 10-minute walk to the surf. There's a range of accommodations here, from loft beds with no shower to cabinas with private baths. It's a surfer hangout with a surfer owner, Pablo, who's been here since 1994.

A good setup if you don't mind driving a short way to the breaks, and you do appreciate a beautiful cliff top setting, friendly hosts, amenities such as a good restaurant, bar, and a fun atmosphere is the Hotel Iguanazul. The picturesque location makes it good for the non-surfing travel companions, too. There are reefs right out front with good waves on the right tides and swells, and they're always empty (see Playa Blanca above). The drive to Negra is only 3km;

7km to Avellanes. Another good thing about the HI: Check out time isn't until 2:00pm, so you can get a good surf in and still have time to eat and pack before heading back to the airport.

Lodging tip: In this whole area you should keep an eye out for scorpions in your room and belongings (shoes, bags, clothes, etc.). It doesn't matter how clean or nice the hotel, they are everywhere, and they like dark, warm, moist places, like shoes. And here's a tip from Alan Weisbecker, author of *In Search of Captain Zero* and the online newsletter, *Down South Perspective*. Don't bother shaking out your shoes to dislodge scorpions, it doesn't work. As soon as you pick up the shoe they dig in with their claws and don't shake loose. Just wear sandals instead.

Lodging Name	Rates High	Rates Low	A/C	Priv Bath	Hot H2O	Facilities	Comments
Castillo (El) Divertido Hotel $ Playa Junquillal castillodivertido@hotmail.com Tel. 506-658-8428	$28s $38d	$25s $32d	No	All	Yes	Bar Restaurant	AE, MC, V. "Castle" overlooking the beach – about 300 meters away. Live music.
Guacamaya Lodge $$ Playa Junquillal Tel. 506-658-8431 www.guacamayalodge.com	$50-70s $55-75d $80t $85-120q	$35-55s $40-60d $65t $70-90q	All	All	Yes	Restaurant Bar Pool Gift shop	On the road to the beach in Junquillal. Nice cozy bar. Swiss owned with some German food on the menu.
Hibiscus Hotel $ Playa Junquillal tel. 506-658-8437 www.adventure-costarica.com/hibiscus	$40d $50d $60t	$40d $50d $60t	No	All	All	Restaurant	V. Includes American breakfast. Four bungalows in a tropical garden across the road from the beach. Laundry service
Iguanazul Hotel $$ Playa Junquillal tel./fax 506-658-8123 tel. 506-658-8124 www.iguanazul.com	$60-80s $70-90d $80-100t	$47-64s $55-72d $64-81t	Not all	All	All	Restaurant Bar Pool Volleyball Ping-pong	Credit cards. Includes continental breakfast. Secluded, beautiful, cliff top setting, but you'll be driving a short way to the surf. All rooms have 2 double beds and ceiling fans. One of the best views anywhere. Rents horses, bikes, videos, mopeds, bodyboards. A/C$. Phones in rooms. Sportfishing and nature tours. Discounts for longer stays. Highly recommended.
Mono Congo Lodge $$ Tel. 506-658-8261 www.monocongolodge.com	$65-95d $75-105t $85-115q	$65-95d $75-105t $85-115q	All	Not all	Yes	Restaurant Bar	In between Negra and Avellanes—a 10 minute walk to the surf. Swiss Family Robinson style lodge with a lookout tower for checking the surf. Recent ownership change.
Pablo's Picasso Cabinas ¢ tel. 609-926-8989 www.pablosplayanegra.com	$10-25pp	$10-25pp	Fans and A/C	Not all	No	Restaurant Bar	1/2km from beach. Venerable surf hangout famous for "burgers as big as your head". All rooms double occupancy. Breakfast included.

Playa Junquillal Hotel $ tel. 888-666-2322 www.playa-junquillal.com	$25s $30d	$25s $30d	Fans	All	All	Restaurant Bar	Four-room hotel with beach right out front. Four miles south of Paraiso. Special deals if your group rents all four rooms and stays awhile. Deep sea fishing, horses, SCUBA, tours.
Playa Negra Hotel $$ Tel. 506-658-8034 www.hotelplayanegra.com	$55s $66d $75t $84q	$50s $60d $70t $80q	No	All	All	Restaurant Bar Pool	On the beach in front of the break. The perfect set up to hover over Negra and get on it fast.
Tatanka $$ Playa Junquillal Tel./fax 506-658-8426 www.crica.com/tatanka	$45s $56d $67t	$35s $47d $58t	Fans and A/C	All	All	Restaurant Bar Pool	AE, MC, V. Good Italian restaurant. Laundry service, tours, horses, kayaking. Group rates. Full meal plan.
Villa Serena Hotel $$$ Playa Junquillal Tel./fax 506-658-8430 www.land-ho.com	$100	$100	Fans	All	All	Restaurant Bar Pool Tennis	AE, MC, V. Across the road from the beach at Junquillal. Rents horses, fishing charters. Armed security guards. Very nice place for the money with beautiful grounds.

Nicoya Peninsula

It is hard to tell where Guanacaste ends and the Nicoya Peninsula actually starts, but in this guide it starts south of Playa Negra. With the exception of the road into Sámara from Nicoya, the roads here are pretty rough, although like everywhere else they've been improving every year. This area is somewhat remote, especially during the rainy season, so it's a bit of a commitment getting in. More paved roads are in the works. In the meantime, the Nicoya area has a lot to offer in the way of uncrowded waves—some points, lots of beach breaks and a few outside reefs. If you travel without a surf partner, you may even wish it was more crowded. On good swells there are outside reefs at places like Playa Garza and Playa Sámara with no one out just begging to be surfed. But as the area develops and the crowds grow those reefs will be put to better use.

One of the disadvantages of the remoteness is that during the off-season services are less available. For example, finding a restaurant open for breakfast away from town centers (of which there are few anyhow) can be difficult, and some hotels shut down their air-conditioned rooms. Even during the busy season you won't find much in the way of surf shops, except in Nosara and now Mal País, so ding repair and supplies are not as convenient.

How to Get There

First, you can come in from the north; that is, hit the Guanacaste area, Tamarindo, all that, then head on down along the coast as best you can. In the rainy season, however, you'll be lucky to make it with all the river crossings. Most will tell you not to try at all.

You can also cover it from the south by taking the ferry across the Golfo de Nicoya from Puntarenas to Playa Naranjo (no, not Witches Rock...it should be so easy to get there) then heading south toward Paquera and Tambor along the coast as best you can. Or you can take the ferry directly to Paquera. The ferry from Puntarenas to Paquera leaves twice daily, at 6:00AM and 2:00PM, and takes at least two hours to make the crossing. The return trips from Paquera leave at 9:00AM and 5:00PM. The "Naranjo" ferry leaves more regularly throughout the day, and takes about an hour and twenty minutes. The drive from Playa Naranjo to Paquera takes about an hour during the dry season, and it's a rough road. The choice depends on your timing getting into Puntarenas.

A third and best way is to head right into the middle of the area by taking the Tempisque Bridge across the northern and narrower part of the gulf. After crossing the bridge head wherever you want, you'll hit the beach eventually. The best roads, however, are those that take you directly to Sámara.

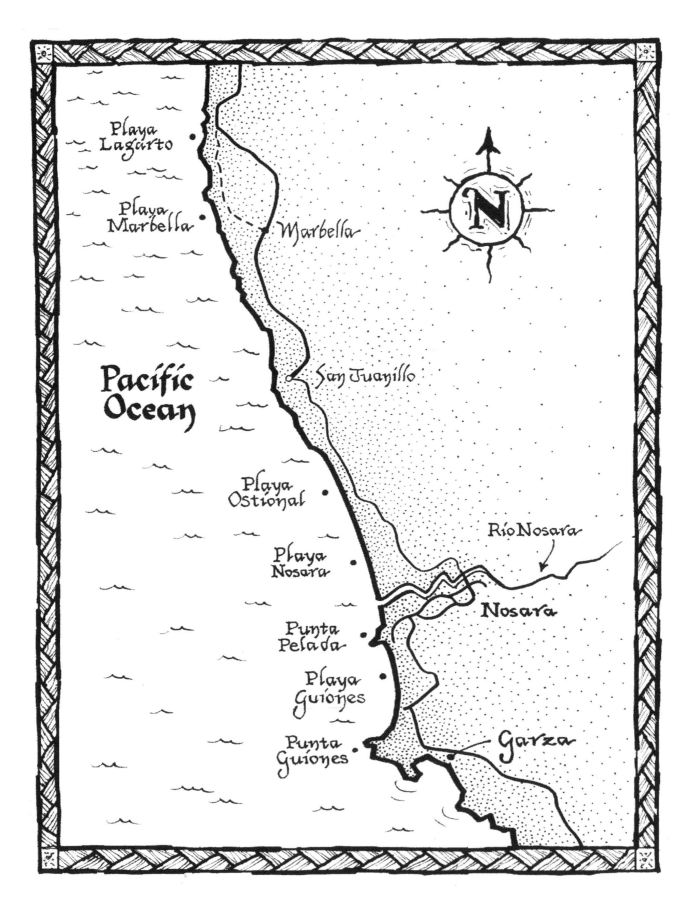

Finally, you can fly in to the airports at Sámara or Nosara via one of the local airlines. Then take cabs and buses. Those local airlines often don't take surfboards, so plan ahead for a rental or loaner.

By the way, if your trip started up north and you've been driving down, you are now far enough south that the weather is a little less dry and wet enough that it sometimes rains even in the dry season. And it just gets wetter from here south.

Playa Ostional

Playa Ostional is known world-wide as the most important nesting site for the protected Olive Ridley turtle, moreso even than Playa Grande. Hundreds of thousands of female turtles come ashore in "arribadas" where they dig holes and lay their eggs, about 100 from each mom. While the gals come ashore year-round, they are busiest July to December, and always at night.

What it is not known for are the good, uncrowded beach breaks and reefs. You'll find surf all along this stretch, and you'll have it all to yourself. Shape is best at higher tides. To get to Ostional you can either fly into the airport at Nosara, or drive there by taking the road from Nicoya toward Samara, or come down from the north. Difficult to reach during the rainy season due to the river crossings. When coming from Nicoya you'll enjoy a nice, paved road all the way to the turnoff for Nosara that is just before Samara. From that point it is about an hour of dirt road driving to Nosara. Ostional is the next town north of Nosara. When coming in from the north (e.g., Tamarindo, Avellanes, etc.), you basically find your way to Playa Lagarto and head south. It's all dirt roads, but not too bad. Just be very careful when approaching bridges. I can't tell you how many times I've almost driven onto a wooden bridge that was collapsed in the middle, averting disaster at the very last second.

Where To Stay for Playa Ostional

Other than very basic cabinas or camping, there are only a couple of places to stay in or near Ostional. One place somewhat near the surf is the new Hotel Luna Azul, which just opened in 2004, but it's still 4km from the beach. It's a nice place that with a health and nature lodge theme. Then there's the Hungarian owned Rancho Hotel Brovilla. You'll need a 4x4 just to get up the steep, rocky hill to the hotel, not to mention back down. The Brovilla has all the comforts, is secluded and relaxing, and it's way up above it all with great views. And it's Hungarian.

Lodging Name	Rates High	Rates Low	A/C	Priv Bath	Hot H2O	Facilities	Comments
Cabinas Ostional ¢ Tel. 506-682-0428	$10pp	$10pp	Fans	All	No		Across from the Soda la Plaza. Patios.
Hotel Luna Azul $$$ Tel. 506-821-0075 www.hotellunaazul.com	$75s $122d $20pp extra	$60s $70d $15pp extra	All	All	All	Restaurant Pool Jacuzzi Internet café Satellite TV	Nicest hotel in the Ostional beach area. Bungalows with patios, refrigerators, phones and room safes. A/C$

Rancho Brovilla Hotel & Resort $$$ tel. 506-380-5639 www.brovill.com	$35-50s $10 add'l person $5 per kid	$35-50s $10 add'l person $5 per kid	Yes, but not all	All	All	Restaurant Bar Pool Sauna	Credit cards. Breakfast included. Nice place up a steep hill just outside town and 1km from the surf. Remote, relaxing, great views. Also rents apartments and houses.

Playa Nosara

Most people call Guiones "Nosara." The real Playa Nosara is north of Guiones and is not surfed much. Playa Nosara is bordered by a rivermouth to the south, and is a long beach with lots of decent beach breaks and no one out. The best surf is near the rivermouth where, depending on tides and conditions, you'll find good lefts peeling off. Locals say it's sharky. To get to the rivermouth follow the signs to "Boca Nosara," which means Nosara Rivermouth. To the surf from this direction you'll have to cross the river. The village of Nosara itself is 5km inland, and you can find supplies and lodging there, but most people stay to the south near Playa Guiones. You can also camp in the Ostional Wildlife Refuge. In this whole area it is best to have a vehicle because everything is so spread out.

Playa Guiones

This is what everyone calls "Nosara," but every map says Guiones, so I'm going by the maps. Guiones is one of the most consistent breaks in Costa Rica, or anywhere. There's *always* surf here, and it's usually pretty fun. Lots of beach break peaks and a left point at the north end that breaks occasionally. The surf can get big, and it's usually bigger and better as you head to the north part of the beach. For its size it's a fairly forgiving wave, but when it gets big it's still big, so beginners should be careful when the surf picks up. Guiones has been getting more crowded due to the consistent surf, the new hotels catering to surfers and especially the surf schools. The surf schools ensure no shortage of kooks in the water.

There are a few surf shops in this little surf vacation village, and more to come I'm sure. The easiest to find, Coconut Harry's, marks the main turnoff to head down to the beach at Guiones. (There are many turnoffs, but this is the most direct and passes other shops.) Proprietor Henry Heinke is a colorful character, and you'll see him most days down at the surf. The Corky Carroll surf school, which used to be run out of the Harbor Reef is now at Coconut Harry's. Another good shop is the Nosara Surf Shop, down the road from Harry's to the beach and across the street from the Casa Tucan Hotel. They have a good supply of boards, at least 60 rentals and about 50 new, along with all the surf gear and t-shirts you expect from a real surf shop. Add the Safari Surf School and ding repair to that.

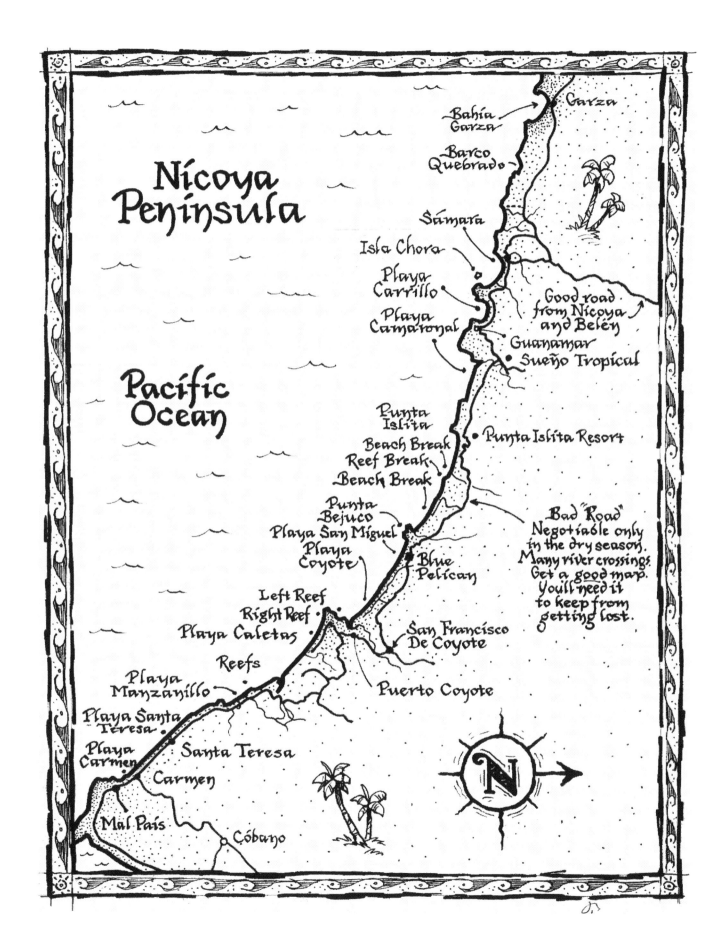

Where To Stay for Playa Nosara and Playa Guiones

There are no hotels right in front of the surf in Playa Nosara or Playa Guiones, but camping is permitted as with most of Costa Rica. The hotels are scattered about in the woods near the beach and up the hills, and you can walk to the surf pretty easily from most of them. Hotel Playas de Nosara (recently renamed the Nosara Beach Hotel) sits atop the point at the north end of Guiones giving you a great view of the surf as well as fairly easy access. But this hotel seems to be always under construction (for over 20 years!), so meals and other services can be spotty, and the place is, well, a wreck. But the owner makes up for the mess with his hospitality and nuttiness. It's weird but cool. But if bugs bug you, go elsewhere.

And elsewhere is the Harbor Reef Lodge. Like most hotels in this area, the Harbor Reef Lodge is set back from the beach in the woods, providing pleasant seclusion. The rooms are spacious and nice with big bathrooms, hardwood floors and great air conditioning. The whole property attracts a friendly group of people—families, couples, fishermen and especially surfers. Owners Randy and Brenda opened the Harbor Reef Lodge in 1997, moving to Costa Rica from Catalina Island off the coast of Southern California, which is where Randy was born and raised. After living 50 years in what most people would consider paradise, Randy found his own paradise in Playa Guiones. And given the consistency of the surf in here, I think he nailed it. I can't say enough good things about the Harbor Reef Lodge.

Randy doesn't surf, but his sons do. Randy's a fisherman, and Brenda has developed the gift shop into a mini surf supply center, with rental boards, rash guards, leashes, wax, repair kits and more. In 2003 they added a general store (beer), so any supplies you need (beer) you can find right there, including beer.

Randy has also gotten into managing house rentals in the area, like the Casa Cortez that's up the hill, walking distance from the surf, and a great place to get some peace and quiet. Casa Cortez doesn't have air conditioning, but breezes and fans keep the four bedroom/2 bath getaway cool enough.

Randy was raised in the hospitality business—his family owned the Two Harbors Resort in Catalina—so he knows how to run a hotel and really take care of guests. He also runs a good little restaurant with mighty fine food and a cozy little poolside bar as a great place to hang and swap surf stories. My only problem with the Harbor Reef Lodge is that I don't want to tell others about it because I want to be able to get a room whenever I want. But Randy and Brenda are so great I just gotta make a huge recommendation. In Guiones, this is the place.

There's also a surf camp a short walk from the surf at the north end of Playa Guiones called Blew Dog's. It was the old Olas Grandes, and it's now owned by an ex-East Coast surfer named Jake. He's been there for a few years now, and is still making improvements, such as a new pool. Jake is a chef of many years, so the food is good and a good deal too at Tico prices. He also has a variety of boards for rent, board repair and surf lessons. Accommodations are inexpensive, including their "flophouse" where you can get a bed for $8-$10 a night. Worth checking out for sure.

Lodging Name	Rates High	Rates Low	A/C	Priv Bath	Hot H2O	Facilities	Comments
Almost Paradise $ Tel. 506-682-0173, 506-223-3200	$45d $55q	$35d $45q	No	All	All	Restaurant	No credit cards. Breakfast included. On the hill with beautiful ocean views and good breezes. Relaxing. 300 meters from Playa Pelada.
Blew Dogs Surf Club $ Tel. 506-682-0080 www.blewdogs.com	$10-35s $45d	$8-25s $35d	Fans	All	All	Restaurant Bar	No credit cards. Full-on surf camp that's a short walk to a good peak at the north end of Guiones. Some kitchens. Board rental/repair/lessons.
Casa Río Nosara $ tel. 506-682-0117 fax 506-682-0182 www.rionosara.com	$15s $25d	$15s $25d	Fans	No	All	Restaurant	Includes breakfast. Singles in dormitory. On the banks of the Nosara River. Canoe tours, kayak rentals, deep sea and river fishing.
Casa Romantica $$ Tel. 506-682-0272 www.casa-romantica.net	$55s $65d $15pp extra	$45s $55d $15pp extra	Not all	Yes	Yes	Restaurant Pool	Under new ownership (Swiss) in 2004. Walk to surf. Includes breakfast.
Casa Tucán $$ tel./fax 506-682-0113 www.casatucan.net	$39-55s $50-65d $5per extra person	$29-39s $40-49d $5per extra person	All	All	All	Restaurant Bar Pool	Short walk to Playa Guiones. Some kitchenettes. Weekly, monthly rates available. American run. Great food. Kind of the happening restaurant in town.
Chorotega Cabinas ¢-$ tel. 506-682-0129	$14s $35d	$14s $35d	No	Not all	All	Restaurant Bar	No credit cards. Private and shared baths. About 4-5km from beach in the town of Nosara near the airstrip.
Estancia Nosara $$ tel./fax 506-682-0178 e-mail estancia@nosara.com	$45-52s $52-62d $60-72t $70-82q	$35-42s $42-52d $48-58t $58-68q	Not all	All	All	Restaurant (sometimes closed in off-season) Bar Pool Tennis	MC, V. All rooms have minibars, some kitchenettes. Three meals included for $25/day plus 15% tax and 10% tip. Lots of activities (not free). Satellite TV in lounge. Phone in reception. About 1km from Playa Guiones. Rents horses, boogieboards, bikes. Snorkel stuff. Tours. Good value. A/C$ Air taxi service. Very surfer-friendly.
Giardino Tropicale $$ Tel. 506-682-4000 www.giardinotropicale.com	$55-105s $60-110d $65-115t	$40-90s $45-95d $50-100t	Not all	All	All	Restaurant Pool	MC, V, AE. Great Italian restaurant. Big portions. Up on the main road.
Guilded Iguana $$ Tel. 506-682-0259 www.gildediguana.com	$45-65d $65-80t $10 per extra person	$30-50d $50-65t $10 per extra person	Not all	All	All	Restaurant Bar Pool Satellite TV	A nice place a short walk from the surf. The newer rooms are big and clean, but basic (i.e., no TV). All rooms have frig's, coffee makers and complimentary coffee in rooms.
Harbor Reef Lodge $$ Tel. 506-682-0059 Fax 506-682-0060 www.harborreef.com	$49-$93+ +$5 per additional person. From standard to 2-room suites that sleep to 6	$25-$75 +$5 per additional person. From standard to 2-room suites that sleep to 6	All	All	All	Restaurant Bar Pool Gift shop with surf supplies General store	Amex, MC, V. Single and group rates available. Kids under 3 free. Cabinas and suites. Walk five minutes to the main break at Guiones. Frig's with freezers Surf school with board rentals. Boogieboard and kayak rentals too. HIGHLY RECOMMENDED

Hotel Café de Paris $$ Tel. 506-682-0087 www.cafedeparis.net	$49-69d $99q $10pp extra Villas $120/day	$49-59d $69q $10pp extra Villas $120/day	Not all	All	All	Restaurant Bar Bakery Internet café Pool Outdoor theater	Credit cards. Continental breakfast included. Some kitchens. At the intersection of the main road and the main turnoff to the surf. The hotel is a 10 minute walk to the waves. Ocean view villas are further; above Coconut Harry's. Great restaurant, bar, French bakery and hangout. A/c$
Hotel Casita Romantica $$ Tel./fax 506-682-0019 www.casaromantica.com	$70s $80d $15pp extra	$55s $70d $15pp extra	Not all	All	All	Pool	Walk to surf. Apartments with kitchenettes. A/C$
Lodge Vista del Mar $ Tel. 506-682-0633 Fax 506-682-0611 www.lodgevistadelmar.com	$39-42s $56d	$39-42s $56d	Yes	All	All	Pool	Breakfast included. $5 extra for a/c. Penthouse has full kitchen, 360 views, $180/day. Up the hill away from it all with great views.
Playas de Nosara Hotel $$ tel. 506-682-0121 www.nosarabeachhotel.com		$50-60s $65-75d	Fans	All	All	Restaurant Bar Pool	No credit cards. Beautiful location at the point at Punta Pelada and Playa Guiones. Great views of both beaches and the breaks. Walkways to the beaches. All rooms have private balconies. Great place to hang. Go online and print out 20% discount coupon.
Rancho Suizo Lodge $ tel. 506-682-0057 fax 506-682-0055 www.nosara.ch	$38s $55d $87	$28s $40d $57t	Fans	All	All	Restaurant (no lunch) Bar Jacuzzi	No credit cards. Includes breakfast. Trails to beach; 5-minute walk to Playa Pelada. Tours arranged. Rents bikes, horses, fishing boats. Peaceful when the caged parrots aren't screaming their lungs out. Good food.
Tortuga Suites $$$ Tel. 506-682-0059 Fax 506-682-0060 www.harborreef.com	$122-133t $160 6-8 $10 add'l person	$110-119t $145 6-8 $10 add'l person	All	All	All	Pool Entertainment center	Credit cards. Kids under 6 stay free. Rented/managed by the Harbor Reef. 3 night minimum. Apartments or house with full kitchens, TVs, DVDs. DVDs, surfboards, bikes for rent. Short walk to the surf.
Villa Taype Hotel $$$ tel. 506-682-0280, 506-682-0333 www.villataype.com	$60-130s $80-135d $115-120t	$60-130s $80-135d $115-120t	Not all	All	All	Restaurant bar Pool Tennis court Ping-pong	Full buffet breakfast included. Fridges and direct TV in rooms. Private terraces. 150 yards from the surf. Private parking.

Garza

South-facing bay with reefs at each end and occasional beach breaks inside. Outside reefs fire on big swells. There is a left off the rock toward the south end of the bay that gets big and juicy. It's way outside and a bit sketchy. Beginners take heed. The north end of the bay has a good right reef. To get to the right you can walk around the bay, or drive up next to the Villagio Hotel where there's beach access. While in Garza, make sure to get some ceviche—conch or lobster—it's the best. (Thanks for the tip, Steve!) As with most of Costa Rica, watch your stuff or it will get stolen.

Where To Stay for Bahía Garza

Lodging Name	Rates High	Rates Low	A/C	Priv Bath	Hot H2O	Facilities	Comments
Villagio la Guaria Morada $$$ tel./fax 506-680-0784	$75d $90t $105q	$75d $90t $105q	No	All	All	Restaurant bar Pool Casino	MC, V. Includes breakfast. Oddly, this place is always empty. On the beach in the bay with the right reef just out front. Was most luxurious in the area but is now totally run down.

Playa Sámara

Some small beach breaks good for beginners, and bigger outside reef breaks for the more experienced. I would not plan my surf trip around Sámara. But if you are passing this way you might want to check it out for those outside reefs. The beach is in a protected bay facing south, about 24km south of Nosara over dirt roads, or an hour from Nicoya over a nice paved highway. Playa Sámara is a favorite beach destination of the Ticos, so it has decent accommodations and food. Campgrounds at the north end of town.

The mouth of the bay has rocky points with good breaks. Reef way outside in the middle of the bay has good rights on south swells. There are other reefs at the north end of the bay, way outside with good rights. And more reefs at the south end of the bay near Isla Chora with good rights on the back side and some lefts. The waves at Isla Chora are the best in the area. You might want to rent a kayak from the guy on the beach and paddle out to check out the reefs first. Or better still, check in with Joel at Camping and Bar Las Olas (on the beach north of town center) for a boat ride out. If you find Joel, ask about "The Blender," the below-sea-level-suck-out-reefbreak-right.

Where to Stay for Playa Sámara

Las Brisas del Pacifico is a pretty good hotel right on the beach with the best beach break right out front (which is not to say good, cuz it's not). It has a good restaurant and bar, and good ocean views. It is also walking distance to town and the nightlife. The staff is friendly and the showers have *hot* water. My only complaint is that the section of the hotel up the hill with the air-conditioned rooms may be closed during the off-season.

A budget, core-surfer option is Joel's Camping and Bar Las Olas. It's a collection of beach huts right on the beach—I mean *on* the beach. Joel will tune you into the local surf, in addition to being your boat captain for Isla Chora trips.

Lodging Name	Rates High	Rates Low	A/C	Priv Bath	Hot H2O	Facilities	Comments
Arenas Cabinas ¢ Tel. 506-656-0320	$8pp	$8pp	Fans	All	No	Restaurant (breakfast only)	

Belvedere Cabinas $ Tel. 506-656-0213 www.samarabeach.com /belvedere	$45s $48-60d $75t $85q	$38s $40-56d $65t $75q	Yes	All	Yes	Bar Pool Jacuzzi	V. Includes continental breakfast. Beds have mosquito nets.
Brisas (Las) del Pacifico Hotel y Villas $$$ Tel. 506-656-0250, 506-656-0723 fax 506-656-0076 www.brisas.net	$70-105s $75-110d $85-125t	$70-105s $75-110d $85-125t	Not all	All	Yes	Restaurant Bar Pools Jacuzzis	AE, MC, V. On the beach south of town in front of the beach break. Great views from balconies. A/C$. No a/c in off-season.
Camping and Bar Las Olas $ Tel. 506-656-0187 www.samarabeach .com/lasolas	$20-25s $25-30d $30-35t $35-40q	$15-20s $20-25d $25-30t $30-35q	Fans	All	No	Restaurant Bar Pool tables Foosball Volleyball Storage lockers	Beach huts right on the beach. Satellite TV in bar. Joel, the surfing proprietor captains boat trips Isla Chora. Good, surfer-budget option. Rents surf and boogie boards and snorkeling stuff.
Casa del Mar $ Tel. 506-656-0264 www.casadelmarsamara.com	$29-65d $39-75t $85q	$29-55d $39-65t $75q	Not all	Not all	Not all	Restaurant Pool	AE, MC, V. Bed & breakfast. AC$.
Marbella Hotel & Apartments $ Tel./fax 506-233-9980	$35s $42-45d $50t $60apt.	$18s $28d $35t $50apt.	No	All	All	Restaurant Small pool	AE, MC, V. Long walk to the beach. Apartments good for families or groups. River rafting. Rents surfboards, bikes and cars.
Villas Playa Sámara $$$$ Tel. 506-656-0104 www.villasplayasamara.com	$155s $190-220d $400q $570 six	$115s $130-150d $280-360q $390-510 six	All	All	All	Restaurant Bar Pool Swim-up bar Jacuzzi Casino Volleyball	AE, MC, V. Kitchens$. Includes 3 meals. Water-skiing and windsurfing (cost extra). Ask for unit 13 right at the edge of the beach. Kids 2-12 only $15/day.
Sámara Beach Hotel $$$ Tel. 506-233-9398 www.hotelsamarabeach.com	$65-75s $75-90d $85-100t $95-110q	$37-47s $47-57d $57-67t $67-77q	Not all	All	All	Restaurant Pool	A/C$. Includes breakfast. Rents bikes. Tours.

Playa Carrillo

The next cove south of Sámara is a south-facing protected bay with some inside beach break and outside reefs. It's also home of the well-known Guanamar sportfishing resort. The gem here is the reef in the middle of the bay's mouth. The reef is way outside, with juicy rights on upcoming tides and a hairball left. It also needs a good swell. Rarely surfed. A good way to check out the break from a distance is with a relaxing lunch at El Mirador, a great little restaurant on the cliff overlooking the bay at the south end.

Where to Stay for Playa Carillo

Your best bet is to stay in Sámara and drive to Playa Carillo. Otherwise, it's the expensive Guanamar or an eco-traveler place up the hill to the north of the bay.

Lodging Name	Rates High	Rates Low	a/c	Priv bath	hot H2O	Facilities	Comments
Guanamar Beach & Sportfishing Resort $$$$ tel. 506-239-2000 www.crica.com/hotels/ guanmar	$110-120s/d $180t $250 suite	$110-120s/d $180t $250 suite	All	All	All	Restaurant Bar Pool Gift shop Tours, fishing charters Airstrip	MC, V, AE. TVs and telephones in rooms. About 15-minute drive south of Playa Sámara above the beach at Playa Carillo. Long walk down to the beach. Has room service. Rents bikes, bodyboards, horses, snorkeling stuff.

Playa Camaronal

Just south of Playa Carillo is this south-facing, secluded beach (not for long—a big development is under way at the time of this writing) long known for its consistent surf. Camaronal has a rivermouth and beach breaks with both rights and lefts. It's never crowded and it can get BIG. In fact, Camaronal usually has the biggest surf in the area. To get here, take the road south out of Playa Carillo, pass the Sueño Tropical Hotel, then take the right fork (about 5 miles out of Carillo) towards Punta Islita. You'll soon come to a river crossing (Río Ora) with no bridge. In the dry season the river is easily crossed with a 4x4. In the wet season you are most likely out of luck, so you can park your car there and walk. After crossing the river, head down the dirt road a bit to the cow pasture. From the high ground you can see the waves. I haven't tried it, but I've heard talk of paddling down the river to get to the beach. If anyone recommends that approach, ignore it. For starters, if you paddle down the river to get to the surf, how do you get back? Paddle up-river? Secondly, there are crocodiles in that river.

South of Camaronal is Punta Islita where smaller waves break in a picturesque cove below the hotel of the same name. The waves are nothing to speak of for the most part as compared to Camaronal to the north, but it's a place to get wet without driving if you plan on staying at the exclusive, secluded and beautiful Punta Islita Hotel. Probably the best thing to say about the surf here is that it's the easiest to get to in the area.

Where to Stay for Playa Camaronal and Punta Islita

The two nearest hotels are the Sueño Tropical to the north, or the exclusive and expensive Punta Islita to the south. Both are long hikes or moderately short drives from the surf.

Lodging Name	Rates High	Rates Low	A/C	Priv Bath	Hot H2O	Facilities	Comments
Punta Islita $$$$ tel. 800-525-4800, 506-231-6122 www.hotelpuntaislita.com	$170-330s/d $385t $400-550q+	-15%	All	All	All	Restaurant Pool w/wet bar Jacuzzi Driving range Gym Tennis Ping pong	Credit cards. Includes breakfast. All rooms have terraces with hammocks, minbars, hair dryers, Direct TV, and coffee makers. Some private Jacuzzis and pools. Fishing and horseback riding. Beautiful setting and views. Great honeymoon spot. Secluded.

Lodging Name	Rates	Rates	A/C	Priv Bath	Hot H2O	Facilities	Comments
Sueño Tropical $$ Tel. 506-656-0151, toll free 877-456-4338 www.elsuenotropical.com	$40-50s $45-55d	$40-50s $45-55d	All	All	All	Restaurant Bar 2 Pools Jacuzzi	Good place in between Camaronal and Carillo. New owners in 2005.

Between Punta Islita and the Mal País area there are few accommodations and nothing very comfortable (especially for the non-surfing companions), but there's lots of uncrowded surf.

Playa San Miguel

As with much of this area, San Miguel is a long stretch of totally uncrowded beach breaks. Here you will definitely surf alone. And the good news is that there's a hotel right there on the beach. This is really getting away from *everything*.

Where to Stay for Playa San Miguel

Dean Mural emailed in March 2001 about a place you might want to check out.

"Just a quick note to let you know of a terrific little place in Playa San Miguel. The name of the establishment is Casa Sultan Pacifico and is run by a couple from Miami, he fishes and she is a trained chef so the combination makes for some of the best food I have experienced in Costa Rica. The rates are $15 for a double in high or low season, there is no a/c, private baths can be obtained and there is no hot h2o. There is a bar and restaurant serving excellent food and the folks who run the place are terrific."

If you don't mind spending a little more and staying off the beach, check out the Italian owned L'Arca de Noe. It's like an oasis in the middle of nowhere. Peace and quiet, and recommended by many. The nicest hotel in the area.

Lodging Name	Rates High	Rates Low	A/C	Priv Bath	Hot H2O	Facilities	Comments
Blue Pelican Inn $ tel. 506-655-8046 www.amtec.co.cr/bluepelican/	$30-40d	$30-40d	All	All	All	Restaurant Bar	No credit cards. Treehouse hotel right on the beach with ocen views from all rooms. Good restaurant.
L'Arca de Noe $ Tel. 506-655-8065	$35-55s/d	$35-55s/d	All	All	All	Restaurant Bar Pool	1km to San Miguel, 4km to Playa Coyote. Continental breakfast included. Horse and kayak rentals. Laundry service. Free transport to/from Islita Airport. $55 from San José.
Casa Sultan Pacifico	$15d	$15d	No	Yes	No	Restaurant Bar	Dean Mural loves it!

Playa Coyote through Mal País

A variety of beach and reef breaks. It used to be that not many surfers came here, but that has changed dramatically, especially from Playa Santa Teresa, south. Most of this coast, however, is still somewhat uncrowded, especially north of Playa Santa Teresa. Take the time and trouble to get in here—in the rainy season it can be completely inaccessible—and you will likely be rewarded.

Playa Coyote

Beach breaks, a reef break, a decent left off of the point, and a good, short right if you walk around the point for a little ways. Here you can drive right down onto the beach. The best place to stay nearby is Hotel Arca de Noe, or inland 5 km at San Francisco de Coyote where there are some cabinas. There's also camping (toilets, shower) at Tanga's beach restaurant (make a left as you drive onto the beach). If this is your main destination, follow these directions: Take the Playa Naranjo ferry from Puntarenas, from Playa Naranjo head to Jicaral, then San Francisco de Coyote, then San Miguel. Find out more at www.playacoyote.com.

Playa Caletas

A long beach with beach and reef breaks all along. At the north end where the main road meets the beach is a rocky right reef break. Needs a good swell.

Where to Stay for Playa Coyote and Playa Caletas

Lodging Name	Rates High	Rates Low	A/C	Priv Bath	Hot H2O	Facilities	Comments
Casa Caletas $$$ Playa Coyote Tel. 506-289-6060 www.casacaletas.com	$120-130s/d $150 t	$100-110s/d $130 t	All	All	All	Restaurant Bar Pool	Boutiquey hotel overlooking the river at Playa Coyote. Includes breakfast. Guarded parking. Special honeymoon package.
Veranera Cabinas ¢ Playa Coyote no phone		$14d	No	No	No	Restaurant Bar	Basic accommodations at the south end of Playa Coyote between the rivermouth and the headland.

Playa Manzanillo

Offshore reef at the north end of the beach breaks on big swells. If you make it to this area, ask around for Owen the surfing Canadian, AKA "Juan Canadiense." He can set you up with lodging rentals and customized surf tours (i.e., secret spots). Owen is just one of the many expats you'll run into as you get lost in this area and start asking for directions—interesting characters who will make you think twice about ever going home.

> Speaking of getting lost.... Besides learning your way, getting lost can teach you other lessons, like one about living "off the land." Once, after making one of many wrong turns driving from Mal País north to Playa Negra, I got directions which included "Go back about five kilometers to the fork with the mango tree and make a left." I headed back, picking up a lost Canadian couple in my dusty slipstream. At the mango tree I did what any traveling surfer would do; I stopped for some free food. The only ripe mangoes had fallen from the tree to the ground, which was fine with me as I used to gather them

from the ground at my house when I lived in Miami. The Canadian couple also joined in the fun. Later at the Iguanazul Hotel after the long, hot, dusty drive, I rinsed off my free fruit and chowed down on those sweet juicy mangoes. The first one was delicious, a little overripe, but juicy and sweet. The second the same, but just a little funny tasting. It also had these small, white, hair-like strands in it. The third was funnier tasting still, so I decided to take a good close look. Upon closer inspection I saw that the hair-like strands were wiggling, because they were worms squirming their slimy little tails off. So I raced to the bar and started knocking down shots of rum hoping to kill the little *gusanos*. I think I did a damn good job. Lesson learned: Don't get lost.

Playa Hermosa (Nicoya)

Beach break with peaks all along. Between Playa Manzanillo and Santa Teresa, 4km north of Santa Teresa. Also lots of reefs in here that are rarely surfed.

The Mal País Area

My how the Mal País area has changed. Just a few years ago it was considered out of the way, and there was only one hotel with air conditioning. Now it is packed with eco tourists, rasta surfers, upscale hotels, roadside junk jewelry stands, internet cafés and a dozen surf shops. In five years it will be Tamarindo South.

Explore this area and you'll find at least three good left reef-points if there's a strong swell, beach and reef breaks when there's not. Mal País, as everyone calls the whole area, actually starts just south of Playa Carmen and goes down to Cabo Blanco. Good waves and moderate (but growing) crowds.

Mal País is not a stop along the way; it's a destination unto itself. That's because the road in and out from the north can be difficult, and sometimes impossible in the rainy season, so much of the year you have to leave the same way you came in. If you want to head to points north and can't drive the beach route you will need to take the backtrack roundabout route—always recommended by the locals—through Paquera and Naranjo. Whether you come straight from the airport in San José or from Tamarindo, plan on six hours to get here during the dry season. Who knows during the rainy season.

The best way to Mal País is via the ferries in Puntarenas: Either the Paquera, which is most direct, takes about 90 minutes, is more expensive (about $11 for a car, driver and one passenger) and runs less often (five times daily); or the Naranjo, which takes about an hour and adds an hour drive over a rough road (*very* rough), but is cheaper and runs more frequently. The locals will recommend the Paquera. If you take the Naranjo ferry, follow the signs to Paquera. From there head toward Tambor then Cóbano, the nearest town to Mal País. Go straight through Cóbano following the signs to Mal País. About 2km out of Cóbano, take the "Y" intersection to the left. About 15km later you will find yourself at a "T" intersection with the break most commonly known as Mal País right in front of you. Technically, that's Playa Carmen, but everyone calls it Mal País. Santa Teresa is to your right and the reef-points for Mal País are to your left. The drive from the Paquera ferry takes a little more than an hour during the dry season. Here are schedules for the ferries. I don't know why I've put them here. They change all the time.

Paquera Ferry / Tambor		Naranjo Ferry	
From Puntarenas	*From Paquera*	*From Puntarenas*	*From Naranjo*
4:15 am	6:00 am	3:00 am	5:10 am
8:45 am	10:30 am	7:00 am	8:50 am
12:30 pm	2:30 pm	10:50 am	12:50 pm
5:30 pm	7:15 pm	2:50 pm	5:00 pm
		7:00 pm	9:00 pm

You can also take the Tempisque Bridge further north, finding your way south to Naranjo and taking the same directions above. I'm not sure if this route is any faster, except when you know there are long lines for the ferries in Puntarenas, such as on holidays. I am sure, however, that it wears you out much more, especially if you've just gotten off the redeye.

If Mal País is your only destination, then you might consider taking a taxi from the airport. The hotels or the Mal País Surf Camp will make those arrangements for you if you book in advance. Another option is to fly to Tambor, a 25-minute flight from San José. Your hotel can arrange for a pickup, or you can get a cab.

Playa Santa Teresa

Hollow beach break that picks up lots of swell—there's always something to surf here. Good rights and lefts, and breaks best at lower tides. The cleanest and best shaped beach break in the area. "Teresa" was once somewhat of a secret, but is now crowded, what with the popularity of the Mal País area and the recent accommodations built practically right on the break. Teresa is about 2km north of Playa Carmen.

There are lots of places to stay along the six kilometer stretch from Teresa to Cabo Blanco, and quite a few withing walking distance of the Playa Santa Teresa. The closest are Point Break and Cbinas Santa Teresa.

Playa Carmen

As mentioned, what is known to most as Mal País is really Playa Carmen, or El Carmen. Beach break peaks with long rights and lefts, and some rock-reefs up and down the beach. Fairly easy break, so it's good for beginners, but not when it gets big. Most of the surfing happens right there where the road from Cóbano meets the Pacific.

Playa Carmen is the closest beach to the Mal País Surf Camp, a great place for surfers who are on a budget or enjoy the camaraderie of other surfers (out of the water). The owner, Doug Packman, is a good guy who has built a pretty cool place with accommodations ranging from camping to houses for rent, and everything in between. They also have a summer camp for kids, including meals, and a video of everyone surfing for $35 per day. If you need to rent a board, stop here. And if you break your board, Doug will buy it. (But you probably won't get much. He gave my buddy Chappy three t-shirts and three beers for his longboard that he snapped at Playa Teresa. Thanks for the beer and the t-shirt, Chap!) See "Where to Stay" below for more information, or book through Surf Express or Tico Travel for convenience.

Punta Barrigona

Punta Barrigona is one of the Mal País left reef-points. It breaks best on strong south and west swells at low tides. Heading south from Playa Carmen, turn right toward Mar Azul Cabinas & Restaurante. The break is right in front of and to the north of the restaurant.

Los Suecos

Further south is Los Suecos, also called Helena's, the last left reef-point. It breaks out in front of the Sunset Reef Marine Lodge. You'll know that you're there when the road runs into a wall then turns to the left; there are fishing boats to the right. You can't see the break very well from the road. You need to walk around the hotel on the lava reef. Los Suecos is a juicy, but needs a strong swell to break. It's juicy enough that some are calling it the Teahupoo of Costa Rica. It's not by a long shot, but it's not a beginner's wave. It's a long paddle out over lava reef, and once you get there you'll find tons of powerful uncrowded waves. Best on mid tide.

Where to Stay for Manzanillo through Mal País

Manzanillo to Mal País is actually a pretty long stretch, but there are really not too many places to stay until you get to the area south of Santa Teresa. The lack of lodging has helped control the crowds…so far. One decent walk-to-surf option near the Santa Teresa break is Cabinas Santa Teresa. The Sunset Reef Marine lodge at the other end of Mal País is another, sitting right in front of Los Suecos, with air conditioning. A few years back the Sunset Reef was the only hotel in the area with air conditioning. Now there are many. The Sunset Reef is still one of the more comfortable hotels around here, which makes it good for families and couples, although more and much nicer hotels are opening all the time. Steve from Islands Surf Shop in Santa Monica took his whole family to Sunset Reef and everyone dug it. Ask for William, and tell him we sent you.

If you drive in from Cobano, the first accommodations you will see are Frank's Place, an old surfer favorite and a good budget option right there at the main intersection at Playa Carmen. Great little restaurant and decent rooms just a short walk to the main surf spot. I always get good letters and emails on Frank's.

One of the long-time favorites is the Tropico Latino. The rooms are clean, big and comfortable. If you are a writer you will appreciate the desks with chair and lamp setup in the rooms. If you are a lounger, you'll love the hammocks on your front porch and the beach. This hotel is owned by a friendly Italian, Massimo, and managed by a surfer who's been in Costa Rica since 1984, Stephen Longrigg. You'll probably surf with Stephen if you stay here. I like it because you can walk to the surf, there's a pool, restaurant and bar, and Stephen and Massimo are great hosts. What I don't like is that it's hard to get a room in the high season. Another thing to think about is I've been getting reports of room break-ins. This is not unique to Tropico Latino, so that's not a reason to avoid these cabinas. But be sure to take advantage of the safe deposit box, to be sure. There are only six rooms, so plan ahead.

Lodging Name	Rates High	Rates Low	A/C	Priv Bath	Hot H2O	Facilities	Comments
Bosquemar Cabinas $ Playa Carmen tel. 506-640-0074 or 619-447-6787(US) www.bosque.malpais.net	$40-45 up to 4 people	$35-40 up to 4 people	Fans	All	All	Pool	Credit cards. A 1000-meter walk to the surf, but a clean and good option. Kitchens. Will arrange airport pickup for $20 per person. Also rents houses.
Casa Azul $$$ Playa Carmen Tel. 506-640-0379 www.hotelcasaazul.com	$60s $90d $350 2br suite	$50s $80d $250 2br suite	Not all	Not all	Not all	Pool Rooftop terrace	No credit cards. Right in front of the surf on the beach 100 meters north of the main crossroads. More of a house with rental rooms. Shared kitchen
Frank's Place $ Tel. 506-640-0096 www.frankplace.com	$12-28s/d $50-85t $60q	$10-22s/d $40-75t $45q	Not all	Not all	All	Restaurant Pool	Credit cards. Surfer favorite. Walk to surf. Some kitchenettes. Some shared baths. Recommended.
Hotel Surf The Place $$ Tel./fax (506) 640-0001 www.theplacemalpais.com	$70-80d $10 per extra person	$70-80d $10 per extra person	Fans	Yes	Yes	Restaurant Bar Pool	Credit cards. Kids under 10 free. Guestrooms with a/c rented in main building. Villa with a/c available for weekly rentals. Horseback riding, mountain bike rentals, jeep rentals, room service, internet access, phone, e-mail, fax, babysitting, laundry service, massage. Very nice place, but the surf photos on the website are not from Mal País.
Mal País Surf Camp $-$$ Playa Carmen tel./fax 506-640-0031; 954-583-5560 (USA) www.malpaissurfcamp.com	$12.50s $30-85d $105t $7pp camping	$12.50s $30-85d $105t $7pp camping	No	Not all	Yes	Restaurant Bar Pool Pool tables Satellite TV	Credit cards. Walk to Playa Carmen. Rents boards, horses, bikes. Also has camping. Laundry service, ding repair, surf tours, surf videos and fishing. A cool place to stay. They'll even video your surf session! Airport ($150 one way) and ferry pickup service.
Mar Azul Cabinas y Restaurante $ Mal País tel. 506-640-0098, 506-640-0075 www.marazul.malpais.net	$30t $60 house for 5 $80 house for 6	$30t $60 house for 5 $80 house for 6	Fans	Not all	No	Restaurant Bar Foosball TV in bar	Mal País. Basic accommodations. Share some baths. Rents horses. Surf Punta Barrigona right out front. Camping $1.50 per person.
Moana Lodge $ Tel. 506-640-0230 www.moanalodge.com	$60-80d $10pp extra	$60-80d $10pp extra	Not all	All	All	Pool Communal kitchen	Small with African motif, despite the name.

Name	Double	Single	A/C	Private Bath	Hot Water	Amenities	Notes
Oasis Bungalows $$ Tel. 506-640-0259	$65-80d $75t $85q	$55-65d $65t $65q	Not all	All	All	Pool	Small, cozy place. 10 minute walk to Playa Carmen. One child under 12 free. Laundry, tours.
Point Break Surf Hotel $ Santa Teresa www.surfing-malpais.com	$40-50d $80q	$40-50d $80q	No	Not all	Yes		Rustic, but the closest accommodations to the break at Santa Teresa. Surf lessons, horse and bike rentals, massage.
Ritmo Tropical $ Tel. 506-640-0174 www.ritmo.malpais.net	$47d $57t $67q $77quin	$47d $57t $67q $77quin	No	All	All	Restaurant Bar	Credit cards. Good location close to Playa Carmen and town center.
Santa Teresa Cabinas $ Tel. 506-640-0137 www.malpais.net/psteresa	$20-25d	$7-20	Fans	All	No		Closest hotel to Santa Teresa, about 150 yards from the surf. 3 kitchenettes with fridges. 2 beds in each room. Spartan but clean. Best "walking" choice for Santa Teresa. Can get rooms as low as $7 during off-season.
Star Mountain Eco Resort $ Mal País tel. 506-640-0101 www.starmountaineco.com	$65s $90d $120t	$65s $90d $120t	Fan	All	All	Restaurant Pool Jacuzzi	Price includes breakfast and taxes. Kids under 3 free; 3-6 50% off. Closed Sept-Oct. 4 miles from the beach, but a nice "hideaway" that's also good for the non-surfers.
Sunset Reef Marine Lodge $$ Mal País tel./fax 506-282-4160 www.sunsetreefhotel.com	$95d $95t $100q	$85d $85t $86q	All	All	All	Restaurant Bar Pool	MC, V. Surf Los Suecos right in front. 2 queen beds in every room. Dive trips including equipment. Fishing trips. Great for families. Good snorkeling out front. Tambor and Paquera ferry pickup. Rents bikes and kayaks.
Tropico Latino Lodge $$$ Mal País tel./fax 506-640-0062, 506-640-0337 www.hoteltropicolatino.com	$86-129d $99-142t $112-155q	$73-107d $86-120t $99-133q	All	All	All	Restaurant Bar Pool Jacuzzi	No credit cards. On the beach at Playa Carmen. Manager Stephen Longrigg has been surfing Costa Rica since the early '80s. Tours and horses. No a/c, but quite comfortable. Recent reports of break-ins, so check your valuables with the management.
Vista de Olas Bungalows $$$$ Tel. 506-6400183 www.vista.malpais.net	$120-150d $130-160t $140-170q	$90-120d $100-130t $110-140q	Not all	All	All	Restaurant Bar Pool Jacuzzi	Private bungalows in the hills with beautiful views overlooking the beaches. Kids under 10 stay free. A/C$
Zopilote Surfcamp Playa Hermosa Tel. 506-390-9148 www.zopilote-surfcamp.com	$75d/q	$50d/q	All	All	All	Satellite TV	View lodging 10 minutes from Playa Hermosa. Check for package prices which include boards, breakfast & dinner, laundry service and Cobano pick-up..

East of Cabo Blanco

Despite what you might think from looking at the map, there's no real surf once you get to the east side of Cabo Blanco. It's common knowledge that there are some breaks in the Cabo Blanco reserve itself, but you'll need a boat and local knowledge to get to them.

Central Pacific

In this guide the Central Pacific is defined as the beaches between Puntarenas in the north to Punta Uvita in the south.

The beaches of the central Pacific coast are generally more accessible than the other regions of Costa Rica. One reason is that it is closer to San José and the main airport, so much of it is better developed. Another is the terrain—it's not as rugged, so the highway can run close to the beach.

This region stays greener than the Northwest during the dry season (winter) because it is more humid. But it is still not as wet and humid as in the South and the Caribbean.

The best-known breaks in this area include Boca Barranca and Playa Hermosa—both great waves, both easily accessible, both crowded. But there are plenty of other great breaks with less exposure and more solitude. In fact, *most* of the other breaks are uncrowded. And here's a plus for goofy-foots: While Guanacaste is known for its great rights, the Central Pacific—especially between Puntarenas and Jacó—is known for lefts.

The best surf season is when the south swells prevail, April through November, but there's always surf in Costa Rica's Central Pacific. *Always.*

Puntarenas

Don't go here except to find a "base camp" hotel to surf Boca Barranca, Doña Ana and the other nearby breaks. There's no surf in this resort/port town that has the charm of a weary, lackluster Tijuana. This is the butthole of Costa Rica.

Boca Barranca

About three miles south of Puntarenas you will find this easily accessed rivermouth with very long lefts, leg burners second in length only to Pavones. Fast and sometimes hollow at low tide, and low tide is best. It gets progressively worse as the tide goes up to the point where there's no wave at all. Site of the annual Rabbit Kekai "Toes on the Nose Longboard Classic" contest held Memorial Day weekend. Since it's less than two hours from San José it gets very crowded—especially on weekends when the locals take over—although I have surfed it alone. During the rainy season the water gets especially brown and dirty and the currents sometimes strong—kinda spooky. Even in the dry season the water is murky. Murky or not, be wary of getting infections. There's usually a sandy bottom all the way in. But sometimes the bottom is all fist-sized, sharp, barnacle-encrusted, algae-coated rocks. So even small cuts get infected. I've also heard stories of dead cows and all sorts of things washing out of the Rio Barranca into the lineup. Makes Huntington look like Perrier. Both Boca Barranca and Doña Ana need good-sized south swells to break. Best in July and August. Walk out alongside the river to the point and paddle out from there. If you try to paddle out down the line the current will take to the Fiesta

Hotel in about 15 seconds. Check the surf from the bridge over the river. Parking, food and beer are right there on the point. But watch out for ripoffs.

Doña Ana

Just across the river to the south of Boca Barranca is another good left (except on high tides). Needs a big swell. The break starts outside easy and gets progressively faster with each section going inside. One way to check it out is to paddle across the river or from the line-up at Boca Barranca, but it's much easier to go through the park. Ed Eaton of Bloomington, New Jersey suggested I recommend wearing reef booties for getting in and out over the rocks. I recommend wearing reef booties for getting in and out over the rocks.

Puerto Caldera

About 3km south of Boca Barranca is another great left that breaks at the mouth of the estuary off the jetty. Easy to find since it's right next to the highway. Also needs a solid south swell. "Puerto" means port, and the smell confirms it.

Where to Stay for Boca Barranca Through Puerto Caldera

As much as I dislike the city of Puntarenas itself, it's the nearest "big city" to these breaks, so I've included Puntarenas hotels in the listing. The Puntarenas hotels here are either at the east end of town (Cocal) nearer the surf, or just outside of town in the suburb known as San Isidro, just a short drive to the surf. The Fiesta is a 20-minute walk from Boca Barranca, a bit expensive, and the point is visible from many of the rooms. It's definitely the best hotel in the area for a non-surfing girlfriend/boyfriend, spouse or kids. It's an upscale all-inclusive resort that doesn't feel much like Costa Rica, but it can be a welcome break. Closer still to Boca Barranca is Hotel Río Mar. It's not as nice as the Fiesta, but you'll save lots of money and hike-to-surf time. Down the same side street as the Fiesta are two hotels, Casa Canadiense and Villa del Roble. And if you want to stay right on top of the break at Boca Barranca and you're OK with the most basic (read not very nice) accommodations theres the Cabinas Oasis (506-663-7934). For Caldera you may want to check out the Marina Resort. It's extra muggy around here, so air conditioning is more welcome than usual.

Lodging Name	Rates High	Rates Low	A/C	Priv Bath	Hot H2O	Facilities	Comments
Casa Canadiense $ Tel./fax 506-663-0287	$50d	$50d	No	All	All	Pool	Security gated parking. ½ km from the Fiesta, but still a drive to the surf. Kitchens in rooms.
Club de Playa Cabinas $ tel. 506-221-1225 fax 506-263-0031		$40-80 for 4-9 persons	No	All ,	All	Pools Playground	Kitchens in rooms. In San Isidro.

Fiesta Resort & Casino $$$ Puntarenas Tel. 506-663-0185, 800-662-2990, 800-228-5050 fax 506-663-1516 www.fiestaresort.com	$120pp	$120pp	All	All	All	Restaurants Bars 3 Pools Casino Volleyball, tennis, gym, jacuzzi, mini-mart, gift shop, boutique	Credit cards. All-inclusive resort that's great for the wife, family or girlfriend. Outside Puntarenas near Boca Barranca—a 20-minute walk. All rooms have telephones and satellite TV. Laundry service. Rents bikes, jet skis, snorkeling stuff, water skis, sailboards. Surfboards for sale in gift shop. Sometimes crowded with conventions. Partyland.
Portobello Hotel $$ Puntarenas tel. 506-661-1322, 506-661-2122 www.portobellocr.com	$45s $55d $65t	$32s $45d $55t	All	All	All	Restaurant Bar Pool	AE, MC, V. One travel guide calls this "the loveliest hotel in Puntarenas." But don't get too excited. Nice grounds and a good restaurant. Drive to surf. TVs in some rooms. Telephones in all rooms. High-speed internet.
Río Mar Hotel $ tel. 506-663-0158	$20s $28d	$20s $28d	No	All	No	Restaurant Bar Kiddie pool	V. Closest to Boca Barranca and Doña Ana. Speedboat available for fishing. Also has larger rooms for families. Relaxing place.
Yacht Club $ Tel. 506-661-0784	$26-45s $38-62d	$26-45s $38-62d	Not all	All	all	Restaurant Bar Pool	Includes breakfast. A/C$

Tivives

Beach break with uncrowded left and right peaks. There are no hotels or cabinas right there at Tivives, but you can camp at the beach or drive from the Hotel Marazul.

There are a couple of ways to get in here. From the north, Caldera, or Highway 27, you will see the sign for the turnoff that will take you to the town (actually a co-op) at the beach. For the less beaten path, take the turnoff to Playa Guacalillo from Highway 34. At the fork with signs for Bajamar, go right, or north, and follow the road about three or four miles until it hits the river. You are there.

Playa Valor

A hollow, left-point type wave that breaks off of a cliff at the south end of the Tivives beach, after you paddle across the river. Long overhead barrels when it's on. It is a little tricky to find but a really fun wave. Some say that it's named "Valor" because there are lots of sharks.

Where to Stay for Tivives

Lodging Name	Rates High	Rates Low	A/C	Priv Bath	Hot H2O	Facilities	Comments
Marazul Hotel $ Tel./fax 506-221-8070		$50d $75 cabinas	Fans	All	All	BIG pool Restaurant Tennis Volleyball	Cabinas sleep up to six. Rents horses and bikes.

Playa Escondida

Excellent, hollow left and right reef 10km north of Jacó accessible only by boat unless you are a member of the private club there. You've seen a million pictures of this place, videos too, and they all say "secret spot." Works best on big south swells—where the left really lines up long—and lower tides. You can rent boats from Jacó or Playa Herradura, where you'll ask the fishermen to take you out. In Herradura ask for Tony. He'll charge $10 per person. There are also charters and other boat options. Herradura is about five kilometers north of Jacó. Escondida has become crowded, often with 20 to 30 guys out. Best bet is to try to beat the crowds by getting on it early. You'll need to anyhow, because the it blows out by late morning. Beginners beware: Juice + reef + mistake = blood.

Playa Jacó

Jacó is Costa Rica's most visited beach. On my first trip to Costa Rica, many advised me not to waste any time there. I don't mind it, but I stay at the south end of town away from the "excitement," as Jacó is Costa Rica's premier beach party town, for Ticos and Gringos alike.

Jacó has a long list of good accommodations and is easily accessible, being about two hours from the airport or San José (about 105km), depending on the traffic. As a result, Jacó (just like Boca Barranca) is the day-trip surf for people from San José, so it can and does get crowded, in and out of the water.

The surf itself can get fun, but it's not worth flying halfway around the world. Playa Jacó is a big, wide and long sandy beach with peaks all along, but it tends to close out when it gets over five feet. The best surf is usually up towards the rivermouth; the smallest down near the south end of the bay. Biggest on south or southwest swells.

One of the benefits of Jacó being a "surf city" is that there are quite a few surf shops for supplies, ding repair and rentals. At the south end of Jacó right off the highway is my favorite shop, Carton Surfboards. The proprietor, a young Tico surfer/shaper named Edwin "Carton" Villalobos, is a great, hardworking guy who will really take care of you. Carton's shop is fully stocked with supplies, accessories and new and used boards. Pura vida, Carton!

Roca Loca

The southern end of Playa Jacó is bordered by a rocky-point headland called Punta Guapinal. About five minutes out of Jacó around the point at the cliff, you will see a couple of car-parking areas and maybe some cars. Here you will find a rock reef with a great right called Roca Loca. It can get very good, but needs a good-sized swell. Breaks best on low to medium tides. The wave breaks over a big submerged rock that's right in the impact zone—beginners beware. To get to the surf, you have to climb down a sketchy cliff. When you get to the water watch out for urchins. And don't leave anything you want in your car.

Where to Stay for Jacó, Roca Loca and Playa Escondida

The most popular option is staying in Jacó and traveling to the other breaks, including Playa Hermosa (below), since everything is nearby. Prices in Jacó can be higher than other areas due to its touristy nature. But if you grab a copy of the local free newspaper, *Jacó Good Times,* available at places like Kimo's sandwich and surf shop you can get discount coupons and find hotels that give surfer discounts. Camping is available near the beach at Camping El Hicaco (506-643-3004), which also has a restaurant and the Cabinas Madrigal (see below).

A relatively new surf camp has come on the scene that you might want to check out. Built and operated by Alvaro Solano, the five-time national surfing champ of Costa Rica (probably six-time by the time you read this), and Ashley Fieglein, a surfer from Palo Alto, California, Vista Guapa Surf Camp opened in the Summer of 2002. You'll find Vista Guapa at the northwest part of Jacó, on a scenic hillside outside the hustle and bustle of town. They have a beautiful camp with three villas, each with two air-conditioned rooms with separate, private baths and hot showers. They also have a swimming pool, a yoga deck, a barbeque area, and a main house where breakfasts are served. Dinner is provided for guests through a partnership with the Jungle Surf Cafe in Hermosa, which is known for its ahi tuna steaks. Alvaro accompanies the experienced surfers to the best local surf twice a day, and also gives beginner lessons once a day. And if that's not good enough, Lisbeth Vindas, the #1 female surfer in Costa Rica also instructs a couple times a year. (She's had to cut back now that she's on the international tour.) Sign up for weeklong or longer packages, with meals and other things included, like airport shuttle transportation which is available every Saturday.

Lodging Name	Rates High	Rates Low	A/C	Priv Bath	Hot H2O	Facilities	Comments
Alice Cabinas $ Playa de Jacó Tel. 506-643-3061	$27d $34-45t	$27d $34-45t	Yes	All	Not all	Restaurant Small pool	MC, V. Some with kitchens.
Amapola Hotel $$$$ tel./fax 506-643-3668 www.barcelo-amapola-info.com	$111+s $180+d $243+t $306+q	$81+s $134+d $181+t $210+q	All	All	All	Restaurant Bar Pool Jacuzzis Casino Disco	Credit Cards. One of the Barcelo resorts. The kind of resorts that are ruining Costa Rica. Telephones, cable TV, refrigerators in rooms. Sport fishing, scuba, jet skis, tours, blah, blah, blah...everything.
Antonio Cabinas ¢ Tel. 506-643-3043	$13pp	$13pp	Fans	All	All	Restaurant	Near the bus terminal.
Clarita Cabinas y Restaurante ¢ tel. 506-643-3013	$20d	$20d	No	All	No	Restaurant	Oceanfront.
Club del Mar Condo/Hotel $$$$ tel./fax 506-643-3194 www.clubdelmarcostarica.com	$132-275d $550 penthouse	$110-242d $440 penthouse	All	All	Yes	Restaurant bar pool	AE, DC, MC, V. A/C$. On the beach and away from the hustle of Jacó. Closer to Roca Loca and Playa Hermosa because it is at the far eastern end of Playa Jacó, but waves are crummy out front. Some kitchenettes. Great place for wife, girlfriend and family.
Cometa Cabinas, La ¢ tel. 506-643-3615		$15-30 up to 5	Fans	Not all	All		V. Private bath$. Hot water$.

Copacabana Hotel $$$$ Tel. (toll free) 866-436-9399 www.copacabanahotel.com	$99-149s/d	$99-149s/d	All	All	Yes	Restaurant Bar w/sat.TV Live music Pool Swim-up bar Internet café	Credit cards. On the beach. Clean. Sportfishing. Rents kayaks, boogieboards. TVs in rooms.
El Bohio Cabinas $ Tel. 506-643-3017		$16-35	No	All	No	Restaurant bar Pool	Some kitchenettes. On the beach.
Emily Cabinas ¢ Tel. 506-643-3513		$11-30	Fans	All	All	Restaurant	Private baths cost extra. Budget surfer favorite. Good hangout. Has surf info and ding repair. Home of the famous Chuck, the surf guide.
Estrellamar Villas $$ Tel. 506-643-3102 www.hotels.co.cr/estrellamar	$63s $77-119d $81-119t $89-119q	$43s $47-77d $61-77t $63-77q	All	All	All	Restaurant Bar Pool Jacuzzi	MC, V. Includes breakfast. TVs in rooms. Some kitchenettes. Across the road from the beach. Private parking Quiet.
Flamboyant Hotel $$ Tel. 506-643-3146 www.apartotelflamboyant.com	$65-85d $70-105t $75-105q	$50-70d $55-90t $60-90q	Yes	All	Yes	Restaurant Pool Secure parking	AE, MC, V. The Flamboyant in Jacó is small and nice with kitchenettes, on beach in the center of town. Good waves out front.
Gaby Cabinas $ tel. 506-643-3080 email: gaby@hotelaeropuerto-cr.com	$25-30pp	$15-20pp	No	All	Yes	Pool	On the beach in Jacó. Includes breakfast. Kitchens. Cable TV. Parking.
Hacienda Lilipoza Hotel $$$ tel. 506-643-3062 fax 506-643-3158		$120s/d $146t $172q	All	All	All	Restaurant bar Pool Bbq Tennis Boutique	AE, MC, V. Rate includes full breakfast and dinner. About a km from the beach in the hills. Most luxurious hotel in Jacó with the best restaurant. TVs, two double beds, phones and bidets! in the rooms. Room service. Tours. Rents mopeds. No kids under 5.
Hotel Cocal & Casino $$$ tel. 506-643-3067, 313-732-8066 www.hotelcocalandcasino.com	$100-130d $150q	$60-85d $110q	All	All	All	Restaurant bar Casino Pools	AE, MC, V. On the beach with good surf out front. Room service. Private parking. No kids allowed. Two beds in each room. Some ocean views. A/C$
Jacó Beach Hotel Best Western $$$ tel. 506-290-2878, 800-352-6406 www.onecostarica.com/jacobeach/jacobeach	$109s $117d/t $15 per extra person	$100s/d/t $15 per extra person	All	All	All	Restaurant bar Pool Casino Disco Tennis Volleyball Gift shop	AE, DC, MC, V. Telephones in rooms. Some have refrigerators and TVs. Includes continental breakfast in green season. Busy, crowded hotel. On the beach. Ask for room with view. Room service. Car, bicycle, moped, sailboat, kayak and surfboard rentals. Room service.
Jacó Princess Villas $$ tel. 506-643-1000	$99s/d/t	$69s/d/t	All	All	All	Pool	Condos for groups of 5 with kitchenettes.
Jacófiesta Hotel $$ tel. 506-643-3147, 800-327-9408 fax 506-643-3148, 407-588-8369		$50-90s $55-100d	All	All	All	Restaurant bar Pools Casino, disco Tennis Volleyball	AE, MC, V. Cable TV and telephones in rooms. Some cabinas with kitchenettes. Tours and car rentals. Get discount coupons at Kimo's for rates starting at $10 per person.

Hotel	Price 1	Price 2	Col3	Col4	Col5	Amenities	Notes
Mango Mar Hotel $$ tel./fax 506-643-3670	$60-120s/d $10 per extra person	$50-90s/d $10 per extra person	All	All	All	Restaurant Bar Pool Jacuzzi Parking	Major credit cards. Oceanfront; waves out front. Kitchenettes. Tours arranged. Security guard in parking lot.
Mar de Luz Garden Suites $$ tel. 506-643-3259 www.mardeluz.com	$75s $80d $95t $110q	$60s $65d $80t $95q	All	All	All	Pool Secured parking	V. Kitchens, cable TV, private terraces. Apartments back in a neighborhood.
Marea Alta Cabinas $ tel. 506-643-3554	$29	$29	Fans	All	No		Kitchen.
Miramar Villas B&B $ tel. 506-643-3003	$60s/d	$40s/d	Yes	All	All	Pool	No credit cards. Includes breakfast. Walk 60 meters to beach. Barbecue grills available. Kitchenettes. Some large rooms.
Naranjal (El) Cabinas y Restaurante $ Tel. 506-643-3006	$28t $38q	$28t $38q	All	All	Not all	Restaurant Pool Parking	Kitchenettes
Palmas (Las) Cabinas $ Tel./fax 506-643-3005	$29-49s/d	$29-49s/d	Not all	All	Not all	Small pool	No credit cards. Some kitchenettes. Good cheap place to stay if you are staying a long time. A/C$
Paraíso del Sol $$ Tel. 506-643-3250 fax 506-643-3137	$50-60 up to 6	$50-60 up to 6	Yes	All	Yes	Pool Bar Parking	Kitchens. Ask for special surfer rate. Free security boxes. Laundry service. Guarded parking.
Pochote Grande $$ Tel. 506-643-3236 www.hotelpochotegrande.net	$60-70s $60-70d $70-80t $80-90q	$40-50s $45-50d $50-55t $55-60q	All	All	All	Restaurant Small pool	MC, V. On the north end of the beach in Jacó near the better surf. Kitchenettes. A/C$
Ranchos (Los) $ Tel./fax 506-643-3070 www.amerisol.com/costarica/lodging/losranchos.html	$25-65 up to 7	$20-50 up to 7	Fans	All	All	Pool Secure parking	Walk to surf—50 yards from the beach in the center of town. Loud at night due to the disco next door. Some kitchens and kitchenettes. Laundry service. Good surfer hangout. Surfer owned.
Sole d'Oro Apartotel $$ Tel./fax 506-643-3172	$70s $80d	less	Yes	All	Yes	Pool	Kitchen.
Tangerí Hotel & Chalets $$$ Tel. 506-643-3001 www.hoteltangeri.com	$94-101d $107-133t $125-157q	$72-87d $88-102t $104-116q	Yes	All	All	Pool Restaurant Bar	V, MC. Includes breakfast. Some kitchens with refrigerators. TVs. On the beach with surf out front.
Villa Caletas Hotel $$$$ Tel. 506-637-0505 www.hotelvillacaletas.com	$150-345d $380 villas	$130-300d $340 villas	All	All	All	Restaurant Bar Pool Boutique Gym	AE, MC, V. Combined mountain and seaside resort. Its location gives seaside breezes along with the mountain air freshness. Its hilltop location more than 1150 feet above the ocean combined with turn-of-the century style make Villas Caletas unique among the resorts, hotels and restaurants of Costa Rica. Spectacular 360-degree views. Score major points with the significant other here.

Vista Guapa Surf Camp $$$$ Tel. 506-643-2830 www.vistaguapa.com	$1050s $1660d weekly inc. meals, surf trans & tours $90s $96d b&b	lower	All	All	All	Pool Yoga deck Satellite TV Armed guards	Credit cards. Package price includes 2 meals, transportation to surf, etc. Discounts for extended stays. Outside the hustle and bustle of Jacó. Surf lessons. Airport shuttle on Saturdays. Owned by 4-time Costa Rica surf champ Alvaro Solano. How could you beat that?
Zabamar Hotel $ Tel. 506-643-3174	$35-55d	$35-55d	Yes	All	All	Restaurant Pool Bar Parking	AE, MC, V. Includes breakfast. Some refrigerators. Laundry service. Try asking for a surfer discount. Good surfer hotel.

Playa Hermosa

When you get tired of Jacó, or you're just plain ready to get deep into some juicy beach break tubes, or you're just looking for a spin cycle pounding, head south to Playa Hermosa. Here you will find seven kilometers of strong beach breaks in a beautiful (Hermosa means "beautiful") setting of black sand beach surrounded by mountains, and waves that, with a little size, love to hold you under, break boards, and drill you into that beautiful black sand. But those hollow beach breaks make it all worthwhile.

Playa Hermosa is probably the most consistent break in Costa Rica, so it is usually bigger than most other breaks. It is hard to get out the back when it gets overhead, and starts closing out when double overhead. Nearly everyone you talk to has a story about getting hammered at big Hermosa. Best on the higher tides, and it loves a southwest swell. Crowded, especially on weekends, but since the beach is long the crowds are spread way out and it's easy to find empty peaks all along. The favorite sandbar is in front of the big tree known as the Almendro. But why paddle out here when there are sandbars all up and down the beach? Bring your buds and you'll dominate your own peak in heaven.

Tulín's and Boca Tusubres

Consider these breaks part of Playa Hermosa since they are on the same stretch of sand. Tulín's (too-leenz) is down the beach, past the little ranch and development, and toward the rivermouth (Boca Tusubres). It's a beach break much like Hermosa, but bigger. It breaks best at lower tides, which is when Hermosa closes out more, and it holds its shape better. Best of all, the crowd is smaller. There's a price to pay for the smaller crowds: Tulín's breaks harder and farther out than Hermosa, which is pretty hard and pretty far out. This is definitely not for beginners.

Drive a bit further and the dirt road becomes a sand road and you start to see logs and piles of driftwood, signs that you are nearing a rivermouth. That rivermouth is from Río Tusubres. Here the waves get even bigger and juicier, and totally empty—except for the vultures hanging out on the beach. Perhaps it's a sign...

Playa Hermosa

- Road to Jaco
- Roca Loca
- Terraza Del Pacifica
- Ding repair
- David Hotel
- Public Phone
- Cabinas Las Arenas
- Cabinas Las Olas
- Cabinas Vista Hermosa
- Restaurante Pipasa
- Villa Ballena Cabinas
- Waves
- Waves
- Waves
- Almendro
- 34
- Road to Esterillos, Quepos & Dominical
- Waves
- Ranchita & Development
- Océano Pacífico
- Soda & Cabinas Tulins
- Waves (Tulin's)
- Driftwood and vultures mark the spot for big juicy tubes.
- Waves
- Boca Río Tusubres

N

Where to Stay for Playa Hermosa

There are lots of good places to stay right on the beach in front of surf that cater especially to surfers—possibly more than anywhere else in Costa Rica. Cabinas Las Olas has always been the core surfer's choice. It's right on the beach in front of very good, consistent surf. It was there before Costa Rica became the comfortable surf trip it has become, nurtured by surfer/owner John O'Toole, and it's still there, now under new ownership. O'Toole did it all right, making sure his guests had a great Costa Rica surf experience. (O'Toole is now with Wavehunters surf travel agency.) And it looks like the new owners, Jason and Carie Garris, are carrying on the tradition, even stepping it up a notch, adding some new rooms with air conditioning, airport transfers, a small surf shop with board rentals and guided tours to nearby surf breaks and surf lessons. The food situation is great, with one of the best breakfasts around and a restaurant right on the beach. If you are interested in staying here, ask about the Skybox suite, or check out the all inclusive Cazadores de Olas Surf Camp package at www.wavehunters.com.

A great choice if you are traveling with wife or need more upscale accommodations (air conditioning) is the Fuego del Sol (formerly Hotel David). It's nicer than Terraza del Pacifico next door by virtue of its being newer (the weather rots everything in Costa Rica pretty quickly). And the folks here are very nice. Cool thing about Terraza, however, is that it's the title sponsor and home base for Il Campeonato Internacional de Surf, one of the Vans Surfing Magazine Airshow Series contests. Right in front of these hotels is good surf, including a juicy right that bowls in front of the rocks and a left down the line from that.

I have been remiss not including the Loma del Mar Surf Camp in the last couple of editions, probably because I have yet to actually visit it. But there's so much of it online I figure it's pretty well covered. Besides, for some reason I don't often stay at surf camps; I don't have a good reason. I think they are great for those who may not drive, are on their first surf trip to a particular region, are short on time or wanderlust. And those who have the ability to commit. I can't sit still, or commit. Anyhow, since I haven't visited Loma del Mar I'll point you to their extensive web site at www.rovercam.com/lomadelmar. The site is also home to The Rovercam, the best web site for checking the surf in Costa Rica. The camp itself sits up on a hillside overlooking Playa Hermosa, ensuring guests of this camp will never lose out on surf. They offer everything a surf camp should, and more, including encouragement and support to make sure your surf time is maximized.

Lodging Name	Rates High	Rates Low	A/C	Priv Bath	Hot H2O	Facilities	Comments
Backyard, The $$$$ Tel. 888-535-8832 http://centralamerica.com/cr/hotel/backyard.htm	$120-170d-q $10 per extra person	$115-165d-q $10 per extra person	All	All	All	Pool Secure parking	No credit cards. Right in front of great surf. Next door to the Backyard Bar.
Brisa del Mar $ Tel. 506-643-7078	$35s $40d $45t $50q	$35s $40d $45t $50q	All	All	All		TVs and frig's in rooms. Walk to surf.

Name/Contact	Single/Double/etc (High)	(Low)	A/C	Hot water	TV	Amenities	Notes
Cabinas las Arenas $ Tel. 506-643-7013 www.cabinaslasarenas.com	$30-35s $40-45d $50-55t $60q	$25-27s $32-35d $42-45t $47q	Fans	All	No	Restaurant/bar with surf videos Surf shop Camping	No credit cards. Walk to surf. Also offers all-inclusive plans. Tours.
Cabinas Las Olas $-$$ tel./fax 506-643-3687; 888-899-TUBE, www.cabinaslasolas.com, www.wavehunters.com	$40s $60d/t $75 Skybox $100/quad - six	$40s $60d/t $75 Skybox $100/quad - six	Yes	All	All	Restaurant Pool	Surfer hangout. Highly recommended. Great surf out front. Also surf camp with guides. Kitchenettes with frig's. Good intro to Costa Rica surfing. Boat trips to secluded breaks.
Costanera B&B $ Tel. 506-643-1942 www.costaneraplayahermosa.com	$20s $30d	$20s $30d	All	All	No	Restaurant	No credit cards. Small place on the beach.
Destiny Resort & Spa $$$ Tel. 506-643-3385 www.destinyresort.com	$100 up to five	$100 up to five	All	All	All	Pool Jacuzzi	Bungalows with full kitchens, balconies with great views and three beds. Managed by top female surfer Giannina Coto. Tours, massage, facials, body wraps, yoga, airport transfers and more. Website bills it as a "couples paradise".
Fuego del Sol $$ Tel. 506-289-6060 www.fuegodelsolhotel.com	$69s $79d $89t $129-145 suites	$59s $69d $79t $99-115 suites	All	All	All	Restaurant Bar Pool Gym	MC, V, AE. Right on the beach with surf out front. Watch it from the bar or patio. Clean hotel with good air conditioning and cool touch-activated lamps. Perfect for girlfriend/wife/family. Tours.
Jungle Surf Café & Cabinas ¢ Junglesurf69@hotmail.com	$10	$10	Fans	No	No	Restaurant	Bargain place. Includes breakfast. Owner Tom has lived and surfed in Costa Rica since 1991.
Loma del Mar Surf Camp $$$ Tel. 506-643-1423 www.rovercam.com/lomadelmar/	Per week/ per person $795-1295s $695-1195d $1095t $995q		Yes	Yes	Yes	Dining room Pool Game room	All inclusive surf camp. A/C$. Includes meals, airport transfers, surf guides and transportation to the surf. Surf lessons with video review. Villas for rent.
Terraza del Pacifico $$ Tel. 506-643-3222, 506-643-3444, 212-213-2399 (NY) Also home of the **Jim Hogan Surf Camp** www.jimhogansurfcamp.com	$80d $10 for extra bed	$65d $10 for extra bed	All	All	All	Restaurant Bar Pool Swim-up bar Casino (high season only)	AE, MC, V. Great hotel for non-surfing partner or family. Lots of surfing families. At the north end of Playa Hermosa with surf right out front, or walk south to the more popular peaks. You could also probably walk to Roca Loca from here. Satellite TV and phone in room. Free internet access for guests.
Tulín Surf & Beach Resort ¢ tel. 506-643-1617 ottomoto@sol.racsa.co.cr		$7-10pp	No	Not all	No	Restaurant	No credit cards. Pay extra for private bath. Surfer-owned, Texas hospitality. Recent ownership change. Great surf right out front (Tulín's). Kayaks, tours, darts, volleyball, horseshoes. Secluded.
Vista Hermosa Cabinas $ tel. 506-643-3422 www.vistahermosa.20m.com	$60d $70t $90q	$60d $70t $90q	All	All	All	Restaurant Bar Pools Parking	No credit cards. Right in front of surf. Restaurant owned by Italian surfers. Frig's in rooms.

Esterillos Oeste

Just south of Playa Hermosa around Punta Judas and less than a mile from the highway is a rivermouth beach settlement flanked by a long sandy beach. It's a great, out-of-the-way place to kick back, with cheap cabinas, bars, friendly locals, and a popular surf camp. Oeste has all sorts of surf, with beach breaks breaking on the inside to reefs breaking way outside the rivermouth. The best surf and some good bowls can be found on mid to upcoming tides. The waves are, for the most part, mushier at the north end of the beach and get more hollow and walled as you move south, where it's all beach break. The whole Esterillos area faces due south, as opposed to Playa Hermosa, which faces southwest. Can get crowded on weekends with locals.

Where to Stay for Esterillos Oeste

Lodging choices are simple: Either cheap cabinas or the Rancho Coral Surf Camp. Rancho Coral is a "soup to nuts" sort of deal, starting with airport pickup. They offer surf lessons, like most surf camps, but also personalized instruction for the more experienced surfer looking to fix bad habits. Video review is part of the program. The rooms are very comfortable for the area, having air conditioning, kitchens and satellite TV. The rates include breakfast and dinner as well as transportation to and from the airport. Weekly, group and off-peak discounts available.

Lodging Name	Rates High	Rates Low	A/C	Priv Bath	Hot H2O	Facilities	Comments
Caleteras Cabinas ¢ Tel. 506-717-2143		$12d $15t	No	Yes	No	Restaurant Disco	On the beach. Kitchen.
Don José Cabinas $ Tel. 506-238-1876		$20-40 up to 8	No	All	No	Kiddie pool	
Famoso Cabinas $ Tel. 506-779-9184		$24 +$8 extra persons		All	No	Restaurant	
Hotel La Dolce Vita www.resortladolcevita.com	$55d $15 per extra person	$45d $15 per extra person	All	All	All	Restaurant Bar Pool	Apartments with kitchens 100 meters from the beach.
Rancho Coral Surf Camp $$$ Tel. 506-778-8648 www.ranchocoral.com	$50-90s $65-100d	$50-90s $65-100d	All	All	All	Restaurant	Credit cards. Includes breakfast. Full on surf camp with lessons. Meals and airport transportation included with packages. Rooms have TVs and kitchenettes. Laundry service. Fishing and other tours. Ding repair.

Esterillos Centro, Este and Bejuco

More rivermouths and beach breaks, and fewer crowds. Make that *no* crowds. The turnoffs are only a few kilometers south of Esterillos Oeste. If you are coming from the beach at Esterillos Oeste you neet to head back to the coast road and go south, because the beach road doesn't go through. There's really not much more to say about these beaches. Just miles of empty waves.

Where to Stay for Esterillos Este and Bejuco

A great place to stay in seclusion with empty, hollow beach breaks right out front is Alberque "La Felicidad."

Lodging Name	Rates High	Rates Low	A/C	Priv Bath	Hot H2O	Facilities	Comments
Alberque La Felicidad $$ Esterillos Centro Tel./fax 506-778-6824 www.lafelicidad.com	$55-80d $15 per extra person	$40-65d $15 per extra person	Yes	All	All	Restaurant Bar Pool	Credit cards. On the beach in front of good surf (or "the best spot for the surf in Costa Rica) as their recent letter read. Discounts for longer stays. Full meal plans available. A/C$
Delfin Hotel $$ tel. 506-717-1640, 407-367-9306, 506-770-8308 fax 407-367-9308		$50d	All	All	No	Restaurant Pool Tennis	Good food.
Fleur de Lis $ tel./fax 506-779-9141 fax 506-779-9108		$65d	Fans	All	No	Restaurant Small pool	Kitchenettes
Pelican Hotel $$ Esterillos Este Tel./fax 506-778-8105 www.pelicanbeachfronthotel.com	$60-80s/d	$40-50s/d	All	All	All	Restaurant Bar Pool Pool table	Cash only, no credit cards. On the beach. Board rentals, surf lessons, boogie boards, massage, tours.

Palo Seco

Heading south from Esterillos you'll come to a rather large town called Parrita. And guess what, just like the rest of this area you will find a decent beach break just south of town at Playa Palo Seco. Follow the turnoff sign just south of Parrita to the beach. On the way you will pass through the town of Palo Seco where you can get food and supplies. The surf is totally uncrowded. And if there are guys out you can drive either way along the beach road to find a peak to yourself. This is a great place. Black sand beach. Breaks best on higher tides.

Damas Rivermouth (Boca Damas)

A little over a mile north of the Quepos Rivermouth you'll find another rivermouth break with lefts and rights. (This is getting repetitive.) It's usually bigger here than the nearby breaks, especially Quepos and Manuel Antonio. As with other rivermouths, it's best to surf here when the tide is coming in. When the tide is going out the currents can get strong enough to take you with 'em. Another common feature of rivermouths that Boca Damas enjoys is the presence of crocodiles. The right on the south side of the rivermouth is long, fast, sectiony and sometimes hollow. The north side has a long left that is best reached by boat from Damas or Quepos. It is possible to walk in from Quepos, but it's a long walk and you'll have to paddle across the scummy Quepos estuary. (That freaked me out.) Your best bet is to hook up a boat ride. Ask any boat captain or fisherman in Quepos or Damas. The locals know the drill.

Quepos

Look out at the jetty and you'll see a small, perfect left that's easily accessed. It needs a lower tide and a good swell to work well, otherwise, get your log. There is also beach break inside. The waves here are best on big south swells.

Quepos (pronounced kay-pos) is a good-sized town with many restaurants and hotels, due in good part to having the Manuel Antonio National Park nearby, a popular tourist destination with good night life, but also to the deep sea fishing. As a "big city," Quepos is not a particularly nice place (one friend calls it "Crapos"), and it is also more expensive than most of the less developed areas. Quepos is kind of a pit, with lots of mosquitoes breeding in lots of stagnant water. If you want to walk to surf, stay in Crapos. Otherwise, stay up the hill toward Manuel Antonio where it's cooler and cleaner.

Quepos is about a four-hour drive from the airport at Alajuela. (In years with heavy rains the drive is longer due to the frequent washing-out of a few of the bridges. And sometimes the bridges simply collapse from overloaded trucks. Heck, some of those bridges could collapse under a skateboard.) From the airport follow the signs to Jacó and Hwy 1 south.

Manuel Antonio

Five km south of Quepos is this internationally famous national park with beach break lefts and rights. Good shape when the swell is big enough. The beaches here are beautiful, but good surf is inconsistent. That said, there's still usually something to surf pretty much every day. Don't leave anything in your car here (or anywhere else, really) as thievery is pretty popular here.

The main road takes you through town past all the hotels and down to the main beach, Playa Espadilla. Right out front is a fun beach break with fair to good shape on higher tides and better swells. Walk north along the beach a couple hundred yards and you'll see either a rock reef or a boil offshore, depending on the tide, where a wave pops up and often breaks, reforming on the inside. This is the beginning of "Playitas." Keep walking past the big rock and you'll come to a rocky little cove with the biggest waves along this beach and good, juicy barrels on decent swells, lefts and rights. Everything breaks best here on higher tides. Keep an eye out for rocks on lower tides. La Playita, aka Playa Silvia is also a gay hangout.

As mentioned, Manuel Antonio is an internationally famous eco-tourism park. That means it's a place where tourists go to look at exotic flora and fauna. And fauna includes crocodiles, with a couple of them hanging out near the northern end of Playa Espadilla. One is a nine-footer the park rangers named *Juancho*. So if a big croc starts tailing you in the water try addressing him respectfully by name (that's *Señor* Juancho) and maybe you'll be spared. They haven't attacked any people yet, but one ate a dog in 2001. Between 1999 and 2000 the park rangers relocated 13 crocodiles from Manuel Antonio to Playa El Rey to the south, where there are better waves and smaller crowds. Much smaller crowds.

Where to Stay for Manuel Antonio and Quepos

There are hotels on the beach right in front of the breaks, the Arboleda and Nature's Retreat, or something like that. You can also walk to the beach from many of the other hotels up on the hill, like Villas El Parque and Byblos. It's nice to stay up on the hill as it's cooler and there are lots of food options.

Lodging Name	Rates High	Rates Low	A/C	Priv Bath	Hot H2O	Facilities	Comments
Almendros (Los) Cabinas $ Quepos tel. 506-777-0225		$50 w/fan $70 with a/c	Yes	Yes	Yes	restaurant bar pool	200 meters from Manuel Antonio beach. Rents horses, tours and fishing trips. $a/c
Arboleda Hotel $$ Quepos tel. 506-777-0092 fax 506-777-0414		$65-85d	Not all	Most	yes	restaurants bar pool pool table	AE, MC, V. Right on the beach in front of the surf. Lower-priced cabinas have shared bath. Higher-priced rooms have A/C and patios. Rents surfboards, catamarans, horses, boogieboards. Fishing charters. Tours.
Byblos Hotel, El $$$ Quepos tel. 800-333-9361, 506-777-0411 fax 506-777-0009	$140-170 a/c extra$, 2 kids under 12 free	$75-115 a/c extra$, 2 kids under 12 free	Yes	Yes	Yes	restaurant bar pool jacuzzi	AE, MC, V. Includes breakfast. Telephones and cable TV in rooms. Refrigerators. Newer rooms have a/c and some ocean views (suites). Laundry service. Good French restaurant.
Casitas Eclipse Hotel $$ Quepos 6350 tel. 506-777-0408, 619-753-6827 (San Diego) fax 506-777-0408	$65s/d $85-100/1br $150/2br	$40s/d $50-60/1br $90/2br	All	all	yes	snack bar pool bar	V. Little houses on a hill sleep up to 5. Serves breakfast only. Units with kitchens cost extra.
Ceciliano Hotel ¢ tel. 506-777-0192		$15s/d $20t		not all	no	restaurant	Private bath$. Laundry service.
Colibrí Apartotel, El $-$$ Manuel Antonio tel. 506-777-0432	$49s $60d $69t $79q	$26s $35d $44t $53q		all	yes	pool	V. Secluded and peaceful. King-size beds. Barbecues. Some kitchenettes. No kids under 8.
Colina, La $ Quepos tel. 506-777-0231	$29s $40d	$18s $25d		all	yes		V. Includes continental breakfast (bed and breakfast) served in room.
Costa Verde Condominios $$ Quepos tel. 506-777-0584 fax 506-777-0560	$60-90s/d	$40-70s/d		all	yes	restaurant bar pool	AE, DC, MC, V. All rooms have kitchenettes, balconies, ocean views.
Dorado Mojado, El $ Quepos tel. 506-777-0368 fax 506-777-1248	$53s $66-109d $118t	$35-66s $44-66d $66t	All	all	yes	pool	MC, V. Includes breakfast. Has 4 villas with kitchens and TVs. Good place for fishing fans.

Espadilla, Cabinas $ Manuel Antonio tel./fax 506-777-0416		$47-60 up to 3	not all	all	no		No credit cards. Near the beach. Some kitchenettes. All with refrigerators and laundry sinks.. A/C$
Hotel California $$$ Quepos tel. 506-777-1234 www.hotel-california.com	$90-$115d +tax		All	All	All	Restaurant Pool Jacuzzi	Credit cards. Breakfast included. Beautiful ocean views. Great place for the girlfriend/ wife. Fridge's, telephones and cable TV in rooms. Balconies with views of Boca Damas surf in the distance. Tours, snorkeling, kayaks, rafting, horses, fishing.
Kamuk Best Western Hotel $$ Quepos tel. 506-777-0811 www.kamuk.co.cr	$60s $75d $90t	$45s $50d $60t	all	all	yes	restaurant bar	Credit cards. Right across the road from the beach at Quepos. Walk to the left at the jetty.
Karahé $$ Quepos tel. 506-777-0170 fax 506-777-0152		$70-100s/d $90-125t	not all	all	all	Restaurant bar pool jacuzzi	AE, DC, MC, V. Includes breakfast. Walk to beach. Newer rooms are closer to the beach. Fishing charters. Laundry service. Kids under 12 stay free. Private, cozy atmosphere. Ocean views.
Lirio, El $ to $$ Quepos tel./fax 506-777-0403	$80 up to 3	$35 up to 3	all	all	yes	Pool	No credit cards. Includes breakfast. Good deal in summer. Lots of room.
Makanda-by-the-Sea $$$ email: Makanda@sol.racsa.com tel. 506-777-0442 fax 506-777-1032	$150d $210q	$110d $150q	fans	all	yes	restaurant bar pool jacuzzi	No kids. All rooms have kitchens and king-size beds. Villas and studios.
Malinche (EL) Hotel ¢ Quepos tel./fax 506-777-9993		$8-30s $15-35d	not all	all	not all		V. Hot water and A/C$.
Mariposa (La) Hotel $$$ Playa Manuel Antonio tel. 800-416-2747 (US), 506-777-0355 www.lamariposa.com	$130-$280	$90-$180	All	All	Yes	restaurant bar pool	No credit cards. Villas and double rooms. The best in Manuel Antonio. Lots of room. Best views in area. Walk down the trail to Playitas. All tours arranged. No kids under 15 allowed.
Mimo's Apartotel $$ Tel. 506-777-0054 www.hotelmimos.com		$50 d/q $85 suites	Yes	All	All	Restaurant Bar Pool Jacuzzi Covered parking	Kids under 12 free. TVs. A/C$. Standard rooms sleep up to five. Suites have air conditioning. Italian owners.
Mirador del Pacifico Hotel $$ Quepos tel./fax 506-777-0119		$55-75s/d $100 villa for 2 $130 villa for 4		all	yes	restaurant bar pool	AE, MC, V. Extra charge for credit cards. Includes continental breakfast. Villas have kitchens.
Mogotes Villas $$ Quepos tel. 506-777-1043 tel./fax 506-777-0582		$60-95s $80-110d $95-125t	yes	all	yes	restaurant bar pool	Late singer Jim Croce's home includes breakfast. Some kitchens. Telephones. Ocean views.
Nicolas Villas $$-$$ Quepos tel. 506-777-0481 tel./fax 506-777-0451		$50-90d		all	yes	Pool Bar	Condos, some with kitchens. Some balconies with great views. No restaurant, but dining is across the street. Quiet.

Name / Contact						Facilities	Notes
Palmas (Las) Bungalows $ tel. 506-777-0051		$33-70		all	yes	restaurant bar pool	Kitchens. Kids under 6 free.
Parador, Hotel El $$$$ Tel. 506-777-1411 Fax 506-777-1437 e-mail parador@sol.racsa.co.cr	$172-671d add $30 per extra person	$122-476d add $30 per extra person	All	All	All	Restaurants Pools Tennis Gym Helicopter pad	If money is no option… Breakfast included. Kitchenettes, cable TV, views. Weddings a specialty. Tours, free shuttle to National Park.
Parque (El) Villas $$ Quepos tel. 506-777-0096 fax 506-777-0538		$71-82	not all	all	yes	Restaurant bar pool jacuzzi	Credit cards. One suite has a kitchen. Nice breezy restaurant with views of Playitas. Walk down a long trail to the surf. A/C$.
Pedro Miguel Cabinas $ Manuel Antonio tel. 506-777-0035		$20s $27d $54t		all	no	restaurant (winter only) pool (small)	No credit cards. Ask for an upstairs room. Some kitchenettes.
Piscis Cabinas ¢ Quepos tel. 506-777-0046	$20s/d $24t/q	$17s/d $20t/q		all	no	restaurant	No credit cards. About 150 yards from the beach.
Plinio Hotel $ tel. 506-777-0055 fax 506-777-0558 www.hotelplinio.com	$35-40s $50-55d $65-90 suite		not all	all	yes	restaurant bar pool pool bar rec room	AE, MC, V. Includes buffet breakfast. Great restaurant. Fantastic place to stay. Excellent views. Low-season surfer discounts. A/C$.
Quepos Hotel ¢ tel. 506-777-0274		$9-13s $17-20d		not all	no		No credit cards. Private bath$. Laundry service.
Quinta (La) Cabinas $$ Quepos tel. 506-777-0434		$65s/d $72t $80q	not all	all	not all	restaurant pool	Some kitchenettes. Hot water$.
Rancho Casa Grande Hotel $$$ tel. 506-777-0330 fax 506-224-0738		$95d $110-125 cabins	All	all	yes	restaurant pool jacuzzi tennis	Near the airport. Has its own private beach. Rents horses. Kitchens$.
Romántica Villa Hotel $$ tel./fax 506-777-0037		$60-80		all	yes	pool	Includes breakfast.
Si Como No $$$ Manuel Antonio tel. 800-237-8201, 506-777-0777 fax 506-777-1093 email sicomono@sol.racsa.co.cr		$140-175d inc tax	All	all	all	restaurants bars pool jacuzzi movie theater	Includes breakfast. "La-di-da." Great place to make your lady happy. Kayaking, rafting, sportfishing. Conference facilities.
Sirena Hotel $$ tel. 506-777-0528 fax 506-777-0171		$60-80	yes	all	yes	pool	Kids under 12 free.
Sula Bya Ba Hotel $ Quepos tel./fax 506-777-0547 fax 506-777-0279	$28s $35d $45t			all	no	restaurant bar	AE, MC, V. A ways from the beach. Includes breakfast. Tours.
Teca Villa $$$ tel. 506-777-1117		$120-140	All	all	yes	restaurant pool	Includes breakfast.
Tres Banderas, Las $ Tel. 506-777-1284 or 1871 Fax 506-777-1478 www.hotel-tres-banderas.com	$55s $60-65d $95q suite $15/per additional person	$35s $40-45d $75q suite $15/per additional person	All	all	All	Pool Jacuzzi Restaurant Bar	All major credit cards. Secluded tropical setting away from the city hustle and bustle between Quepos and Manuel Antonio.

Tulemar Bungalows $$$$ Tel. 506-777-0580, 506-777-1325 www.tulemar.com	$269-389d plus $25pp	$178d plus $25pp	All	All	All	Restaurant Bar Pool	Credit cards. Includes breakfast. Kids under 12 free. Kitchenettes, TVs, VCRs, minibars. On the beach, but there's no surf. Kayaks and snorkeling no charge.
Villas El Pájaro Azul $$ tel. 506-777-1046 fax 506-777-1241		$80-100		all	yes		Houses with kitchens.
Villas Mymosa $$$ Manuel Antonio Tel. 506-777-1254 www.villasmymosa.com	$75-$122	$52-87	All	All	All	Restaurant Bar Pool	Private terraces. Some good views. Each villa has kitchen, living room, TV.

Playa El Rey

Secluded beach break peaks with rights and lefts that break best on lower tides. Take the road south from Quepos toward Dominical. After about a half-hour drive you'll come to Roncador where you'll turn right and drive about 11 kilometers. Not much in the way of hotels, but there's camping. Alacran Surf Tours (www.alacransurf.com or www.surf-costarica.com) offers daily-guided trips to El Rey including board rentals, bilingual guides, and a barbecue lunch. As mentioned above, crocodiles have been relocated to Playa El Rey from Manuel Antonio, but I haven't heard of any attacks or even sightings.

Playa Matapalo

(Not to be confused with Cabo Matapalo.) About halfway between Quepos and Dominical is the village of Matapalo, which is also inland from the surf about 3km. Head to the ocean and you'll find a very long (45km), secluded, unbroken sandy beach with good, uncrowded beach/rivermouth breaks favoring higher tides. Everyone from the Manuel Antonio/Quepos area heads to Playa El Rey to escape the crowds, so it's even less crowded further south at Playa Matapalo.

Where to Stay for Playa Matapalo

The Playa Matapalo hotels are almost right on the sand, with just a strip of trees between you and the waves. Most of them are European owned and run, with pride taken in their restaurants and wine offerings.

Lodging Name	Rates High	Rates Low	A/C	Priv Bath	Hot H2O	Facilities	Comments
Coquito del Pacifico Hotel $ Tel. 506-787-5029; 506-384-7220 www.elcoquito.com	$45s $55f $65t $75q	$31s $41d $49t $57q	All	All	All	Restaurant Bar Pool	No credit cards. Cabinas. Rents bodyboards, bikes, horses. On the beach.
Matapalo Cabinas ¢ Tel. 506-779-9255	$26	$26	Fans only	All	No		Cabinas. Shared kitchen.
Oasis Cabinas ¢ Tel. 506-777-1984	$15-20	$15-20	Fans only	All	No	Restaurant Bar Pool	Rustic cabinas. Good burgers.

Piedra Buena Cabinas $ Tel. 506-779-9255	$40-45	$40-45	Fans only	No	Yes	Restaurant/bar	Rustic cabinas.
Ranchito, El ¢ Tel. 506-779-9255	$12-20	$12-20	No	All	No	Restaurant/bar	TV.
Terraza del Sol Hotel $ Tel./fax 506-779-9255	$45d	$20d	Fans only	All	No	Restaurant	No credit cards. Cabinas. Gourmet French cuisine at decent prices. Rents kayaks.

Dominical

The town of Dominical is a mini, laidback surf-city, actually a hamlet, with surf shops, surf bars, and surf-oriented hotels. Actually, one of Costa Rica's first surf ghettos. There are several breaks to pick from around Dominical—beach, rivermouth and reef—in what is probably the most consistent surf region in Costa Rica. Dominical is a wave magnet known for its hollow, powerful, shapely beachbreaks that get heavy with size and is surfable up to 20' faces. Michael McGinnis, proprietor of Cabinas San Clemente and a damn good surfer, likens the beach break at Dominical to Mexico's Puerto Escondido, and I've seen the pictures to prove it. There are plenty of peaks and bowls up and down the beach with the best (and most crowded) right in front of Cabinas San Clemente and Tortilla Flats Hotel & Restaurant. While these are the most crowded, nobody dawn patrols here, so it's uncrowded until about 8AM, and the sun is up before 6am and offshores blow until about 10. The waves are more forgiving at higher tides, which is also when the shape is best. Grinds and closes out at low tide, especially when big.

While Dominical waves may sometimes be forgiving, it is also the site of frequent drownings due to the waves, currents and rips. If you are a beginning surfer, or are not a strong swimmer, this is not your spot.

When it gets big, head south of town and you'll find a left-breaking reef/point that goes off—Punta Dominical. Works best on medium to high tide and needs a decent swell. This left can get long and hollow, and there's a short right too. Breaks from shoulder high to triple-overhead.

Just south of Punta Dominical are more reefs with some rights and longer lefts. Fun, uncrowded waves. Good for longboards.

And whether it's big or not, be sure to check out Mike McGinnis' San Clemente Restaurant and Bar for good food, fun, and a decent surf shop. Mike runs the Dominical Information Center and also has a program where he'll video your group surfing in the day and show the videos in the bar at night. (So don't start bragging about your double-overhead, 10-second barrel too early in the evening.) Mike is a good guy to seek out in Dominical. He can also set you up with trips, like the one to the Nauyaca Waterfalls for cliff jumping and other life-threatening fun.

Where to Stay for Dominical

As soon as you pass the bridge and approach town (when coming from the north or east) you'll see an information center on your right. Not a bad place to check on hotels, tours, car rentals, real estate, etc. Dominical is great in that there are places to stay right at the beach and in front of the waves, such as the previously mentioned San Clemente and Tortilla Flats, AKA Cabinas Nayarit (tiny rooms with two beds squeezed in like a 2-foot tube) and Green Iguana Surf Camp. Many are dark, dingy, and just plain crummy, so check them out first. There are many other cabinas within a short walk to the surf, such as the Diuwak, which has a surf bar with videos and air conditioned rooms.

One nice place is about 2km south of town. It's called the Coconut Grove Cottages, and as the painted rock sign says, it has a pool and air conditioning—the latter being a luxury in these parts. Most of it is relatively new, a real plus in these parts where things rot quickly. The cabinas are small, but they're big enough for two or three, depending on your sleeping arrangements. Each has a refrigerator, coffee maker (with coffee!), toaster, plates, flatware and other kitchen stuff so you can make yourself at home. Rooms are about a 100 meters from the beach, and there's some surf just out front and to the south. If you first check it out at high tide, beware, there are lots of rocks hiding under there. Punta Dominical can be seen from here, and the beach break at Dominical is a 15-minute walk up the beach to the north.

The Río Mar is also a pretty good Dominical choice, especially for the non-surfers in the group, but it doesn't have air conditioning and is about a kilometer from the surf. The setting is beautiful and the hotel is secluded and peaceful, right on the Río Baru. The pricing is pretty good, too, especially if you grab the coupon out of *The Tico Times*.

Another nice option is the Punta Dominical Cabinas. It's high on the cliff right over the point—a benefit when the surf is on—with great views, cool breezes (no air conditioning) and a good restaurant. Great for the wife or girlfriend due to the beautiful, secluded setting.

A good low budget choice is Antorchas Camping, where you rent a tent right off the beach. One reader, Tim Pryor, calls Antorchas his favorite place to stay in Costa Rica. Showers and toilets are shared among campers. And they provide facilities to cook your own food. There are also a few rooms to rent for $8. The crowd is a little older, and "a little more interesting," per Tim. A really sweet woman named Cecilia runs the place. There are other camping options; just ask around. You might want to avoid Backpackers Hostel, per Aaron Nardella. He and his buddy had their stuff stolen while they were out for a surf. (By the way, ripoffs are not unique to the Backpackers Hostel.)

South of town about 4km and up a 4wd-only trail is Escaleras. Here there are great views and a few cool places to stay, but it's farther away from the surf than other choices and you should probably take a horse up the trail (check with lodge owners).

Lodging Name	Rates High	Rates Low	A/C	Priv Bath	Hot H2O	Facilities	Comments
Bella Vista Lodge $ Tel. 506-787-8069 www.bellavistalodge.com	$55s/d $75d+	$45s/d $75d+	Fans	Yes	Yes	Restaurant	No credit cards. Actually up the Escaleras road 4 km south of Dominical overlooking Dominicalito. Includes breakfast. Great views.
Camping Antorchas ¢ Tel. 506-787-0307	$8pp	$8pp	No	No	No		Recommended budget option. Camping, dorm rooms and private rooms.

Coconut Grove Cottages $$$ tel. 506-787-0130 www.coconutgrovecr.com	$75s $85-125d $10per extra person	$65s $75-100d $10per extra person	Yes	Yes	Yes	Pool	Cash only. Rates include taxes. Great place 2km south of town and a short walk to the surf. Newer rooms in good shape. Small, equipped kitchenettes. Be careful with reservation deposit policy.
Escondidas Cabañas $ Tel. 506-721-2904	$45-70d	Less	No	Yes	No	Restaurant	No credit cards. Includes breakfast. New Age place. Tranquil. Vegetarian restaurant, Tai Chi classes, massage, tours. Rents bikes. 9km south of town, secluded location overlooks the ocean.
Green Iguana Surf Camp $ Tel. 506-787-0192 www.greeniguanasurfcamp.com	Check for package rates	Check for package rates	Not all	All	All	Restaurant Bar	Surf camp packages put guest up at various hotels. Packages can be all-inclusive or customized: Lesson, equipment, airport transportation, breakfast and dinner included in one of three local restaurants. Also Spanish instruction.
Pacific Edge Cabinas $$ Tel./fax 506-787-8010 www.dominical.biz/pacificedge	$50-75d $68-92t $108q	$50-75d $68-92t $108q	Fans	Yes	Yes	Restaurant Pool	Credit cards. Spectacular beach views 4km south of Dominical and up the hill. Small kitchenettes available. Make reservations.
Punta Dominical Cabinas $$ Tel. 506-787-0016, 506-787-0017 www.laparcela.net	$55d +$12 per extra person	$55d +$12 per extra person	Fans	All	Yes	Restaurant Bar	No credit cards. 5km south of town overlooking the point. Great views over the coves. Great restaurant (La Parcela). Horseback tours. Cabins sleep 7. On Punta Dominical. Secluded.
Río Lindo Hotel $ Tel. 506-787-0078; U.S. 305-294-6313 www.riolindo.com	$65-98s/d $10 extra bed	$45-65s/d $10 extra bed	Yes	Yes	Yes	Restaurant Bar Pool Jacuzzi	No credit cards. Ask for upstairs room and special surfer rates. Tours.
Río Mar Hotel $$ Tel. 506-787-0052 www.villasriomar.com	$70-125d	$55-100d	Not all	All	Yes	Restaurant Pool Gym	On the river about 1km from the surf. Horseback and canoe tours. Rents bikes, kayaks. One of the nicest hotels in Dominical, but still no a/c. Internet access and room service.
Roca Verde Hotel $ Tel. 506-787-0036 www.rocaverde.net	$85d	$75d	Fans	Yes	Yes	Restaurant Pool	Credit Cards. South of town central just off the highway.
San Clemente Cabinas $ Tel. 506-787-0026 fax 506-787-0055	$25-65d $10 pp shared bath	$25-65d $10 pp shared bath	Not all	Not all	Not all	Restaurant Bar	Credit cards. Surfer-owned. Spacious cabinas on the beach in front of best waves. Not a bad place to stay.
Tortilla Flats (Nayarit Cabinas) $ tel. 506-787-0033 www.tortillaflatsdominical.com	$35-55d/t	$25-40d/t	All	All	All	Restaurant Bar Laundry	No credit cards. Right in front of the best waves here. Part of Green Iguana Surf Camp/School. Rents bikes. A/C$. Also rents houses with kitchens. Tiny rooms. Also offers package deals.

Playa Hermosa (Dominical)

Head south from Punta Dominical and before you get to Punta Uvita you'll find a good beach break called Hermosa—not to be confused with the way more recognized and crowded Playa Hermosa de Jacó further north. It's generally a little smaller than the beach break at Dominical, but it's a good place to go when the swell's on and it's getting crowded elsewhere. Best on mid to high tides.

Punta Uvita

Seventeen kilometers south of Dominical is the costal village of Uvita, which is at the base of a huge reef that juts way out into the Pacific. If you have time and maybe even a boat you might check it out. There's surf out on that reef. It goes way, way out and there's no one out there. There's some fun surf exploring to be had. If there isn't any surf, this is also the gateway to Ballena National Park, the only marine park in Costa Rica. The park is home to the largest coral reef on the Pacific side of the country. There's a fee of about a buck per person to get into the park, plus a small parking fee. There is also an offshore island, Isla Ballena, with reefs and surf. And if reefbreaks aren't your thing, there are decent, uncrowded beachbreaks in the cove just north of Punta Uvita.

Boca Coronado

Want to know where there's tons of good to excellent uncrowded surf—as in no one out at all? Here it is. And even though the word is just now getting out, it will be years before it even starts to resemble crowded. In fact, you'll probably wish there were other guys out just to help get a read on the place. Boca Coronado, aka Playa Tortuga, is a big rivermouth that catches lots of swell and with surf everywhere. On the north side of the rivermouth you'll find long lefts with great shape. And on the south side are the rights. And a few sandbar peaks on both sides. This is a big rivermouth with a lot of water moving around, so watch it on dropping tides.

Where to Stay for Boca Coronado

Up the hill from the beach and the highway is a great little place with views of the surf called The Lookout at Turtle Beach. A nice, clean place for the non-surfing partner or family with a very good restaurant, bar with satellite TV and pool. Villa El Bosque and Villas Gaia are both relatively close to the surf.

Lodging Name	Rates High	Rates Low	A/C	Priv Bath	Hot H2O	Facilities	Comments
Lookout at Turtle Beach Hotel $$ Tel. 506-950-9013 www.hotelcostarica.com	$85d	$85d	Fans	All	All	Restaurant Bar Pool Gift shop	No credit cards. Breakfast included. Great views of the surf, but a long walk to the waves. Nice, clean hotel. Extra single beds available.
Villa El Bosque $ www.catchtravels.com /CR_Villaselbosque	$35-60d $60-70t $75q	$30-50d $50-60t $65q	Fans	All	All	Restaurant Pool	No credit cards. Two night minimum.

Villas Gaia $$ Tel. 506-786-5044 www.villasgaia.com	$75-85d $15 extra bed	$75-85d $15 extra bed	Yes	All	All	Restaurant Bar Pool	Tours, snorkeling and fishing. Offers all-inclusive packages. A/C$

Río Sierpe

The Costa Rica issue (Vol.18#2) of *The Surf Report* describes a rivermouth break at the mouth of Río Sierpe that "can be excellent." (Their map, however, points to Boca Guarumal, north of Río Sierpe.) Truth is, it's not. It's difficult to reach and usually closed out. To check it out, catch the boat for Drake's Bay at the town of Sierpe.

Pacific Southwest

Let's define the Pacific Southwest as the region along the Pacific Coast south of Punta Uvita to the Panamanian border. The Pacific Southwest has progressively more rain and humidity as you move south. Parts of the region receive 150-300 inches of rain annually. Even the so-called "dry" season gets torrential downpours, turning the jungle into a steaming sauna. But let's not forget, this is also the region that is home to the legendary Pavones, probably the longest left in the universe. And across the gulf is Cabo Matapalo with its remote, long, excellent rights.

How to get there

If you're coming straight from the airport just head south on CA2. It's a long and winding road, but scenic. If you are going to the Osa Peninsula exit CA2 at Piedras Blancas heading toward Rincón. To reach Pavones you'll continue on and exit at Río Claro to head toward Golfito. If you are driving along the coast from Dominical just keep driving. You will meet up with CA2 at Palmar Norte. Note for the old-timers: The road south out of Dominical is now paved all the way. Nice!

Osa Peninsula

Moreso than other more heavily touristed sections of the country, the Osa Peninsula is what you expect from Costa Rica: dense jungle, beautiful scenery, tons of wildlife, and secluded surf. National Geographic magazine says the Osa Peninsula is "the most biologically intense place on earth."

One problem here is that communications can be difficult, making it harder to make reservations, although with the Internet and cell phones the situation has improved much. You still may want to talk with a surf travel agent who has a working relationship with some hotels down there. Surf Express, for example, works with Lapa Ríos.

It's tough to get around Osa since there isn't much of a road system, so getting to surf sometimes means going by boat. That also means that the Osa Peninsula has fewer of the other comforts one may require. This ain't no Manuel Antonio.

Drake Bay

Remote break with big, long, powerful waves when there's a swell. It can break up to 10', way, way outside. No crowd as this is way off the beaten surf path.

Contact the Drake Bay Wilderness Camp (tel. 506-717-2436) to find out about a charter service that can take you to some excellent, remote breaks.

Getting There: You can take the road in from the east starting in Rincón, but it still doesn't get all the way to Drake Bay. The traditional way in is by boat. Most of the hotels in the area arrange boat transportation with your reservation. You can also hook up a boat ride from the dock in the village of Sierpe, 15km south of Palmar. There's no regular service that I know of, but it's not hard to find a ride for a fee. The trip down the Sierpe River and out into the Pacific is beautiful. From the south, or the long way around the Osa Peninsula, is a "road," so to speak. I've heard of people hiking in from the south, but not driving. The fastest and easiest way in is with Nature Air (506-220-3054, www.natureair.com), flying right into Drake Bay daily from San José.

Drake's is remote, but popular with eco-tourists (ecoids). Make sure you have reservations before you arrive.

Where to Stay for Drake Bay

You don't just drop into Drake Bay and start looking for a place to stay, not just because it's difficult to get here, but because many of the hotels are on all-inclusive resort plans with minimum stays. Drake Bay Wilderness Resort and Aguila de Osa are two good examples. Read the listings below carefully and be sure to check ahead. One of the few surfer-friendly places is the Corcovado Adventures Tent Camp. It's also one of the more reasonably priced.

Lodging Name	Rates High	Rates Low	A/C	Priv Bath	Hot H2O	Facilities	Comments
Aquila de Osa Inn $$$$ tel. 506-296-2190 www.aquiladeosa.com	$641s $1056d kids $304 2-night minimum; rates drop a lot with each added night	$617s $972d kids $304 2-night minimum; rates drop a lot with each added night	Fans	All	All	Restaurant Bar	MC, V. Minimum stay is 2 nights, and rates improve with each added night. Check web site. Rates include three meals. Reservations required. Wilderness comfort; most "luxurious" in the area. On the hill over the ocean with great views, next to the Río Aguijitas. Caño Island trips for divers. Rents horses. Sportfishing and scuba. Closed October.
Casa Corcovado Jungle Lodge $$$ Tel. 506-256-3181 www.casacorcovado.com	$865s, $1530d for 2 nights $50/kid Includes meals and air/car/boat from San José	$715s, $1230d for 2 nights $50/kid Includes meals and air/car/boat from San José	Fans	All	All	Dining room Bar Pool Gift shop	2-night minimum. Rates drop with added nights. Tours. Situated right next to Corcovado National Park.
Cecilia Cabinas $ tel. 506-771-2336	$25pp	$25pp	Fans	not all	no	restaurant	No credit cards. Includes three meals. Two of the cabinas have private baths. Can arrange cheap boat trips here.
Cocalito Lodge $$$ tel. 506-786-6335, 519-782-3978 (Can.) fax 506-786-6150 email: barrybend@aol.com	4 day/3 night packages, per person: $463-573s $426-481d $389-445t		No	All	No	Restaurant	No credit cards. Rates include three meals and tours. Rustic hardwood cabinas right on the beach. Run by two friendly Canadians, Mike and Marna. Nice clean place with good food. Tours for divers to Caño Island, rents horses, bikes, local tours, sportfishing.

Corcovado Adventures Tent Camp $$ tel. 506-384-1679, 506-396-2451 cell www.corcovado.com	$65s Includes meals. Package options.		No	No	No	Dining hall	Reserve with credit card, pay with cash or travelers' checks. Surf nearby at the Rio Claro rivermouth. Includes three meals. Shared baths. Near the beach. Tours, trips to Caño Island, sportfishing. Rents snorkeling stuff, kayaks, horses.
Drake Bay Wilderness Camp $$$$ tel./fax 506-770-8012 www.drakebay.com	$740s for 3 nights Includes meals and air charter from San José	$680s for 3 nights Includes meals and air charter from San José	Fans	All	All	Restaurant	MC, V. Includes three meals and air charter from San José. Rates drop with added nights. Open since the mid-1980's. Rooms and tents right on the beach. Shared bath. Trips to Caño Island, tours, sportfishing. Good food. Loans snorkeling stuff and canoes. Make sure you have a reservation.
Jinetes de Osa $$ Tel. 800-317-0333 (US) www.drakebayhotel.com	$70-100s $120-150d $195t meals included	$60-90 $100-130 $165 meals included	Fans	Yes	Yes	Restaurant	Credit cards. Includes three meals. Was shared bath, but I believe this has changed. Big with the dive crowd.
Marenco Biological Reserve $$$ Tel. 506-258-1919, 800-278-6223 (U.S.) www.marencolodge.com	$75s $150d $225t	$75s $150d $225t	No	All	No	Restaurant	Credit cards. Includes three meals. Good food. South of Drake Bay. Rooms have ocean views from the hillside location. Eco-tourism place. Packages include transportation.
Paloma (La) Lodge $$$$ Tel. 506-293-7502 www.lapalomalodge.com	Packages per person, 3 night minimum, includes meals and transport from San José: $1050-1270s prices drop with extra nights		Fans	All	All	Restaurant	No credit cards. Package price includes three meals and transportation from San José. Hilltop location with great views. Tours, trips to Caño Island, sportfishing. Rents horses, kayaks. Loans snorkeling stuff. Good food. People love this place, due in part to the owners.
Poor Man's Paradise Resort $ Tel. 506-771-9686 www.poormansparadiseresort.com	$50-60s	$50-60s	Fans	Not all	No	Restaurant Bar Campgrounds	Includes 3 meals. Modest, but clean. Owned and run by a native Tico family. Not an ecotourist trap.

Puerto Jiménez

The jumping-off point for Cabo Matapalo and Corcovado National Park is Puerto Jiménez. It's about 50 km off the Pan-American Highway and reachable by car, bus, or ferry from Golfito, or by plane from San José—but by plane or bus your surfboard-carrying options are limited by space. The plane flight from San José takes about 45 minutes. There is surf outside Puerto Jiménez on the way to Cabo Matapalo, but this town is best used as a place to find lower-priced accommodations since the places closer to the surf are on the high side.

Cabo Matapalo

The area leading to and including the southeast tip of the Osa Peninsula is generally known as "Matapalo." Here you will find a variety of remote points and reefs, mostly rights that can get incredibly long on a good south swell. And it needs swell; it's not like Dominical or Playa Hermosa where there is always something to surf.

In addition to a good swell you'll need time. It takes a full day to get to this area from the airport, unless you catch a flight to Puerto Jiménez. If you are on a one-week trip to Costa Rica, spending two of your seven days traveling in and out of Cabo Matapalo may not be the best use of your time. Another option is to "surf" your way down and back, which usually gives you 2-3 days in Matapalo out of a 7-day trip.

Cabo Matapalo is very special, but as a surfer, you are not welcome in the line-ups here. Local surfers are not pleased with Matapalo's newfound popularity. There is a community of ex-pat surfers who have bought land near the surf. But since this place is not easy to get to or stay at—like say Tamarindo or Playa Hermosa—the crowds have not yet completely taken it over. Maybe the fact that this is the sharkiest part of Costa Rica will help their cause.

Respect the private property of the Matapalo locals; you'll be surfing their waves and they'll be in the line-up. If you think you are the aggro-rippa-"me and my bro's dominate" type, don't even think about coming here. The locals here are escapees from the real world and are not about to let you ruin their paradise. You are way too far from decent medical care to upset them, so lay low, don't come in crowds, and show a lot of respect. And, as with the rest of Costa Rica, don't leave any valuables in your car or on the beach; they'll get stolen.

Getting There: The road from Puerto Jiménez is tough, gradually getting narrower, bumpier and muddier. There are many streams to cross. This is definitely 4x4. Taxis will take you to and from Puerto Jiménez. You can also get there by boat from Golfito. (Of course, you can get *anywhere* by boat.) To get here, drive south out of Puerto Jiménez about ten miles, or 30 to 45 minutes. You'll know you are getting close when the road enters the jungle. At that point take the left fork in the road after you cross the rocky stream in the steep ravine. (You'll know you've missed the turn if the road becomes a steep uphill and you see the sign for Lapa Ríos.) At the concrete entry gate, go straight for Playa Carbonera or go through it for the rest of the Matapalo breaks.

Playa Carbonera

Easy, long, slow rights and lefts. Less sensitive to tide than some of the other Matapalo breaks. Carbonera is just before you reach the jungle area of Matapalo.

Pan Dulce

This is the first break you come to inside the cement gate. Excellent rights that can go on for 200 yards on good swells. Holds size well and the waves get fast. Low tide is too sketchy due to the exposed reef; medium to high tide is best. This will be your "walk-to-surf spot" if you stay at Bahía Esmeralda—it's about a ten-minute walk from the lodge.

Backwash

South of Pan Dulce is Backwash, another long, fast right, but this one comes with a left too. Best at low tide.

Hog Hole/The Point

Also called Matapalo Beach. A 20-minute walk from Backwash, or one mile from Pan Dulce is the break that picks up the most swell around here. This is the juiciest wave in the area, and it's yet another good right reefbreak with an occasional left. There's always someone out here, and it gets crowded when the swell is because it's likely to be the only break working. The wave breaks between two rocky reef outcroppings, with rocks in the middle on the inside. It pops up on the outside and races in toward and past the next set of rocks—be careful. On a four-foot day I cracked a fin on my favorite Al Merrick when I straightened out at the wrong spot. You quickly learn to wait for the good swells, when the waves break outside the reefs, or take care when it's small or low tide.

You may have heard you can camp here. You can, but there are no facilities, not even a trash can, so go lightly. The last time I was there, there was a lot of thievery.

Where to Stay for Cabo Matapalo

One way to control crowds is to make surfing expensive. And while that actually has not been the plan, economics have been on the side of the locals as the accommodations here are mostly not in the price range a surfer normally expects in Costa Rica. And that's because this place caters more to the eco-traveler, and less to the surfer. The good news is that, if you have the money, there are some fantastic places to stay—like Lapa Ríos (long walk to the beach) and Bosque del Cabo—that would make for the ideal surfer's honeymoon: excellent surf and a secluded, romantic, magical resorts. And if all goes well, you may be able to talk your wife into going back every year to celebrate your anniversary. (Advice to the young: There are also no restaurants here, except at the Lapa Ríos resort, and that's muy expensive.

Most of the hotels in Cabo Matapalo only take cash. If you run short, stop by the bank in Puerto Jiménez on your way in and use your credit card to get more. You'll need a lot.

Lapa Ríos is the most expensive and luxurious hotel in the area. The wife or girlfriend will love you for taking her on a surf trip if you cough up the bucks to stay here. In fact, I hear that up to 40 percent of the guests here are honeymooners. In addition to the honeymooners, you'll also be hanging out with a lot of blue-haired eco-tourists looking for that perfect combination of adventure and luxury. The coolest thing about the Lapa Ríos, though, is that you can watch the waves wrap around the points from your perch high above the gulf.

My favorite place to stay is Bahía Esmeralda. Eighteen kilometers south of Puerto Jiménez and up on a lush hillside overlooking the Golfo Dulce and owned/managed by a long-time local surfer (since 1987), Brett Harter, this gem of a lodge is the place to stay if you like great food, partying with the locals, and attentive service. Did I say "great" food? Make that the *best* food in Costa Rica, and maybe anywhere you've been. Brett's an excellent cook, and host, and the digs are comfortable. No air conditioning, but there's none in the area anyhow. Strong fans in the rooms, though. Back to the food…. There's no real restaurant, per se, because there's no menu. The food served is up to Brett, and he'll probably ask what your preferences are too. If you go, ask Brett about the "pig's milk cheese." Esmeralda is a short walk from Pan Dulce and within a mile of the rest of the breaks.

An alternative is to stay in Puerto Jiménez and commute in and out. Puerto Jiménez has cheap lodging, cheap restaurants and bars, a bank, a gas station, and more. It's quite an interesting place, especially compared to Matapalo where it's secluded and can get boring. There's also a ferry here that will take you across the gulf to the Pavones side.

Lodging Name	Rates High	Rates Low	A/C	Priv Bath	Hot H2O	Facilities	Comments
Bosque del Cabo Wilderness Lodge $$$ tel./fax 506-735-5206 www.bosquedelcabo.com	$125-170s $95-130d $85-115t $85-100 Per person inc. three meals daily		Fans	All	No	Restaurant Pool	AE, MC. Perched on the cliff over the surf (long hike, 10 minute drive) at the tip of the peninsula. Tours, horses, kayaks, sport fishing. Bungalows with great views. Beds have mosquito netting.
Encanta La Vida $$ Tel. 506-735-5678, cell 506-376-3209 www.encantalavida.com	$75-125pp Per person inc. three meals daily		Fans	Yes	Yes	Restaurant	Secluded group of large cabinas. Great for families or groups. At the tip of Cabo Matapalo. Meals included. Laundry, horses, kayaks, transport to/from Jiménez.
Hacienda Bahía Esmeralda $$$ Tel. 506-381-8521 www.bahiaesmeralda.com	$120pp incl. taxes and 3 meals daily	$105pp incl. taxes and 3 meals daily	Fans	Yes	Yes	Restaurant Spring fed freshwater pool	No credit cards. Prices include three meals daily. Luxury guesthouse or private cottages with decks facing the ocean. Gourmet meals. Horses, kayaks, scuba, hiking, gold panning! And fishing. 10-minute walk to Pan Dulce. My favorite.
Lapa Ríos $$$ Tel. 506-735-5130, 800-948-3770 www.laparios.com	$308s $408d $585t $736q	$240s $328d $465t $592q	No	Yes	Yes	Restaurant Bar Pool	AE, MC, V. Credit card surcharge. 12 miles south of Puerto Jiménez. INCREDIBLE. Includes 3 meals and transportation to and from Jiménez. No TV or phones. Great food. On a hill 350 feet over the surf. Tours, trips to Caño Island, Corcovado, etc. Sportfishing, kayaking, horse riding. Surf lessons. Popular with honeymooners as romance rules the air here. American owners.

Parrot Bay Village $$-$$$ Puerto Jiménez Tel. 506-735-5180, 5748 www.parrotbayvillage.com	$90s $110d $130t $150q	$70s $80d $90t $100q	Yes	Yes	Yes	Restaurant Bar Volleyball Gift shop	Credit Cards. Price includes full breakfast and dinner as well as free kayak use. On the beach in Puerto Jiménez. Remodeled in 2001. Sportfishing.
Tierra de Milagros $ Tel. 506-735-5062 www.tierrademilagros.com	Contact for current pricing		No	All	All		No electricity or running water. Supply own linens or sleeping bag. Vegetarian meals served $10/day. "Holistic" place. Open air showers.

Carate

Beach breaks on the west side of the tip of the peninsula, the south-facing coast. No crowds.

Getting There: Drive around past Cabo Matapalo and just keep going. It's at the end of the road. Takes about 90 minutes from Puerto Jiménez. There's also a taxi that leaves out of Puerto Jiménez three days a week from Cabinas Puerto Jiménez. Truck drivers also leave from Puerto Jiménez and will take you for a few bucks. Or for a lot of bucks you can fly in via air taxi to the Carate airstrip from Puerto Jiménez.

Where to Stay for Carate

Lodging Name	Rates High	Rates Low	A/C	Priv Bath	Hot H2O	Facilities	Comments
Corcovado Lodge Tent Camp $$ tel. 506-257-0766 www.corcovadotentlodge.com	$89-99s $66-71d per person includes meals	$67-82s $47-62d per person includes meals	No	No	No	Restaurant Bar	AE, MC, V. Includes three meals. Right above the beach. Tours.
Lookout Inn $$$ Tel. 506-735-5431 www.lookout-inn.com	$99-109pp inc tax	$99-109pp inc tax	Fans	All	All	Dining room Bar Pool	All-inclusive. Popular bar for local expats. 300 meters east of the Carate airstrip.

Burica Peninsula

Burica Peninsula mostly means one thing to surfers: Pavones. But there are lesser-known spots here that are much less crowded with fantastic surf.

Playa Zancudo

Nice, mellow town spread along a long stretch of good to excellent beachbreaks. Popular with the fishing crowd, but slowly being discovered by surfers. It's nicer here than Pavones, and there are more and better amenities, including an internet café. If you like, you can stay in Zancudo and take boats to Pavones and other spots, but it's become way expensive—costing $80 to $100—when you consider there's great, uncrowded surf right here in Zancudo. To get to Zancudo just pretend like you are going to Pavones (see directions below), but you'll take a right where the clearly marked fork in the road tells you to.

Where to Stay for Playa Zancudo

Accommodations in Zancudo are pretty basic. Cabinas Sol y Mar is next door to Zancudo Boat Tours—a good guide to the area that also rents surf and boogieboards. Or the Zancudo Beach Club can also set you up with tours to Pavones. They also have decent surf right out front. There are lots of other places to stay right on the beach. One place to check out that actually has air conditioning is the Latitude 8 Lodge. Another air-conditioned option is Palmera de Oro. A newer place right on the beach in front of surf and having a decent Italian restaurant and a pool table is Iguana Verde Cabinas.

Lodging Name	Rates High	Rates Low	A/C	Priv Bath	Hot H2O	Facilities	Comments
Almendros, Los, Hotel $ Tel. 506-776-0008	Call for current	$15-25	Yes	Yes	Yes	Restaurant	V. On the beach. Fishing trips. Satellite TV in restaurant.
Cocos (Los) Cabinas $ Tel. 506-776-0012 www.loscocos.com	$55-60d	-20%	Fans	All	All	Restaurant	V. On the beach. Weekly rates are better. Kitchenettes. Owners operate Zancudo Boat Tours.
Coloso Del Mar $ Tel. 506-776-0050 www.coloso-del-mar.com	$40-45s $5 per extra person	$25-30s $5 per extra person	Fans	All	Yes	Restaurant Gift shop	Cash only. 100 meters to beach. Meal packages available.
Latitude 8 Lodge $ Tel. 310-776-0168 www.latitude8lodge.com	$50 d/t $60 with a/c	30% less than high season	Yes	Yes	Yes		No credit cards. Surf out front. 2 air-conditioned beachfront cabinas remodeled in 2001. Cabins have 3 beds, frig's and cooking stuff. Also a smaller non-a/c cabin available for less. Rents surfboards. Sportfishing. Used to be the Luna Linda. A/C$
Oasis on the Beach $$ Tel. 506-776-0087 www.oasisonthebeach.com	$50-65s	$30-45s	Not all	All	Yes	Restaurant Bar Gift shop	Credit cards. On the beach with surf right out front. Rooms have refrigerator, solar hot water, queen-sized beds, screened windows and ceiling fans. A/C$. Surf tours, sportfishing, eco tours, laundry service and email available. Formerly Zancudo Beach Club.
Palmera de Oro $ Tel. 506-776-0121	$49s $78d	$49s $78d	Yes	Yes	Yes	Restaurant Pool	Includes breakfast. TVs in room. Small, slightly strange place across the road from the beach.
Roy's Zancudo Lodge $$$$ Tel. 506-776-0008, 877-529-6980 toll free US www.Royszancudolodge.com	$745-845s $1112-1423d $1393-1790t	$745-845s $1112-1423d $1393-1790t	All	All	All	Dining room Bar Pool Hot tub	Located on the beach. World-renowned fishing lodge with over 50 records. Boat available to lodge from Golfito. Frig's in rooms. Includes fishing, tackle, meals, open bar, laundry service, internet service—all free.
Sol y Mar Cabinas $ tel. 506-776-0014 www.zancudo.com	$20-41d $5 per extra person	-30% $5 per extra person	Fans	All	Yes	Restaurant/bar Volleyball Horseshoes Camping	No credit cards. Good food. Good place to stay. Next-door is Zancudo Boat Tours (see above). Great fish burgers.

Pavones

This place is legend. Excellent, world-famous series of cobblestone, rivermouth left points that, on a good swell connect up into what is probably the longest left in the known universe, with rides over a kilometer long on a strong south swell. And it needs a *strong* south swell to work. The waves start out way around the rivermouth and wrap all the way past the restaurant and into the bay (the best place for beginners). Excellent shape and tons of speed, so much that it's difficult to make on smaller days, especially for regular foots. Blows out most afternoons, destroying most of the shape. As you would expect, it draws crowds from near and far. The best season for the south swells that Pavones needs is the rainy season, April through October.

There are many breaks between Pavones and the end of the peninsula, Punta Burica. For example, there's a reef about three miles south of Pavones that takes the same swells and can be twice as big. Boats available in the area to reach other spots.

The town of Pavones isn't much. It's actually pretty dingy. But there's surf, enough places to stay and eat, and there's a surf shop just outside of town about a mile called Evergreen. While Pavones isn't at the end of the earth, it still doesn't have hard-wired phone service, so everyone is on cellular, and phone numbers change often.

"Land disputes in Pavones have spurred murders, arson, sabotage and other violence for the past 20 years, every since the United Fruit Company packed up in 1985 and hundres of jobless banana pickers became land squatters." This quote comes from an article in *The Tico Times* about recently released from prison/surfer Dan Fowlie (convicted for drug violations and famous locally for flying over town flinging cash out of the plane to the locals), fugitive financier Robert Vesco and other interesting folks who help give Pavones its colorful history. Currently, Pavones' most famous resident is "*In Search of Captain Zero*" author Alan Weisbecker, whose email newsletter keeps us all posted on the continuing saga surrounding this fantastic break.

Pavones is about 410km from San José. If you drive it takes seven to ten hours. To get here from the airport catch the Pan-American Highway south to the town of Rio Claro and head right. (If it's getting late you may want to consider staying in Rio Claro and not risk missing the ferry, which operates from 5am to 8pm, or getting lost in the dark. There's a decent little hotel at the intersection called The Impala. Good restaurant, too. Rooms are $25 and less, and some have air conditioning. Or you can bypass the ferry by taking the long way around, driving straight through Rio Claro, past Paso Canoas at the Panama border and around to where you are heading back west.) The sign to Pavones is easily missed, so pay attention. Look for the intersection with the Rodeo Bar. You'll know you've missed the turn if you get to the town of El Rodeo or even El Mono. This is also where the potholes begin. Soon you'll arrive at the ferry crossing—it costs 400 colones. Once past the ferry just keep following the signs. Along the way there's a good lookout point where you can check out Playa Zancudo. Just past that is a fork with a Cabinas Ponderosa sign where you'll bear left to Pavones.

You can fly or take a bus to Golfito, and take a taxi, boat or bus (costs about $2) in from there. Catch the bus in Golfito at the La Bomba Bar at the municipal dock at 2PM. Water taxis are about $65 each way; car taxis cost about $50. Heck, you can take a taxi all the way from the airport in San José, too. There are a ton of ways to get to Pavones, as every surfer who comes to Costa Rica gets here sooner or later.

Where to Stay for Pavones

Pavones is one of those "out-of-the-way" places mentioned in the "Renting Cars" section. While more lodging options pop up every year, it's still far from having all of the conveniences of Tamarindo, Nosara, Dominical or Jacó. For example, there still isn't any wired phone service, but most folks have cell phones. Anyhow, it now has enough of the conveniences for any surfer wanting to surf one of the best lefts in the world.

There are a few places to stay at or near the break. One decent surfer-owned place to check out is Cabinas La Ponderosa. Built and owned by the McCarthy family—Marshall, Brian and Angela—in 1994, these cabinas have air conditioning, a big plus in this part of the world. (At least one of the rooms doesn't have a bathroom inside, so the walk-to bathroom is not air conditioned.) They also rent a two bedroom house with three beds (two doubles and a king) and air conditioning that goes for $75 per person, including three meals. There's surf you can walk to from the Ponderosa, but you'll have to drive or hoof it a long way to the rivermouth. Another good option that's a lot closer to the surf and was featured in the *Transworld Surf* article is Josue's Cabinas. These are newer cabinas with air conditioning and kitchens. Another pretty cool option that's a good deal is Cabinas Mira Olas Pavones. It's quite a walk down to the surf, but you can check it all out from on high. And the cabinas have fully equipped kitchens.

Camping right near the surf is an option, too. One popular camping area is just to the west of the main break at the top of the point.

Lastly, if you don't mind driving every day you can stay in Golfito where there's more comfortable lodging, much better restaurants and bars, and a lot more to do. The drive is probably no worse than your drive to surf at home, and is certainly a lot shorter than boating in and out of Witches. Pavones is sort of a dreary place, so Golfito is a nice break. This option works better in the dry season.

Lodging Name	Rates High	Rates Low	A/C	Priv Bath	Hot H2O	Facilities	Comments
Cabinas Mira Olas Pavones $ Tel. 506-393-7742 www.miraolas.com	$25-45d inc. taxes $8 per extra person	Lower	Fans	Yes	Yes		Sits up above Pavones with a good view of the surf and a 10-minute walk to everything. Porches with hammocks. Some cabins have fully equipped kitchens.
Casa Siempre Domingo $$ Tel. 506-820-4709 www.casa-domingo.com	$80d $120t includes taxes	$80d $120t includes taxes	Yes	Yes	Yes	Restaurant	Bed & breakfast on the hill with great views. Long ways from the surf. Best if you have a car. Price includes breakfast. Only 4 rooms.

Lodging Name	Rates High	Rates Low	A/C	Priv Bath	Hot H2O	Facilities	Comments
Esquina del Mar ¢ Tel. 506-394-7676	$10-20	$10-20	No	No	No	Restaurant Bar	Cheap rooms right at the break on top of the cantina.
Gaviotas (Las) Hotel $$ tel. 506-775-0062 fax 506-775-0544	$42d $80 2br apt. w/kit	$42d $80 2br apt. w/kit	Yes	Yes	Yes	Restaurant bar TV room pools private dock security	Special rates for surfers. Just outside of town. Good restaurant. Tours. Weekend barbecues.
Pavón Tico ¢		$7	No	no	no	Bar	Shared bath.
Ponderosa Cabinas $$ tel. 954-771-9166 (US), 506-824-4145 (messages) fax 506-775-0631 www.cabinaslaponderosa.com	$50-55 per person meals included $30-35 without	same	Yes	All	All	Restaurant Bar Ping-pong Satellite TV Volleyball Basketball	Cash only. Cabinas a couple of miles south of the point. Air conditioning costs $5 extra. Owners surf. Board rentals. Fishing, diving, horses and boats to Matapalo arranged. Bar/rec room has TV. Not all rooms have baths.

Punta Banco

About 10km south of Pavones what I think is the official Punta Banco. Here you'll find reefs and some beachbreaks that break bigger than Pavones and with no crowds at all. You may decide to just avoid Pavones altogether and stay in one of the all-inclusive lodges. May as well, there are few places to eat around here anyhow. Whether or not it's 10km doesn't matter. West of Pavones you'll find lots of totally secluded reefs with fun to great surf.

Where to Stay for Punta Banco

Lodging Name	Rates High	Rates Low	A/C	Priv Bath	Hot H2O	Facilities	Comments
Casa Punta Banco $$$$ tel. 506-388-1395 www.costaricacpb.com email: holidays@elysianholidays.co.uk	$1540d $1740q $1950 six $2150 eight	$1540d $1740q $1950 six $2150 eight	No	No	Yes	House	6-bedroom/2 bath house for rent. Has everything, including cook, maid, washer, dryer, seclusion.
Tiskita Jungle Lodge $$$$ tel. 506-296-8125 www.tiskita-lodge.co.cr	$145s $120d $105t per person per day, 3 meals included	$135s $115d $100t per person per day, 3 meals included	No	Yes	Yes	Pool Dining room Ping pong Foosball	AE, DC, MC, V. Includes three meals. Packages available including charter flights from San José, saving a day of car travel each way. Right near the beach up on the hill with fun surf right out front. Highly recommended by many who want more than surf out of their Costa Rica trip. Has cabins with outdoor, private attached bathrooms overlooking the rainforest. One kitchenette. Horses, snorkeling.

Sotavento Plantanal Lodge $ Tel. 506-308-7484 www.sotaventoplantanal.com	$60-80 up to six; $10 per additional person	$60-80 up to six; $10 per additional person	No	Yes	No	Bar	Two rustic lodges perched a couple hundred feet above the ocean available for rent to parties from 2-6 persons. Full kitchens, or can hire a cook to take care of you for $30/pp/day. Discounts available for weekly stays. Rents surfboards, horses. Free boogie boards. Sportfishing and kayak expeditions.

Punta Burica

Remote reef breaks at the tip of the peninsula near the Panama border. Accessible only by four wheel drive or boat. Total isolation. Big, deep-water waves. There's also an island near Burica with excellent surf. Until recently, this area was either a secret or a rumor, depending on who you knew. Today it's being publicized by at least one of the surf travel companies as part of their secret spot "promotion." And an article in the April 5, 2002 *Tico Times* reviewed the only accommodations, Rancho Burica.

Caribbean Coast

If your first surf destination is on the Pacific coast, you will not see much change following your arrival at the airport. But you will after you take the three-hour drive from San José to the Caribbean. The humidity gets higher. The slow pace gets even slower. Rooms get dingier. The food gets greasier. And the look and feel becomes more Caribbean, less Latin American, as it should considering that the surf here originates in the places you usually envision when thinking Caribbean.

Here you will find fewer upscale accommodations (only a handful of hotels offer air conditioning), especially south of Limón, assuming that you are looking for them. At the same time, there are times when it will be difficult to find a place to stay at all, such as during Carnival in October. So make reservations if you want to stay at the nicer hotels.

Hotels are one thing, the surf is another. Here you will find true coral reef juice and the biggest and best waves in Costa Rica. And you will find them in winter, when the Pacific averages smaller waves. But we speak of the southern coast only; the north is probably not your first choice for surfing.

Barra Del Colorado/Tortuguero

There is little solid information about surf in this area, mostly rumors, and I haven't bothered to check it out myself. It has potential for good beach breaks and rivermouths. But knowing that the area is crammed full of sharks and that there are excellent waves to the south is enough to keep most surfers out. Add to that the difficulty in getting there as access is limited to boats and planes since the road north ends at Moín. But if you have the time and huevos you may want to check it out. Rent a boat at Moín to do some exploring.

Parismina

I don't know if there's surf here. I haven't been to Parismina and know of no other surfers who have either. There is, however, a rivermouth here with big waves, according to guidebooks and non-surfers who have gone. Sportfishing is big here, so there's good accommodations if you have the time and spirit to check it out.

Potrete

A small cove just north of Playa Bonita (walking distance) with good, hollow, shallow rights breaking on coral reefs. Easy access. It's kind of a weird scene here with a soda, seedy characters, eco-travelers catching tour boats, and vultures waiting for scraps from the fishermen.

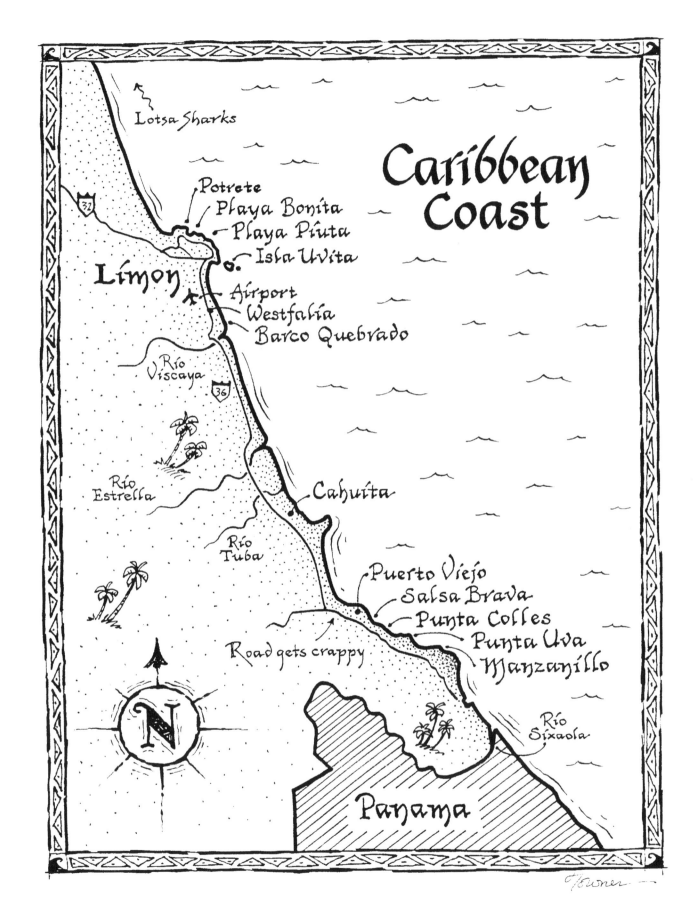

Playa Bonita

Four km north of Puerto Limón is a sandy beach popular with the Limónians. There is good, if sketchy surf here that can get big, but it's inconsistent and often closed out. The best wave here is the thick, juicy left breaking on the coral reef point at the north end of the cove. There is also a thick, fast, hollow right on the right side of the same bay (sometimes known as Cocaine Point). Best on an incoming tide. If you are not staying at one of the hotels within walking distance, you can park right in front of the sandy beach. No camping here.

Roca Alta

A rock reef off the Playa Piuta point is the site of an excellent right that can get big and juicy.

Where to Stay for Potrete, Playa Bonita, etc.

Your best bet for comfort and proximity to surf is the Hotel Matama. It's upscale for the area, but once you cram your buddies in the price can be pretty reasonable, especially considering the amenities. If you are traveling with wife or family, it's also a good bet. It doesn't have the view of Maribú Caribe or Cocori, both on the beach, but it's the best deal if you want air conditioning. And by the way, on the Caribbean you will probably want a/c.

Lodging Name	Rates High	Rates Low	A/C	Priv Bath	Hot H2O	Facilities	Comments
Hotel Cocori $ Tel. 506-795-1670	$40-45d	$40-45d	All	All	All	Restaurant	AE, MC, V. Rates include breakfast. Apartments looking out at Playa Bonita. Kitchenettes, TVs and refrigerators in rooms. Closest hotel to the break.
Maribú Caribe Hotel $$ Tel. 506-795-2543	$68s $78d $88t $112 suite	$60s $66d $88t $112 suite	All	All	All	Restaurant Pool Bar Snack bar	AE, MC, V. Scenic setting overlooking the sea. Hotel and parking are well protected by armed guards. Telephones in rooms. Boat trips to Isla Uvita. Laundry service. Tours.
Hotel Matama $$ Tel. 506-758-1123 www.matama.com	$35-75	$35-75	All	All	All	Restaurant Bar Pool	AE, MC, V. Good choice for the area. Across the street from the left, but walking distance to the breaks. Room service. Phones and TVs in rooms. Rooms for up to six. Armed guard; locked gate at night.

Puerto Limón

The Puerto Limón area (from San José about 160km or three hours' drive) is home to most of Costa Rica's true coral reefs. It is also a bustling, colorful Caribbean port town full of contrasts—uniformed school kids playing in the streets among unsavory, seedy, modern-day "Pirates of the Caribbean" characters. Stay away from Limón altogether if you are traveling with a woman (per mine).

From Puerto Limón south is where most of the Caribbean surf is, at least the explored surf with more typical shark populations as compared to Tortuguero in the north. (It's been said that if surfers could see under the line-up as well as above, we would never surf.)

Isla Uvita

There is a small island right off the coast of Puerto Limón with a long juicy left breaking over a live coral reef—and it can get big. You can see the waves wrapping around the island from Westfalia beach. It is a short boat ride from Limón or Piuta. Catch a boat from the Hotel Maribú Caribe at Playa Bonita or Cabinas Grant in Puerto Viejo. There are no accommodations or drinking water on the island, but you can camp there. When leaving your car in Limón, be sure it's safe, that is, with an armed guard.

Where to Stay for Puerto Limón and Isla Uvita

Puerto Limón is not a "la-dee-da" resort area, so you won't find the Four Seasons in town. Then again, there is no shortage of cheap lodging here. If you are looking for upscale, resort-type hotels, head north about 10 minutes out of town (see "Where to Stay for Potrete and Playa Bonita"). On weekends, holidays and especially Carnival, starting October 12 (Columbus Day), it can be difficult to get a room anywhere around here. Also, be aware that some hotels around here will try to charge you a higher rate if you're a tourist, which you are. Crime can be a problem here, especially at night. Breaking into cars is the local hobby, so if you absolutely need to keep things in your vehicle, consider the Hotel Acón, which has a security-parking garage for no extra charge.

Lodging Name	Rates High	Rates Low	A/C	Priv Bath	Hot H2O	Facilities	Comments
Acón Hotel $ Tel. 506-758-1010	$22s $28d $34t	$22s $28d $34t	All	All	Yes	Restaurant Disco	AE, MC, V. Good choice for in-town, reservations recommended. Disco busy on weekends (noisy).
Hotel Park $ Tel. 506-798-0555	$35-75	$35-75	All	All	All	Restaurant	AE, MC, V. TVs. Overlooks the sea. Ask for room on the seaside.

Westfalia

Miles of hollow beach breaks running south of Puerto Limón along the beach road. Can't handle larger swells, closes out when big, but nearly always has waves. As it grows in size so go the rips and other currents, which can get real nasty. While there are good sandbars all along this stretch, the area at the southern end of the airstrip often has good shape and gets some good offshores. Be sure to check out the rivermouths such as Río Banano. You will definitely surf alone here in contrast to what's waiting for you at Cahuita or Puerto Viejo.

Barco Quebrado

South of Limón near Boca del Banano. More uncrowded beach breaks and sometimes has waves when other nearby spots do not.

Cahuita (Black Beach)

Decent, uncrowded beach breaks with live coral reefs and waves year-round. Can get very good. Near the entrance to the Cahuita Coral Reef National Park is a good break with a current to the left for an easy paddle out. Largest coral reef and some of the best diving in Costa Rica. Camping is permitted.

The road out of Limón south to Cahuita is good; nicely paved with few potholes. The drive is about 45 km from Limón.

This area has developed a reputation for crime that is exaggerated, but not completely undeserved. It's a good idea for women not to walk around alone at night. And don't leave your things on the beach or in your car unattended (that goes for most of Costa Rica).

One of the best places to stay is the Hotel Jaguar. There's a beach break right in front of the hotel, or you can walk to the reef break about 200 yards to the south. The restaurant has great food. More good food can be found nearby at Edith Soda, with a great Caribbean menu that includes vegetarian items.

Where to Stay for Cahuita

Lodging Name	Rates High	Rates Low	A/C	Priv Bath	Hot H2O	Facilities	Comments
Alby Lodge $ Tel. 506-755-0031 www.albylodge.com	$40d $45t $50q	$40d $45t $50q	Fans	Yes	Yes	Shared kitchen and bbq	No credit cards. Rooms sleep up to four.
Algebra Cabinas $ Tel. 506-755-0077 www.cabinasalgebra.com	$18-33d $5 extra person	$18-33d $5 extra person	No	All	All	Restaurant	No credit cards. Laundry service.
Arrecife Cabinas $ Tel. 506-755-0081	$20-30d	$20-30d	Fans	All	All	Restaurant	AE, MC, V. Closest to the reef.
Atlántida Cabinas $$ Tel. 506-755-0115	$45s $55d $65t	$45s $55d $65t	Fans	All	Yes	Restaurant Bar Pool Jacuzzi	AE, MC, V. Includes continental breakfast. North of town near Playa Negra and right on the beach. Good food. Nice place. Small rooms. Pretty and clean. Friendly people. Laundry service. Tours.
Chalet y Cabinas Hibiscus $ tel. 506-755-0021 www.hotels.co.cr/hibiscus.html	$45d $55t/q more options up to 10	$35d $45t/q more options up to 10	Fans	All	All	Pool Volleyball	Credit cards. 1 house; 2 cabins. Good for long-term stays. 2km north of town on Playa Negra. Laundry service. House has kitchen, laundry sink and garage. Good choice.

El Encanto Bed & Breakfast Inn $$ Tel. 506-755-0113 www.elencantobedandbreakfast.com	$49-59s $59-69d $69-79t 3br house $160-175	$49s $59d $69t 3br house $160	Fans	All	All	Restaurant	Amex, MC, V. Three private bungalows. Prices include breakfast and taxes. Snorkeling, horses, kayak tours, fishing. Low season rates include taxes.
Jaguar Hotel $$ Tel. 506-226-3775 www.hoteljaguar.com	$35-40s $55-70d	$35-40s $55-70d	No	All	All	Restaurant Bar Pool Volleyball Guarded parking	MC, V. Rates include taxes and full American breakfast. Book online for a discount. Bigger than usual rooms. Mosquito nets. Walk out front to good surf; watch it from the rooms. Hot water$. Great food.
Kelly Creek Hotel $$ Tel. 506-755-0007 www. kellycreekhotel.com	$45d $10 extra person	$45d $10 extra person	Fans	All	All	Restaurant	Credit cards. On the beach. Surf out front.
Magellan Inn $$ Tel/fax 506-755-0035 www.magellaninn.com	$59-79s add $15 for extra bed	$59-79s add $15 for extra bed	Not all	Yes	Yes	Restaurant Bar Pool Parking	AE, MC, V, DC. Includes continental breakfast. Nicest hotel in the area; about 2km north of town near the end of Playa Negra. Tours. A/C$
Malú Bungalows $ Tel. 506-755-0114 www.bungalowsmalu.com	$40s $50d $55t $60q	$40s $50d $55t $60q	All	All	All	Restaurant Bar	Credit cards. Refrigerators in rooms. Italian owned.
Margarita Cabinas $ Tel. 506-755-0205	$20-30	$20-30	Fans	All	All		MC, V.
National Park Hotel $$ Tel. 506-382-0139 www.Cahuitanationalparkhotel.com	$39-110	$32-110	All	All	All	Restaurant Travel agency Gift shop	Tours.
Safari Cabinas $ Tel. 506-755-0078	$20-40	$20-40	No	All	Yes		Some kitchens. 150 meters from beach.
Surfside Cabins $ Tel. 506-755-0246	$12-20s $15-20d $18-25t $30q	$12-20s $15-20d $18-25t $30q	Fans	All	Yes	Restaurant	No credit cards. Includes breakfast. Some rooms on the water. Lots of concrete.
Tito Cabinas ¢ Tel. 506-755-0286	$30-40d	$15-20d	Fans	Yes	Yes		No credit cards. Some refrigerators in rooms.

Puerto Viejo (Salsa Brava)

Puerto Viejo's Salsa Brava is a serious surf break.

The town of Puerto Viejo is about 220km from San José or a four-hour drive. To get there you drive first to Puerto Limón, then head south. The highway from Puerto Limón going south is great until you turn off for Puerto Viejo where you have about five kilometers of rough dirt and gravel road.

Most surfers come here for the legendary break in front of Stanford's Restaurant, Salsa Brava ("angry sauce" in Spanish)—the big, thick and hairy wave that comes from deep water onto a shallow, sharp coral reef. Probably the best and biggest right in Costa Rica; certainly the most powerful. The left is good too, but you rarely hear about it. Also known as the Caribbean Pipeline, with island-style power and pain. Starts working at 4' and cooking over 6'. Two peaks:

First Peak is the one to the south and walls up toward Second Peak, which is easier to make. First Peak also has a short hollow left good for quick tubes.

Before you paddle out sit at Stanford's upstairs restaurant, have a Coke and check out the line-up. It's also a good vantage point to check out the reef and how to paddle out. Or you can just dive in to the lagoon to the right of Stanford's parking lot and find your way through the reef by aiming for the south end of the lefts. Once you reach the line-up you'll see guys with helmets and booties, both for the reef. If that hasn't convinced you that this is serious surf, then the below-sea-level suck out over the reef will. But oh those tubes!

On my first trip here I met a guy in the water, a Redondo Beach transplant who had been living in Puerto Viejo and surfing Salsa Brava for four years. While lining up near him I suggested to him that after four years he must have it wired, to which he laughed, "Not yet!"

Winter is best—December through March—and also most crowded, as Puerto Viejo is an international traveling surfer magnet. June through August can get good too. But with a little luck you can catch it good any time of the year.

Puerto Viejo has the nightlife and other things you might miss in other smaller, sleepier Caribbean coastal towns. Get ding repairs and boogieboard rentals at Salsa de Talamanca, which is also a restaurant. And don't forget the seafood and disco at Stanford's.

Where to Stay for Puerto Viejo

Lodging Name	Rates High	Rates Low	A/C	Priv Bath	Hot H2O	Facilities	Comments
Black Sands Cabinas ¢ Tel. 506-750-0124 www.cabinasblacksands.com	$17s/d $50 up to 6	$17s/d $50 up to 6	No	Sort of	No	One small cabin	No credit cards. Cabina at the beach, which you can have all to yourselves. Away from it all, including restaurants. But you can do your own cooking. Walk to loo.
Cabinas Casa Verde $ Puerto Viejo Tel. 506-750-0015 Fax 506-750-0047 www.cabinascasaverde.com	$25-34s $32-59d $67-82t	$22-29s $26-68d $54-60t	Fans	Not all	Yes	Pool	Credit cards, but lower rates for cash. Short walk to Salsa Brava. Private bath$. Clean rooms with clean towels and sheets daily. Recommended. It's simple, rustic and the people are great. You even get your own private hammock. Frig's in rooms.
Cashew Hill Lodge $ Tel. 506-750-0256 www.cashewhilllodge.co.cr	$15-30s $20-35d $25-40t	$15-30s $20-35d $25-40t	Fans	Not all	Yes	Banquet facilities	No credit cards. On a hill overlooking Puerto Viejo.
Chimuri Lodge $ Tel. 506-750-0119 www.greencoast.com/chimuribeach.htm	$31s $39d $44t	$31s $39d $44t	No	All	All		No credit cards. Shared bath. Beach cottages away from town. Kitchens available. Tours.

Lodging Name	Rates High	Rates Low	A/C	Priv Bath	Hot H2O	Facilities	Comments
Coco Loco Lodge $ Tel./fax 506-750-0281 www.cocolocolodge.com	$30-45d $45-50t $50-55	$25-40d $30-45t $45-50	No	Yes	Yes	Restaurant	Set back from town in the jungle away from the noise of town. Tours, mosquito nets on beds. Buffet breakfasts $5pp. Apartments available for rent.
El Pizote Lodge $ tel. 506-750-0088 www.elpizotelodge.com	$46d $57t $68q	$39d $49t $57q	Yes	Not all	All	Restaurant Bar Pool Volleyball	MC, V. Just south of town set back from the beach. Bath$. Rents kayaks, horses, snorkeling and scuba stuff. Bungalows have private baths. Kids under 4 free.
Escape Caribeño $$ www.escapecaribeno.com Tel. 506-750-0103	$45-55s $50-70 $60-80	$35-45s $40-60d $50-70t	Yes	All	All		MC, V. Outside town towards Punta Uva. Clean and comfortable. Refrigerators and mini bars in rooms. Italian owners. A/C$.
Jacaranda Cabinas ¢ Tel. 506-750-0069 www.cabinasjacaranda.com	$12s $20d $25t $30q	$12s $20d $25t $30q	No	Not all	No	Restaurant Gift shop	No credit cards. Bath$. Excellent food at low prices in the Garden Restaurant. Laundry service.
Kaya's Place $ Tel. 506-750-0690 www.kayasplace.com	$19-40s $21-45d $28-55t $35-55q	$14-35s $21-45d $28-55t $35-55q	Fans	Not all	No	Restaurant	Credit cards. Cool, rustic eco-lodge right on the sand.
Pura Vida Hotel ¢ Tel. 506-750-0002 www.hotelpuravida.com	$19-25d $24-30t $20-35q	$16-22d $21-27t $26-34q	No	Not all	Yes	Shared kitchen	Private and shared baths. Rents bikes.
Salsa Brava (La) Cabinas $	$20-30	$20-30	No	All	No	Restaurant	On the beach in front of THE break. Where did you think?
Tamara Cabinas ¢ Tel. 506-750-0148 Fax 506-750-0309	$7-30	$7-30	Yes	Yes	Yes	Restaurant Bar	Costs extra for stove or kitchen. A few streets from the beach. Known for the restaurant.

Long Shoal

When Puerto Viejo gets really big there are waves breaking a couple of miles outside at offshore barrier reefs like Long Shoal. Check with Aquamore Talamanca Adventures, a dive outfit, for a boat ride out (aquamor1@racsa.co.cr, tel. 506-759-0612).

Playa Cocles

A decent beach break a few kilometers south of Puerto Viejo. Best on low to mid tide. You can actually walk here from Puerto Viejo by taking the beach trail, or you can stay right out front. Worth checking out when Puerto Viejo isn't on or is crowded. Cocles Beach is the winner of the Costa Rican government "Blue Flag" for clean beaches.

Where to Stay for Cocles

Lodging Name	Rates High	Rates Low	A/C	Priv Bath	Hot H2O	Facilities	Comments
Cariblue Hotel $ Tel. 506-750-0518 www.cariblue.com	$65-75	$55-65	Fans	Yes	Yes	Restaurant Gift shop	Credit cards. Rooms sleep 2-6 people. House available with furnished kitchen.

Casa Camarona $$ Tel. 506-750-0151 www.casacamarona.co.cr	$64s/d $79t $99q	$52s/d $72t $87q	Yes	Yes	Yes	Restaurant Bar Parking	No credit cards. Breakfast included. A/C$
La Costa de Papito $ Tel. 506-750-0080 http://greencoast.com/papito.htm	$44-50d $8 add person	$34-40d $8 add person	Fans	Yes	Yes	Bar	Using credit cards costs extra. Surfboard rentals. Room service breakfast. Directly across from the beach. Tours available.
Kashá $$ Tel. 506-750-0205, 800-521-5200 (US) www.costarica-hotelkasha.com	$75s $90d $100t $120q	$65 $75d $95t $115q	Not all	All	All	Restaurant Bar Pool Jacuzzi	V, MC. Rates include breakfast. Also offer all-inclusive plans. Known for great service.
La Isla Inn $ Tel. 506-750-0109 Email: islainn@racsa.co.cr	$40-90s $55-90d $70-105t $85-120q	$40-90s $55-90d $70-105t $85-120q	Not all	All	All	Restaurant	At the beach break. No crowds here. a/c$
Miraflores Lodge $$$ Tel/fax 506-750-0038 www.mirafloreslodge.com	$90d	$90d	Fans	All	All	Restaurant	Credit cards through PayPal. Bed & breakfast. Good choice if you get an upstairs room. Private home.
Playa Chiquita Lodge $ Tel. 506-750-0408, 506-750-0062 www.playachiquitalodge.com	$60-72d $15 extra pp	$45-50d $15 extra pp	Fans	All	All	Restaurant Bar	AE, MC, V. Breakfast included. Right across from Playa Chiquita. Tours. Rents bikes, horses, snorkel stuff. Nice place, a little rustic.
Punta Cocles Best Western Hotel $$ Tel. 506-220-1171, 506-750-0117 www.costaricareservation.com/cocles.html	$65 s/d/t/q $105 w/kitchen	$60 s/d/t/q $100 w/kitchen	Yes	Yes	Yes	Restaurant Bar w/ent. Beach hut Pool Playground	Credit cards. Nice upscale place. Short walk to the surf. Kids under 12 free (max 2). One of the few hotels here with a/c. 5 kitchenettes. Phones in rooms. Laundry service. Rents bodyboards, bikes, horses, snorkel stuff. Tours.
Shawandha Lodge $$$ tel. 506-750-0018 Shawandhalodge.com	$100-115d	$85d	No	All	All	Restaurant	AE, MC, V. Includes breakfast. French owned.
Villas de Caribe $$$ Tel. 506-233-2200 www.villasdelcaribe.com	$82-127d	$80-104d	Not all	All	All	Restaurant Pool Ping-pong Volleyball	Credit cards. On the beach. Includes breakfast. Nice place. Rents surfboards, boogers, bikes, snorkeling equipment. Kitchens.
Yaré $ Tel. 506-750-0420 www.hotelyare.com	$35s $60d +$10pp extra	$30s $50d +$10pp extra	Fans	All	All	Restaurant Bar	Some kitchenettes (extra$). Tours.

Punta Uva

One of the most beautiful coves in Costa Rica. Beach breaks north of Manzanillo along the Manzanillo Refuge coastline. Rights breaking off the reefs north of the point facing the cove. A great place to relax and catch some confidence-building waves (if Salsa Brava got the better of you). Seven kilometers south of Salsa Brava and much less crowded.

Where to Stay for Punta Uva

Lodging Name	Rates High	Rates Low	A/C	Priv Bath	Hot H2O	Facilities	Comments
MinOtel Las Palmas $$$ Tel. 506-759-9090 www.laspalmashotel.com	$60-70s $85-105d $105-135t +$30pp	$50-70s $75-90d $95-120t +$30pp	Yes	All	Yes	Restaurant Bar Pool Tennis Dive shop	AE, DC, MC, V. Includes breakfast. Higher prices include dinner, too. On the beach. Tours, horseback rides, dive trips, rents snorkeling stuff. Good place.
Walaba Lodge $ Tel. 506-641-8095 recahji@racsa.co.cr	$10-20 pp	$10-20 pp	Yes	All	Yes	Restaurant Bar Pool	Credit cards. Kitchens. Laundry service.

Manzanillo

A fast right break about 7km south of Punta Uva. Easy access since it is near the dirt road, but there are few accommodations. Never crowded.

Where to Stay for Manzanillo

Lodging Name	Rates High	Rates Low	A/C	Priv Bath	Hot H2O	Facilities	Comments
Cabinas Maxi $ Tel. 506-759-9042 Restmaxi@racsa.co.cr	$35d	$35d	Yes	All	No	Restaurant Bar	Big rooms. Busy restaurant. The place to go for lobster.
Dolphin Tour Lodge $ Tel. 506-759-9115 http://www.dolphinlink.org/Tours.htm	$80-115pp depends on group	$80-115pp depends on group	No	All	All	Restaurant	Dolphin tour package. Includes breakfast and dinner. Proceeds go to Talamanca Dolphin Foundation.

Panama

Here are a few tips if you decide to keep going south on to Panama where there's tons more surf, and it's less crowded. In addition to your passport, you'll need a visa from the Panamanian Embassy, which costs $5. You can also buy a stamp for $10 from the National Bank of Panama on Isla Colón. While you are there, change your colones for Panamanian dollars (balboas) as they don't take colones over the border. Don't be surprised if the immigration officers aren't working when you arrive at the border; they're not always there, so be prepared for a delay.

Back to the Airport

Sooner or later, most of us have to get back on that plane and head home. Never a happy time. If you are flying out any time before noon, you'll likely need a place to stay near the airport. The two closest hotels are the Hampton Inn and the Hotel Mango. You can walk to most of the car rental offices from the Hampton. The Hotel Mango is another 200 meters away.

By the way, this is one airport you definitely want to arrive at two hours early, as the agents recommend. The lines are long, it's crowded and disorganized—nothing like when you arrived. And again, be sure to have $26 for the departure tax, or a credit card.

Where to Stay for Near the Airport

Lodging Name	Rates High	Rates Low	A/C	Priv Bath	Hot H2O	Facilities	Comments
Hampton Inn $$$ Tel. 506-442-3320 www.hamptonhotel.co.cr	$105s $101d	$92s $98d	All	All	All	Restaurant Bar Pool	Credit cards. Free breakfast. Phones, TVs and everything else in rooms. Free airport shuttle. Get a reservation; always booked.
Hotel Brilla Sol $$ Tel. 506-442-5129, 506-443-5326 www.hotelbrillasol.com	$40s $50d $60t	$40s $50d $60t	No	All	All	Pool	Credit cards. Two miles from airport in Alajuela. Rates include breakfast. Free airport shuttle. Cable TV. Tours.
Hotel Herradura $$$$ Tel. 506-239-0033 www.hotelherradura.com	$130s $140d	$120s $130d	All	All	All	Restaurants Bar Pool Casino Business center	Credit cards. Published rates much higher than deals available. Upscale business travel type hotel. Nice place with big rooms. Phones, TVs, safes in rooms. Ask about in-room Internet access. Free airport shuttle.
Hotel Mango $$$ Tel. 506-443-1200 www.mangocr.com	$75s $85d	$75s $85d	All	All	All	Restaurant Bar	Credit cards. Small, quiet, more personal hotel near the airport. Tiny rooms. Kids under 10 stay free. Free airport pick-up and drop-off. Cable TV and phones in rooms.

SOUTHWESTERN NICARAGUA

Background

While Costa Rica has been the darling of Central America for surfers, tourists, retirees and investors for the past decade or so, Nicaragua is quickly becoming the new belle of the ball. Surfers have heard about the uncrowded breaks, investors have found an alternative to overpriced Costa Rica real estate, and more adventurous tourists are finding the raw, unspoiled Central America they once found in Costa Rica. (As mentioned in the Introduction, surf tourism in Costa Rica more than doubled in the three years from 2001 to 2004, reaching 222,659.) The skittish now know that Nicaragua is Central America's safest country. And everyone is marveling in the country's economic and political turnaround. Nicaragua is no longer a surfer's secret or the new frontier. It is now mainstream, or nearly so, with surf contests, Century 21 and golf condos.

And some pretty good surf.

The result is a surge in tourism, up 17% in 2005 to over 700,000, and more to come in 2006. (Lonely Planet just put Nicaragua at #3 on its Top 10 countries to visit in 2006.) And with tourism now the economy's leading income source it is likely the successful politicians will be those who favor policies that make Nicaragua increasingly comfortable for visitors—more and better infrastructure, hotels and other things that make it easier for you to get to the surf and enjoy more of it.

Now for the reality check: You've undoubtedly heard or read about empty surf and year-round offshores. Well, don't get too excited yet. Sure, there are uncrowded and even totally empty breaks, but you'll need a boat to reach them, and many of the boat-in spots are crowded anyhow. And yes, southwestern Nicaragua gets offshores roughly 320 days each year. But subtract the flat days during the height of the offshores and the days where the offshores are just plain blowing too hard and you can cut that number by about a third. But that's still pretty good. How many offshore days do you get where you live?

Nicaragua is Central America's largest country, so it stands to reason that it should have a lot of surf potential, especially with over 250 kilometers of Pacific coast line. And it does. So "reality checks" aside, Nicaragua is definitely worth a look. In fact, the surf is awesome.

In many ways Nicaragua is like Costa Rica. The weather pattern is pretty much the same. Most of the surf comes from the Southern Hemisphere. The surf is consistent and the water is warm. Travel costs are low and it's way less crowded than your local break. But Nicaragua is also different than Costa Rica.

Surfwise, one of the biggest differences between Nicaragua and Costa Rica is that most of the breaks are not yet accessible by vehicle, because there's no coast road to speak of, so getting to the surf via boat is pretty typical. Additionally, there's little in the way of lodging, so even if there was a coast road you would still need to travel to the surf. All of this is changing, though, as surf camps, beach lodges and condos are sprouting up everywhere. The real estate market is going hog wild, and there's a coastal highway in the works. So the Nicaragua you visit today is changing dramatically.

It's also poorer than Costa Rica. Much poorer. The literacy rate is lower and the unemployment rate is higher. It's all residual from the U.S. sponsored civil war and the U.S. sponsored political regime preceding it. The socio economic differences are readily apparent from the minute you set foot in Nicaragua.

Leave your Imperial beer, Pura Vida and Iguana Surf tee shirts at home. And don't bother bragging about how many times you've been to Costa Rica. No one cares. You see, the Nicas and Ticos don't get along very well. Without going into the history of it or some kind of diatribe, just know that the Nicas, being poorer and less educated, are looked down upon by the Ticos. The Nicas are the migrant workers in Costa Rica. They do the work many Ticos won't, they make up the largest group of illegal immigrants and suffer prejudice and humiliation as a result. There is also a history of border disputes and other things that have kept the Ticos and Nicas apart. All you really have to know is that showing off your love for Costa Rica won't get you any brownie points.

One last difference: They speak less English in Nicaragua, so you really should brush up on your Spanish. Then again, there are fewer cops and radar traps, so you may not need to use that Spanish as much.

Getting There

These days, most surfers fly in to Managua for a Nicaragua-only trip. It's actually quicker to the surf from the airport than in Costa Rica, assuming you don't get lost, and everyone gets lost. There aren't many road signs, and few that help, so if a friend volunteers to show you the way out of Managua to the surf accept the offer. If you're doing the surf camp thing, "help" is usually part of the package, so you won't have to worry. If you're going to rent a car at the airport and drive yourself don't try to take what looks like the shortest route, i.e., don't try to head west to the Panamerica Highway. Everyone will give you the same advice: Head east toward Tipitapa, then south to Masaya (don't drive through Masaya, drive around it) and work your way to Nandaime where you'll meet up with the Panamerica Highway. These directions assume you're heading to the Rivas province, which is where most surfers head and the only part of Nicaragua this guide covers. When you check the map these directions will seem ridiculous, but they work, ask anyone.

If you come up from Costa Rica (which has always been popular as a means of renewing 90 day visas), you'll have to endure an hour or so of border crossing red tape at Peñas Blancas—much more if you go on weekends or holidays, especially Semana Santa, Easter Week. You can expedite that by hiring one of the "coyotes" there who will speed you through for a fee, roughly $20 to $40 per person. (Try to find one who speaks English. It's a sign of experience.) That's for the Costa Rica side. You'll want to hire a Nicaraguan on that side, too, but they are much cheaper, $5 or less. If you have a rental car know that most rental car companies won't allow you to take the car out of the country. You can also take a bus or taxi to the border then catch another bus or taxi on the other side. Like everything else, taxis are much cheaper in Nicaragua. Border crossing office hours are 6:00am to 8:00pm.

A good option, but more expensive by comparison, is to fly in from Costa Rica from either San José or Liberia. Check with Nature Air (www.natureair.com). You can fly in to either Managua or Granada, then you'll still need to arrange transportation.

Whichever way you're coming in you'll need the usual: A passport (that doesn't expire for six months), and cash for entry and exit fees.

The Surf Breaks

Following are some of the surf breaks of Southwestern Nicaragua, the Rivas province, from north to south, from closest to Managua to closest to Costa Rica.

Quizala

The closest break to Managua; about a 90 minute drive. (In this case, don't head towards Tipitapa.) Rivermouth beach break with lefts and rights. The right breaks closer to the rivermouth and is often long and ripable. The left gets better on the big days. Very consistent.

Take the highway from Managua to the Montelimar Resort. When you think you're getting near the resort start looking for a little sign and a guard shack. Tell the guard you own a lot or house, be friendly and he'll let you in. About five kilometers up the road go left to the beach.

Montelimar

Stay at the resort and surf the lefts out front. Nothing great, but it's one of the few breaks with a hotel in front and it's close to Managua.

Guasacate

The closest beaches to Las Salinas and just north of the now world-famous breaks of Popollo (or Popoyo). Guasacate encompasses a stretch of beach breaks bordered by two rivermouths. Quality depends on tides and seasons, but much of it is good and none of it is crowded as everyone bypasses Guasacate for Popoyo (and crowds) to the south. Access is a bit limited due to the beach houses sprouting up everywhere and the new condo development (Bella Vista), but it's not too difficult to find your way to the surf. (Due to the great surf Guasacate has become one of the hottest real estate markets.) With the influx of beach houses there are rentals to be found, or you can stay at the Popoyo Surf Camp (www.surfnicaragua.com) or the basic hotel at the south end of the beach road near the rivermouth ($5/night). On the higher end is the Hotel Punta Teonoste (www.puntateonoste.com) a few kilometers to the north. It's an all-inclusive, expensive (for Nicaragua), upscale eco resort, and it has surf right out front, too.

Popollo/Popoyo

This is the place putting Nicaragua in the surf mags the past few years, especially following the Quiksilver Crossing's visit. Playful to hollow, juicy, reef breaks with rights and lefts. Usually bigger than most other spots. Stand up tubes when it gets bigger. Outside left reef starts at about eight feet and grows to tow-in material. If you want to see how big it gets go to the Popoyo Surf Camp's web site at www.surfnicaragua.com. As probably the best known spot in Nicaragua Popoyo draws a crowd. Good on most tides. Stay in nearby Guasacate across the rivermouth and walk to surf every day, or at one of the surf camps, like the previously mentioned Popoyo Surf Camp and get a ride in. Hang at the Tiltin' Hilton.

To get to Guasacate or Popoyo take one of two roads in to Las Salinas. The road that looks shorter is sometimes called the Ochomogo road since you pick it up just south of Nandaime at the Ochomogo bridge. This route is a dry season only choice, as there are about nine river crossings. The most common road in is the road that goes through Tola. You pick that up from the Pan Am highway at the north end of Rivas.

Rancho Santana

Juicy left breaking reef/point break and rivermouth beach breaks. The reef (Rosada) is often compared to La Jolla's Big Rock, hollow and juicy, and when on it breaks for over 100 yards. The rivermouth has both rights and lefts and is better for the less experienced, but it still gets hollow, and breaks best on higher tides. The rivermouth is fairly popular and sometimes crowded. Rancho Santana is a private development, "The Cadillac of beachfront communities," as International Living describes it, but you can get in here. House rentals are available, so unlike most of the Nicaragua breaks you can stay right there, with clubhouses, wireless internet and all sorts of goodies, if you have the dough. Check out Casa Ensueño (www.casaensueno.com) for a two bedroom house to rent in front of the left reef. And there's a surf camp here too, the Surf Sanctuary (www.thesurfsanctuary.com). Otherwise, since it's private you won't be able to just drive in and surf. But there's a road to the rivermouth just north of the Rancho Santana gate.

Panga Drops/Ponga Drops

Breaks on any swell, including northwests, and never closes out. Outside A-frame reef that looks mushy from shore but can actually get pretty juicy and bigger than it looks. Rights better than lefts. Hard to get out on big days. Hard to get in on all days, as it's inside the private Iguana Beach development. Either buy property, rent a condo or house, or boat in, the most popular option. (Guess how it got its name.) With smaller swells it's best on low to medium tides. When it's big it doesn't matter. A bigger board is the call as it's not easy to get into these waves.

Colorados

Well known beach break just north of the rivermouth that provides the sand that gives shape to these barreling rights and lefts. Best on mid to higher tide. Like Panga Drops, Colorados is either accessed through the private Iguana development or by boat. When you see Nicaragua featured in surf magazines, you are usually looking at shots from Colorados or Popoyo, but mostly Colorados, as the accommodations here are pleasant and private, and much more comfortable than those up north near Popoyo. Check online for condo and house rentals in the Iguana development, or you can rent the author's condo at www.vrbo.com/232104 or by emailing info@thesurfersguides.com.

Manzanillo

Long lefts off a rocky point. Needs a bigger swell to really shine, but closes out when it gets too big. Best on medium tide. Boat in only as the road is blocked. All of the boat captains know how to find it. It's also called The Left and Punta Reloj (in *The Surf Report*).

Playa Ocotal

Not known for surfing, but it's where you'll find the Morgan's Rock resort (www.morgansrock.com), a comfortable, secluded place to stay. Makes a good base camp for driving or boating (they'll set you up) to the breaks. Find it along the Chocolata road (see Maderas below); just look for the "MR" signs.

Playa Majagual

There is surf here, on occasion, but it's mostly walled beach breaks and rarely good. It is better as a base for either walking to Maderas (long walk) or taking boat trips. In the day Majagual is a relaxing place to hang away from the hustle of San Juan; at night it's a crazy party. The Bahia Majagual Eco Lodge (www.sanjuandelsur.org.ni/majagual) is a good place to stay, with dorm and private rooms, and a panga. Camping at Camping Matilda. Easy to find from the Chocolata road, just follow the signs. Or you can take water taxis from San Juan del Sur.

Playa Maderas

Maderas is the social center of Nicaragua surfing. It's the beach nearest to San Juan del Sur with consistent surf, and also serves as the headquarters for the NSR (Nicaragua Surf Report) boys. The latter means Maderas is prominently featured in the popular daily surf diary at www.nicaraguasurfreport.com. The former means it's crowded, and the crowd includes everyone from total beginners on their first surf trip to local pros. Beat the crowds by getting in the water early.

Playa Maderas is a picturesque cove with beach and reef breaks. It picks up most swells and holds shape to well overhead. Right and left beach breaks with good shape and occasional barrels are the main fare. Mostly sand bottom with reefs to the north and south. Works well on all but low tide, depending on the swell. On the south end of the cove is a left reef break called Machete Point that produces big, hollow barrels on the right swells.

Maderas is about a 15 to 30 minute drive from San Juan del Sur, depending on the road conditions. If you're not staying in San Juan del Sur you can camp on the beach or stay at the hostel on the beach for $5/night. There are also houses for rent, the Villas Playa Maderas. Or stay at the next cove up, Playa Majagual, at the Bahia Majagual Eco Lodge and walk in.

Heck, may as well give directions; it's already a zoo. From San Juan del Sur take the Chocolata road north. The turnoff is just outside of town; you can't miss it. At first follow the signs to Playa Marsella and Morgan's Rock ("MR"), but watch closely as you're really looking for the tiny signs to Villas Playa Maderas. You'll know you went the right way if you reach a fork with two steep hills. The fork to the right, the taller, steeper hill is the right road. You'll know you went the wrong way if you end up at Playa Majagual or Marsella. Plan on giving a ride to locals on your way out. Make friends, get waves.

San Juan del Sur

Not really considered a surf spot, but if you're a local with no transportation or time, or a visitor in the same situation, you can find waves at the north end of the bay near the rivermouth. Mostly closeouts, and lots of locals in the water, but it's something to do, especially if you are immune to unsanitary runoff.

San Juan del Sur is Nicaragua's main beach tourism destination and has the most lodging options. The three most popular hotels are (from highest price down) Piedras y Olas, aka Pelican Eyes (www.piedrasyolas.com), Hotel Villa Isabella and the Hotel Casablanca (both found at www.sanjuandelsur.org.ni). There are probably 50 other hotels, hostels and B&Bs, and most are inexpensive. The Pelican Eyes resort (not inexpensive) is up on the hill looking down on everything San Juan del Sur, which is fitting because it's the only truly upscale hotel in the area. (More are coming soon.) The Casablanca is down on the beach road, right in the middle of the restaurants and boardwalk. A good surfer's option.

My favorite is the Hotel Villa Isabella. It's more of a bed & breakfast than a hotel or resort, and it's sort of smack dab in the middle of town but away from the nighttime party noise. The Isabella is surf tour and real estate central. The patio is always piled high with board bags and the veranda buzzes with land speculators. As such, you'll probably run into Nicaragua's best known expat, Dale Dagger, who runs surf tours and sells property (www.nicasurf.com) or Tom Eberly, the prodigious shaper who owns a surf shop in town (Nica Surf) and also does surf tours (www.nicasurfinternational.com). I like it because the owner Mike is a great guy who takes good care of you. His breakfasts are great and conversations on the veranda are better. The hotel's tagline says it all: "Consider yourself at home."

Playa Remanso

Closest surf to San Juan del Sur, so it's easy to check. Check it often enough and you will catch it good. Beach and reef breaks, but walled much of the time. Good place for beginners to learn. Houses available to rent. Check with San Juan Property Management (www.sjpropmgt.com).

Playa Tamarindo

Yes, there's also a Playa Tamarindo in Nicaragua. But it's not nearly the same as Costa Rica's. Walk in from Remanso. You'll find rights breaking off the headland to the north. Beach breaks to the south. Better on smaller swells.

Playa Hermosa

And there's a Playa Hermosa, too. Beach breaks with best shape on smaller swells and when the swell direction is more south. Boat in only.

Playa Yankee/Yanqui

May be best known for land ripoffs, but it's still a good surf spot. Fickle right breaks off the point at the north end. The beach breaks are all walled. The main break is a reef with lefts and rights found where the road with the high grey walls and barbed wire (you'll find it) meets the beach. It's a wedgey reef break with makeable barrels. Crowded on weekends with locals and traveling surfers.

Playa Coco

A large picturesque bay with mostly walled up beach breaks and a right breaking off the north headland that is occasionally good. There's a resort (their description) a short walk from the beach, Parque Maritimo El Coco (www.playaelcoco.com.ni, 505-892-0124), with houses, bungalows and apartments for rent, all with kitchens. There's also a restaurant on the beach, La Puesta del Sol, so it's not a bad place to hang. Easy to find; just follow the signs from the road just outside San Juan del Sur pointing to the resort. No crowds here. Maybe a local kids or two in the water on a Sunday.

Los Sueños

A totally uncrowded left point off the headland at the south end of Playa La Flor, a big bay in a national park (turtle reserve). Needs a bit of swell, but lines up and barrels. Even the straight souths wrap around in here. There's a parking lot for the turtle reserve, and an entrance fee for camping or just spending the day. The point is a long walk to the south, so bring water, etc.

Pochote

A decent right point that can get good but needs north/northwest swells. Down here it's well-shadowed by Punta Blanca in Costa Rica.

Surf Tour Guides

One doesn't typically think of a surf trip to Central America as a boat trip, like the Mentawaiis or Maldives, but Nicaragua is different. As mentioned previously, there's not much of a coast road, so accessing the beach is often difficult. Additionally, many of the good breaks are blocked by private developments, so boating in is often the best option. Two good boat tour operators are Dale Dagger and Tom Eberly.

Dale's been in Nicaragua for a long time, probably the longest of anyone who can help you find surf. He lives in San Juan del Sur a couple doors down from the Hotel Villa Isabella and he's often dropping by for breakfast or a beer. I believe Dale knows more about surfing in Nicaragua than anyone, and he may even share a bit of that knowledge if you catch him on the right day, but probably not. He will, however, put that knowledge to use to make sure you have a good surf trip. You can reach Dale at www.nicasurf.com where you'll also learn a whole lot more. Or check the Quiksilver Crossing site (thecrossing.quiksilver.com) entry number 1195.

Tom Eberly is another expat who's been in Nicaragua since 2001. A well respected shaper from Southern California and Hawaii, Tom's operating a surf shop (Nica Surf) and surf tour operation (Nica Surf International) out of San Juan del Sur, putting guests up at the Hotel Villa Isabella and the Colonial. Tom is very involved in the local surf scene, which includes sponsoring the local surf contest. Learn more about Tom and his surf tour operation at www.nicasurfint.com.

For the ultimate guide to Nicaragua check in with the boys at www.nicaraguasurfreport.com, AKA NSR Surf. They have a daily surf report with pics mostly from Playa Maderas, but often from Colorados, Popoyo and Playa Yankee. Great guys.

A Final Word on Nicaragua

These last few pages have given a taste of what Nicaragua has to offer. One look at the map will show you that SW Nicaragua is only small portion of what there is to find here. It's going to be awhile before the secrets are revealed, so in the meantime there is still a lot of discovery and adventure to be had – a true rarity! Check for updates on Nicaragua in future editions and at www.thesurfersguides.com.

Index to Maps

Northwest Coast (Ollie's to Langosta)	37
Tamarindo	45
Playa Lagarto to Punta Guiones	57
Nicoya Peninsula (Playa Garza to Mal País)	61
Playa Hermosa	83
Golfo Dulce	101
Carribean Coast	112

Map art by Bob Towner

APPENDIX

Book List

Ahrens, Chris. *Surfer's Travel Guide, The,* Cardiff-by-the-Sea, CA, Chubasco Publishing
Baker, Christopher P. *Costa Rica Handbook,* Chico, CA, Moon Publications
Blake, Beatrice and Anne Becher. *New Key to Costa Rica, The,* Berkeley, CA, Ulysses Press
Samson, Karl with Jane Ajkshunas. *Frommer's, Costa Rica,* New York, NY, MacMillan Travel
Renneker, Mark et al. *Sick Surfers Ask the Surf Docs & Dr. Geoff,* Palo Alto, CA, Bull Publishing

Travel Agencies and Surf Tour Operators

ALACRÁN SURF TOURS, San José, Costa Rica, 011-506-777-1868, www.alacransurf.com or www.surf-costarica.com
COSTA RICA EXCURSIONS, Ft. Lauderdale, FL, 800-630-6225, www.costaricaexcursions.com
COSTA RICA TRAVEL AND REAL ESTATE, Ft. Lauderdale, FL, 866-502-3883, www.crtre.com
LOHE LANI CATAMARAN SAILING CRUISES, 714-957-8144, fax 714-957-8499, email lohelani2@aol.com
MORRIS OVERSEAS TOURS, Melbourne Beach, Florida, www.morrisoverseastours.com, 800-777-6853, 407-725-4809, 213-481-1966, fax 407-725-7956
PURA VIDA ADVENTURES, San Francisco, California, www.puravidaadventures.com, 415-425-465-2162, Specializes in surf tours for women
RICA ROADTRIPS, Tamarindo, Costa Rica, tel. 011-506-653-0874. Specializes in drive-in trips to Witches and other spots from Tamarindo.
SURF EXPRESS, Satellite Beach, Florida, 407-779-2124, fax 407-779-0652, email www.surfex.com
TICO TRAVEL, Fort Lauderdale, Florida, www.ticotravel.com, 800-493-TICO (8426)
TOURTECH INTERNATIONAL, Irvine, California, 949-476-1912, 800-882-2636. Specializes in "eco-travel" in Central America.
WATERWAYS TRAVEL, Malibu, California, www.waterwaystravel.com, 888-669-7873, 310-456-7744.
WAVEHUNTERS, Oceanside, California, www.wavehunters.com, 888-899-8823
WORLDWIDE ADVENTURES, INC., Florida, 800-796-9110, 407-773-4878

Car Rentals

ACTION CAR RENTAL, 506-256-2136, www.rentacarincostarica.com
ADA RENT A CAR (Alamo's agency in Costa Rica), 011-506-233-7733, fax 506-233-5555, http://centralamerica.com/cr/tran/ada.htm

ADOBE RENT-A-CAR, 800-826-1134, 506-442-2422 (airport), 011-506-221-5425, fax 506-221-9286, www.adobecar.com
AVENTURA RENT A CAR, 506-293-4821; fax 506-293-4104
BUDGET, 506-223-3284, 800-472-3325, fax 506-255-4966, www.budget.co.cr/
BUDGET, Hotel Kumak, Quepos, 506-777-0186
DOLLAR RENT A CAR, 506-257-1585 (San José office), 506-443-2078 (airport), www.dollarcostarica.com
ECONOMY RENT-A-CAR, Sabana Norte, San José, 506-231-5410, www.economyrentacar.com
ELEGANTE RENT-A-CAR (now part of Payless), 800-582-7432, 506-257-0026, email www.eleganterentacar.com
ELEGANTE RENT-A-CAR, El Ocotal Hotel, Playa El Ocotal
ELEGANTE RENT-A-CAR, Quepos, 506-777-0115
EL INDIO, 506-223-3284
EXCELLENT CAR RENTAL, www.excellentcarrental.com
EXOTICO RENT-A-CAR, San José, 506-283-7533, www.costaricareisen.com/firmen/autoverleih/exotico/index_eng.htm
FLAT RATE TRAVEL, 506-289-6243, www.orbitcostarica.com/carrentals.htm, or www.flatratestravel.com
HERTZ RENT A CAR, 506-221-1818, 506-223-5959, fax 506-233-7254, 506-221-1949
HOLA RENT-A-CAR, San José, 506-231-5666, 800-HOLA-800, www.hola.net
JEEPS "R" US, San José, 506-289-9920
MEIR RENT-A-CAR, San José, 506-257-4666
NATURISTAS DEL CARIBE RENT-A-CAR and Camping Equipment, 506-256-9657
PAYLESS CAR RENTAL, www.paylesscr.com
POAS, 888-607-POAS, www.carentals.com
PREGO RENT A CAR, San José, 506-257-1158, fax 506-255-4492
PRONTO, 506-255-4458, fax 506-223-3225
SOLID CAR RENTAL, 886-884-8949, 506-442-6000, www.rentacarcostarica.com
TRICOLOR RENT-A-CAR, 506-440-3333, 800-949-0234, www.tricolorcarrental.com
TOYOTA, 506-223-2250, www.carrental-toyota-costarica.com (only rents Toyotas, as you would expect)

Surf Shops & Ding Repair

ARENAS SURF & SKATE SHOP, Plaza Los Colegios, 506-283-3508; Centro Comerical Los Colegios, 506-240-8485; email fashion@sol.racsa.co.cr
BANZAII, Pavas, 506-296-3417, fax 506-290-1021
BEACH SURF SHOP, Jacó, 506-643-3036
BIYOBIS SURF SHOP, San Isidro, 506-771-2270
BLUE TRAILZ, Tamarindo, 506-653-0221, www.bluetrailz.com
CHOSITA DEL SURF, Jacó, 506-643-1308, www.surfoutfitters.com
COCONUT HARRY'S SURF SHOP, Nosara, 506-682-0574, www.coconutharrys.com
CARTON SURFBOARDS, Jacó, tel. 506-643-3762, fax 506-643-1308, email cartonshaper@hotmail.com

IGUANA SURF, Tamarindo, tel./fax 506-653-0148, www.iguanasurf.net
JASS JACÓ SURF SHOP, Jacó, 506-643-3549, fax 506-643-3046
KAUKA SURF SHOP, Heredia, 506-260-8182
KEOLA SURF, San José, 506-225-6041
KIMO'S, Jacó
MANGO SURF SHOP, Alajuela, 506-442-5862; San Pedro, 506-225-1067
MATOS FILMS, Playa Tamarindo, 506-653-0845, www.matosfilms.com
NOSARA SURF SHOP, Nosara, 506-682-0186, www.nosarasurfshop.com
PACIFIC SURF, Jacó
PARADISE SURF SHOP, Jacó
PICO SURFBOARDS, Playa Jacó, 506-643-1087
ROBERT AUGUST SURF SHOP, Tamarindo Vista Villas Hotel, Playa Tamarindo, 506-653-0114
TAMARINDO ADVENTURES, Playa Tamarindo, tel./fax 506-653-0640, email tamaquad@sol.racsa.co.cr
TICO SURF, Heredia, 506-235-2915
TULE, Manuel Antonio, Costa Rica, Central America, tel/fax: 506-777-1721

Local Air Travel

Aero Costa Sol Air Taxi, tel. 800-245-8420, www.westnet.com/costarica/aerocs.html
Macaw Air, tel. 506-653-1362, www.macawair.com
Nature Air, tel. 506-220-3054, www.natureair.com
Paradise Air, tel. 506-231-0938, 506-296-3600, www.flywithparadise.com
Sansa, tel. 506-221-9414, www.flysansa.com

Online Information

Alan Weisbecker's Down South Perspective: www.aweisbecker.com
Costa Rica.net: www.costarica.net
Costa Rica Discovery: www.costaricadiscovery.com
Costa Rica Home Pages: www.costaricahomepages.com
Costa Rica's Weekly Surf Report: www.crsurf.com
Drive Me Loco: www.drivemeloco.com
Go Visit Costa Rica: www.govisitcostarica.com
The Tico Times Online: www.ticotimes.net
Lonely Planet: www.lonelyplanet.com/destinations/central_america/costa_rica/
www.tamarindo.com
RoverCam: www.rovercam.com
Surfline/Wavefax: 900-976-SURF, 800-940-SURF, www.surfline.com
SURFTV.com global internet surf directory: www.surftv.com
Tamarindo.net: www.tamarindo.net
U.S. State Department: http://www.state.gov
U.S. Embassy: http://usembassy.or.cr

First Aid

NATIONAL AIR AMBULANCE: tel. 0-800-011-0017, 954-359-9900, web site www.nationalairambulance.com

TAMARINDO: Clinica Media, Dr. Hermes Quijada, 24-hour emergency service, 506-653-0544, 506-390-1921

INDEX

Air Transportation, 24
Air Travel, Local, 133
Airlines, 15
Appendix, 131
Avellanas, 51
Backwash, 103
Barco Quebrado, 115
Barra Del Colorado, 111
Battaglia, Tom, 41
Bejuco, 86
Boat Tours, 17
Boca Barranca, 75
Boca Coronado, 96
Book List, 131
Burica Peninsula, 105
Buses, 23
Cabo Blanco, 70
Cahuita (Black Beach), 115
Caldera, 76
Caletas, 69
Callejones, 53
Camaronal, 67
Car Rentals, 131
Carate, 105
Carbonera, 102
Caribbean Coast, 111
Carmen, 71
Carrillo, 66
Central Pacific, 75
Colorados, 125
Coyote, 69
Credit cards, 11
Damas Rivermouth (Boca Damas), 87
Dominical, 93
Doña Ana, 76
Drake's Bay, 98
Driving, 19
Escondida, Playa, 78
Esterillos Centro, Este, 86
Esterillos Oeste, 86
Garza, 64
Guanacaste, 36
Guasacate, 124
Guiones, 60
Henry's Point, 46
Hermosa (Dominical), 96
Hermosa, Playa, 82
Hermosa, Playa (Nicaragua), 128
Hog Hole/The Point, 103
Isla Capitán, 46
Isla Uvita, 114

Jacó, 78
Junquillal, 53
La Flor, Playa, 128
Langosta, 46
Limón, 113
Long Shoal, 118
Los Suecos, 72
Maderas, 126
Mal Pais, 70
Manuel Antonio, 88
Manzanillo, 69, 120
Manzanillo (Nicaragua), 126
Maps, 17
Matapalo, Cabo, 102
Matapalo, Playa, 92
Medical Emergencies, 28
Montelimar, 124
Mosquito repellent, 10
Negra, Playa, 53
Nicaragua, 122
Nicoya Peninsula, 57
Nosara, 60
Ollie's Point, 36
Osa Peninsula, 98
Ostional, 59
Pacific Southwest, 98
packing, 7
packing surfboards, 13
Palo Seco, 87
Pan Dulce, 102
Panama, 120
Panga Drops/Ponga Drops, 125
Pavones, 107
Pico Pequeño, 46
Piedra del Zapo, 46
Playa Blanca, 54
Playa Bonita, 113
Playa Cocles, 118
Playa El Rey, 92
Playa Grande, 41
Playa Hermosa (Nicoya), 70
Playa Majagual, 126
Playa Naranjo, 38
Playa Ocotal (Nicaragua), 126
Playa Remanso, 127
Playa Tortuga, 97
Pochote, 128
Popollo/Popoyo, 125
Portrero Grande, 36
Potrete, 111
Puerto Jiménez, 100

Index

Puerto Viejo, 116
Punta Banco, 109
Punta Barrigona, 72
Punta Burica, 110
Punta Uva, 119
Puntarenas, 75
Quepos, 88
Quizala, 124
Rancho Santana, 125
real estate, 41
Renting Cars, 21
Renting Surfboards, 8
Rio Sierpe, 97
Riptides, 4
Roca Alta, 113
Roca Loca, 78
Salsa Brava, 116
Sámara, 65
San Juan del Sur, 127
San Miguel, 68
Santa Teresa, 71
State Department Travel Advisory, 29
Sueños, Los, 128
Surf Shops & Ding Repair, 132

Tamarindo, 43
Tamarindo Adventures, 43
Tamarindo Rivermouth, 44
Tamarindo, Playa (Nicaragua), 128
Taxes, 26
Telephones, 26
Tipping, 27
Tivives, 77
Tortuguero, 111
Tour Planners, 16
Travel Agencies, 16
Travel Agencies and Services, 131
Tropical Diseases, 4
Tulín's, 82
Tusubres, 82
Uva, 119
Uvita, 96
Valor, 77
Water, 27
Westfalia, 114
Witches Rock, 38
Yankee/Yanqui, Playa, 128
Zancudo, 105

Made in the USA
Lexington, KY
02 April 2015